Monatshefte Occasional Volume Number 5

Monatshefte Occasional Volumes

Series Editor
Reinhold Grimm

Walter F. W. Lohnes and Valters Nollendorfs, editors
German Studies in the United States: Assessment and Outlook

Reinhold Grimm, Peter Spycher, and Richard A. Zipser, editors
From Dada and Kafka to Brecht and Beyond

Volker Dürr, Kathy Harms, and Peter Hayes, editors
Imperial Germany

Reinhold Grimm and Jost Hermand, editors
Blacks and German Culture

Reinhold Grimm and Jost Hermand, editors
Our Faust? *Roots and Ramifications of a Modern German Myth*

Our *Faust*?

Roots and Ramifications of a Modern German Myth

Edited by

Reinhold Grimm
and
Jost Hermand

Published for *Monatshefte*
The University of Wisconsin Press

Published 1987

The University of Wisconsin Press
114 North Murray Street
Madison, Wisconsin 53715

The University of Wisconsin Press, Ltd.
1 Gower Street
London WC1E 6HA, England

First printing

Printed in the United States of America

For LC CIP information see the colophon

ISBN 0–299–97019–1

Contents

Preface

Germany's greatest poet completed his greatest work only toward the end of his life, after decades of creative struggle. This is well known, as is his global concept—proclaimed simultaneously, as it were—of an epoch of *Weltliteratur.* Hence, the fact that precisely *Faust,* Goethe's most universal contribution to "world literature," was to be nationalized, germanized, teutonized to an unbearable, indeed horrifying, degree during the 19th and 20th centuries is not devoid of an almost tragic irony. Though there had been a few dissenting voices, the chorus of those engaged in chauvinistic appropriation and politicization (scholars and sundry cultural philosophers alike) proved to be overwhelming and capable of drowning out any opposition—at least until 1945. Yet even then, under different historical circumstances, the figure of Faust and/or the Faust theme remained a bone of contention among Germans, as witness, for instance, the heated debate surrounding Hanns Eisler's projected *Faustus* opera in the 1950s, and the more than thirty years it took before a definitive edition of its text was deemed publishable (cf. Hanns Eisler, *Johann Faustus.* Fassung letzter Hand. Hrsg. von Hans Bunge. Mit einem Nachwort von Werner Mittenzwei [Berlin, 1983]). Equally telling and equally impassioned, if less prolonged, was the earlier dispute—beginning in 1947—about Thomas Mann's novel *Doktor Faustus* subtitled, significantly, *Das Leben des deutschen Tonsetzers Adrian Leverkühn.*

Such and similar considerations, plus the approaching quatercentenary of the first *Faust* publication in 1587, the so-called *Volksbuch,* suggested the topic of the 1985 Wisconsin Workshop organized by the Department of German at the University of Wisconsin–Madison and held there on October 4 and 5, as well as prompting its title question and that of the present volume of proceedings, *Our* Faust*?*. But whose *Faust* is it anyway? Who are "we," to begin with? And may we really italicize (and thus, in a sense, objectify, even reify) Faust's name? For what is raised by that initial question is not just a host of divergent problems, viewpoints, methods, and interpretations of, say, legend or myth vs. history; a capitalistic vs. a socialist message; a national vs. a supranational relevance (or, perhaps merely a European or a Western one vs. an Eastern or a Third-world one) and so on. Nor is the basic question in any way limited solely to a single towering text, the Goethean drama; in point of fact, the very gender, male or female, of the pronouncers of the seemingly innocent pronoun in "our" question has a decisive bearing on the answers one might arrive at. Likewise, as implicitly indicated already, not only are Faust *(Faust)* and the Faustian roots and ramifications of a "world-literary" nature, but they are thoroughly and genuinely interdisciplinary as well. Contributing lastingly to the development of this multiple and most variegated theme have been both the classical sister arts of literature—i.e., music and the entire pictorial realm—and the modern mass media—such as film.

Granted, the nine essays here assembled—by Klaus L. Berghahn (UW–Madison), Russell A. Berman (Stanford University), Françoise Forster-Hahn (University of California at Riverside), Richard D. Green (Northwestern University), Nancy A. Kaiser (UW–Madison), Françoise Meltzer (University of Chicago), Thomas Metscher (Universität Bremen, FRG), Hans Rudolf Vaget (Smith College), and a student collective (UW–Madison)—do not claim to have exhausted the wide range of topics outlined above, much less to have probed into the topicality at large of the various—thematic and problematical—Faustian aspects. Cases of an emergence, or reemergence, of Faust and Faust-like figures in literatures other than German—to mention but one important area— either call for a supplementary treatment or have in the meantime been discussed elsewhere; they abound in French and Russian letters in particular. Not only did Paul Valéry and Michel Butor, for example, write their "own" specific variations on Goethe's text, but Albert Camus, too, conceived of a "Faust à l'envers," however fleetingly (see his *Carnets mai 1935—février 1942* [Paris, 1962], pp. 138f.). And as regards the formidable influence and, concomitantly, stern rejection of *Faust* and near everything Faustian in Russia, all that is needed is a glance at the second volume (1985) of André von Gronicka's seminal investigation, *The Russian Image of Goethe*.

The organizers and editors hope to provide nonetheless, with the following collection, a vast and stimulating array of studies on some of the weightiest facets of the Faust(ian) theme as it extends from the *Volksbuch* of 1587 to Mann's *Faustus* novel of 1947—and beyond as well as back. They also wish to take this opportunity to thank their friend and colleague Klaus Berghahn for his help in planning the Sixteenth Wisconsin Workshop. Above all, however, their heartfelt gratitude is again due to the Vilas Fund of the University of Wisconsin.

Our *Faust*?

Georg Johann Heinrich Faust:
The Myth and Its History

KLAUS L. BERGHAHN

To unravel the history of the Faust theme, from Spies's *Historia* of 1587 to Goethe's *Faust II* of 1832, is a rather tedious exercise, and a literary scorekeeper could perform such a well-known survey far better. Looking down this treaded path, I see far too many footsteps which I'd have to examine, and which I don't want to follow. Skimming through Henning's intimidating volumes of Faust literature, I am tempted to say that each word *not* written about Faust would be a blessing. And I could continue with Thomas Mann's modest words, spoken during the Goethe celebrations of 1949 in Weimar: "I have nothing new to say." Since Mann didn't stop there, I am going to follow his example; in spite of all the literature, my sense of originality does not allow me to do otherwise. So, what I am going to do is a variation on the theme: I want to present Faust as a modern myth. I'll try to show how it came about and why it changed over two centuries.

Understanding Faust as a myth poses some problems, be they ideological barriers or conflicting definitions. Whoever speaks about myth has to be aware that he sets foot on treacherous ground with warning signs all over the place. The older ones read like gravestones: Myth is dead. The gravediggers—and they are numerous, from Epicur through the Enlightenment to the present—pretend that in the history of mankind, logos/reason has replaced myth, which has become superfluous. The newer signposts warn against the irrationality of myth. Ever since the Romanticists postulated a "New Mythology," so the story goes, mythmaking has replaced a rational understanding of history. The mythologizing of the past, in order to define a national identity or to legitimate the superiority of the German race, nation, and culture, led to the destruction of reason long before the Nazis came to power. This kind of pseudoreligious and pre-Fascistic mythmaking is closely connected with the Faust myth, which seems to be a German myth par excellence.[1] When Thomas Mann, in his California exile, was contemplating the title of his Faust novel, he became aware of the danger "to create a new German myth and even to flatter the Germans with their demonic nature."[2] The

danger was, of course, to re-create Faust as a German myth at a time
when the forces that represented this very myth were threatening civilization. And yet, he did not want to leave this myth to the exploitation of the
Nazis. When he finally added the word "German" to the title one year
later, there was no doubt that his *Doktor Faustus* had to be written
against the German myth; and in so doing, he brought the Faust myth to
an end.

All these cautions are in order as long as they do not limit the
freedom to ignore them. Certainly, there should be skepticism against
any ideological abuse or perversion of myth—and the ideological criticism of myth has run its course. This rationalistic viewpoint should,
however, not lead us to discard myth and mythological concepts to the
rubbish of history or to leave these powerful images to the exploitation of
the Right, as Ernst Bloch warned as early as 1935.[3] Artists disregarded
these taboos, anyway, and in spite of them were fascinated by the unspent
vitality and aesthetic potential of myth.[4]

It seems to be easier to polemicize against myth than to define it. But
define it we must if we want to explain and explore the Faust myth. It
would be naïve even to try to distill one definition out of the many
conflicting ones which are offered by theology, philosophy, ethnology,
and psychology. What we need is a definition which describes myth as a
literary form and at the same time takes notice of its changing function in
history. A glance at Grimm's *German Dictionary* does not help much.
The scholars who worked on volume 6 must have been in haste to finish
this tome, or else they would have produced more than a mere three lines
of synonyms: "MYTHE, f. sage, unbeglaubigte erzählung, aus dem
griech. $\mu\hat{v}\theta os$ umgebildet, das geschlecht nach sage, geschichte, fabel,
erzählung u. ähnl." Here, the reduction of myth through reason has truly
worked. The only element that we can use, if it is useful at all, would be
"unconfirmed narration." This is less than enough, and we look to the
Oxford English Dictionary for more helpful information: "Myth. A
purely fictitious narrative usually involving supernatural persons, actions, or events, and embodying some popular idea concerning natural or
historical phenomena. Properly distinguished from allegory and from
legend." Here, we have at least some elements we can work with: myth is
a fictitious narration, deals with supernatural persons, and its source is a
popular idea of natural or historical phenomena which allows for modern
mythmaking. But this definition, too, is like a dried-up well where one
cannot even smell the water.

Since brevity is not always a guarantee of substance, we turn to a
book which defines simple literary forms morphologically.[5] André Jolles
approaches myth as literature and circumscribes the genre, instead of
giving a definition. At the center of his phenomenological description of

myth, there lies the simple pattern of questions and answers: The questions, as an expression of human curiosity, are directed toward everything that surrounds man, the creation and being of this world; the answers are narrative interpretations of an early perception of the world which in a simple form satisfy the human thirst for knowledge. The advantage of this broad perspective is that the age-old dichotomy of myth and logos is no longer valid; both aim at an understanding of the world: one does so by a simple narrative and the other through concepts and ideas. Myth, then, is enlightenment in its earliest form. Although it is assumed that myth develops only in a prehistoric age and becomes part of our tradition in an epic form only at the edge of recorded history, it can also evolve in modern history, and especially in times of crisis. Here, myth condenses a popular perception of a historical event into an oral history which is much later recorded on paper, as in the cases of Tell or the Maid of Orleans. Faust, as we shall see, is another example of a modern myth. Another of Jolles's many insights is also worth mentioning: namely, the transformation of myth. A myth can die or become a symbol: in the first instance, myth is no longer needed to interpret a riddle of the world; in the second, it crystallizes into a thing which gives this symbol an ambiguous and enigmatic quality.

My last and most important source is Hans Blumenberg's stupendous book *Arbeit am Mythos* (1979). It is a revision of the commonplace that myth has been replaced by logos and science; it attempts nothing less than to reconcile myth and reason; or, at least, it proves that our confrontation with nature is carried out on two different levels, a scientific one and a mythical. In spite of all rationalistic criticism of myth, mythical thinking has not lost its vitality. "The naked truth is not what life can be lived with."[6]

The analytical part of this book can be read as an expansion of Jolles's essay, but it is more indebted to Ernst Cassirer's *Philosophie der symbolischen Formen,* which is both criticized and elevated by Blumenberg; indeed, the subtext of his book is a polemical answer to Adorno/Horkheimer's *Dialektik der Aufklärung.* Blumenberg's agreement with Jolles can be traced in a sentence like the following: "The theory recognizes in myth an ensemble of answers to questions, as to how it is itself or wants to be. This forces it to reject the answers while accepting the questions" (34). However, he differs from Jolles insofar as he is much more interested in the reception history of myth than in its form or genre. This also separates him from Cassirer, their other major difference being the fact that for Cassirer myth is merely an aesthetic form no longer connected with real life. As to Adorno/Horkheimer, Blumenberg agrees that mythical thinking is already a form of enlightenment, but he rejects their philosophy of history. For them, myth is a way to work on history as a remembrance, while for him it is just a story. "Gods make stories, but they have no history" (148). Mythmaking tries to conquer nature and to make it bearable. "Myth represents a world of stories which situates the perspective of the audience in time in such a way that the fundus of monstrosities and intolerabilities diminishes" (131).

What happens to myth over the ages, and how it changes, is "work on myth." Blumenberg is not interested in a timeless and ahistorical Ur-myth, or archetype, as were, for instance, Freud, Jung, or Lévi-Strauss; rather, his focus is on the historicity of myth. It seems to be more interesting to him to pursue the reception and variations of a myth than to conjecture about an Ur-myth or to use mythical archetypes as universal human structures.

Blumenberg's theory about the origins of myth is more anthropological than Jolles's abstract question-and-answer model. Man, confronted with the hostile surroundings of a prehistoric past, "came close to not having control over the conditions of his existence" (9). Anxiety *(Angst)* is the *status naturalis* of myth. It is only slowly overcome by rationalizing it into fear of specific, named powers which can be addressed. Man invented stories to conquer his fear; he personified the threatening forces and separated them in order to deal with them individually. Mythmaking served as a tool to reduce the "absolutism of reality" and to tame the terrible forces of nature. What emerges between the prehistoric past and the edge of our history is the product of a selection process among the many myths through storytelling. By this "Darwinism of words," as Blumenberg calls it, the strongest and most convincing myths were developed. Myth, then, is a form of resistance, serving to conquer reality, to make it familiar and meaningful. Once the myths have reached historic times and have been recorded, they become symbols for the self-preservation of mankind.

After the myths have received their final iconic contours, a new phase begins. Now the artists discover the aesthetic potential of these powerful stories and images, and they create with them their own world. Their work on myth is a constant selection and transformation process which can be understood as the historicity of myth. Myth becomes part of history, and it serves to shape it. Blumenberg uses the Prometheus myth for a case study, tracing its transformation from Hesiod to Kafka. Especially Goethe's lifelong fascination with this myth, comparable only to his work on the Faust myth, offers an excellent example of how his works, his life, and his times are interwoven with this myth. Constantly searching for, and selecting, images, Goethe connected the myth with the changing stages of his own life and with the events of his times. His work on myth gave meaning to his existence and allowed him to interpret the world.

Similar to Jolles, Blumenberg assumes that each myth can be brought to an end. This does not mean that a myth is finally destroyed in order to make room for philosophy, sociology, or science; rather, it implies that during its history of reception each myth can reach a point of its most extreme deformation in which the original myth is hardly recognizable any more. Myth has exhausted its form and its usefulness: "The reception has worked up the story, as if it had not existed" (688). This would be a sign of man's sovereignty over reality—myth is no longer needed to explain one riddle of the world. In the case of the Prometheus myth, Kafka's reflections upon it can be considered as a final myth; his final sentence reads: "Myth tries to explain the inexplicable. Since it comes out of a fundamental truth it has to end in the inexplicable."[7]

It is against this theoretical background that I propose to read the Faust myth and to sketch its reception history. I shall investigate the creative work on the Faust myth in three phases: first, the inception of the myth in Spies's *Historia* of 1587; then, as a paradigm of the Enlightenment, Lessing's *Faust* fragment; and, finally, Goethe's *Faust,* which gave the myth its most artistic and enigmatic form.

Faust is a modern myth, which means that we can trace its history. This does not, however, imply that history can explain why that rather insignificant and obscure Faust, not Melanchthon or Paracelsus, became a mythical figure. What we know about his life does in no way indicate why he reached the mythical quality of someone who transgressed the limits of mankind. There must be more to Faust than meets the eye of the historian.

The extraordinary life of this strange magus began around 1480— let's say near Weimar, since one source mentions Rod being a village near Weimar, not Knittlingen. Georg Faust, as he was called, probably studied in Heidelberg, and many sources even grant him the title of doctor of philosophy. He must have had a wide range of knowledge, from theology and philosophy to natural sciences and medicine. The names for such a generalist was in those days "magician," which could have a positive or negative ring: white or black magic. Doctor Georg Faustus certainly qualified as a black magician, not as a scholar. Since 1506, he had practiced his trade and tricks in many places, such as Gelnhausen, Erfurt, Bamberg, Nürnberg, and Wittenberg. He is mentioned in books or letters of such famous contemporaries as Hutten, Melanchthon, and Luther, who castigated him as a conjurer and sorcerer. The people were warned to follow Faust's example, especially since Zimmer's *Chronicle* reported his unnatural death in Staufen: Rumor had it that he was murdered by the Devil. That's where his myth begins.

Speaking of the historical Georg Faust, one should not forget the times he lived in. It was an age of discoveries and a time of crisis: Nature and universe became objects of human curiosity, and the sciences entered into conflict with the doctrine of the church. The medieval world and feudalism crumbled, Protestantism rebelled against the Church of Rome, and the peasants staged the first unsuccessful revolution in Germany. It was a time of transition—the old powers were weak but still in control, and the new forces were not yet ripe to break through. In times like these, uncertainty rules; a gray area between physics and metaphysics allows creatures like devils, sorcerers, and magicians to populate the imagination of the common people. Faust seems to have been an ideal figure on whom they could project their anxieties and hopes. He tamed the Devil and used him to explore the world. Faust became the symbol of man's restlessness and curiosity—the utopian man par excellence.

The incubation period of this modern myth was rather short, less than fifty years. The time between Georg Faust's mysterious death around 1540 and his literary resurrection as Johann Faust in 1587 is filled with stories and anecdotes which circulated among the people. This rich oral tradition was collected and printed by Johann Spies in Frankfurt under the title *Historia Von D. Johañ Fausten / dem weitbeschreyten Zauberer und Schwartzkünstler.* The chapbook is a collection of stories rather than a history of Faust's life, a montage of episodes which shows a man who seeks knowledge and pleasure at any price—and pays for it with his soul. When the whispering and fearful storytelling of the people had reached its literary manifestation, Faust had already become a myth. Spies's *Historia* is replete with questions formerly unheard-of, and the answers are given in the idiom of the time, full of unbelievable events and fantastic actions. These answers are tainted with the common knowledge of the era; the questions, however, transcend these times since they transgress the limits of human knowledge. Here, popular imagination painted on the horizon images of things to come.

What is the meaning of this mythical transfiguration of a rather marginal character? What is the substance of this new myth and what is its function? The latter question is easier to answer than the former. The function of the *Faust* book is clearly written on its title page, which reads: "Allen hochtragenden / fürwitzigen und Gottlosen Menschen zum schrecklichen Beyspiel / abscheulichen Exempel / und treuhertziger Warnung." It is a warning which is amplified by a "Preface to the Christian Reader." To make sure that nobody is even tempted to follow Faust's example, the dangerous formula to conjure up the Devil is left out. The theological tendency is also quite obvious: The book is written from a Lutheran perspective against the Catholic church and its archdevil in Rome. All this is well researched and therefore equally well known. But it does not explain the substance of the book. Certainly, it can be read as a theological pamphlet or a piece of devotional literature; but a theological reading of the text would overlook the underlying tendencies of popular literature which resists dogmatic rationalization, and it could not nearly explain its origin and the fascination with which Faust occupied the common reader. Popular imagination as it expresses itself in the chapbook undermines the authority of the church, whether Catholic or Protestant—and its agent is Faust. What then is the substance of the book, which transformed the historical Georg Faust into a myth?

Angst is the *status naturalis* of myth. Especially in times of transition and uncertainty, when the traditional values of church and society are in jeopardy, superstition runs wild, and the air seems to be full of demons and devils. Luther himself, as legend has it, contributed to this kind of mythmaking when he threw an inkpot after the Devil. Faust, too, confronted the Devil, conjured him up and made him his servant for twenty-four years. Here, anxiety is slowly overcome and transformed into fear. Myth makes the Devil accessible; he even receives a name and can be addressed and dealt with. Not that the people wanted to follow Faust's example, but they could project their anxiety onto Faust and overcome it. The Faust myth helped them to rationalize their anxiety into fear, distance it, and make it bearable. Faust tamed the Devil and paid with his soul so that the people could lose their fear by listening to his stories. From now on, the name Faust is intrinsically connected with the man who dared make contact with the Devil. But for what reason?

This brings us to the second motif of the Faust myth which is a modern variety of mythical thinking: Faust's thirst for knowledge. From a theological perspective, Faust's guilt and damnation are as much based on his contract with the Devil as they are on his scientific curiosity which endangers the teaching of the church. From a mythical perspective, Faust asks all the questions about the earth, nature, and heaven for which the mythical mind also tries to find answers. Faust, however, does so with the modern curiosity of a scientist. He is not satisfied with the dogmatic and stereotypical answers of theology and thus comes into conflict with the church. That Faust needs the help of the Devil in order to satisfy his curiosity is only an afterthought to demonstrate how dangerous it is to look beyond the horizon of the established doctrine. The warning is clear—not only for those who play with the Devil but for scientists as well. In the age of Copernicus, when the earth was removed from the center of the universe, this warning carried weight. The search for knowledge was now considered a dangerous desire, and Faust went beyond the limits of what was tolerable. He became the symbol of all those who no longer wanted to be led along by the church, whose meager consolation—*sola fide*—was an offense to reason. That is what made Faust so daring and modern.

There is yet another dimension which might explain the origin of the Faust myth. The period when the oral tradition of the Faust stories was sifted and condensed into the *Faust* book was also a time when the old forces of state and church consolidated their power. It was a restoration period: the revolt of the lower nobility *(Reichsritter)* had been squelched; the first German revolution, the so-called Peasants' War, had been drowned in streams of blood; and the members of religious minorities and sects had been murdered or exiled. During this hopeless postrevolutionary period, the people were looking for a way out,[8] for someone they could project their hopes on, even if such a figure became exceptional only by a pact with the Devil. The Faust myth can be read as an answer to the German misery of the times. Faust can be understood as a rebellious figure who dared challenge the authorities when Protestantism had long made its peace with the ruling powers. Although the "official" message of the *Faust* book is a warning by means of a horrible example, the Faust myth contains also a memory of what could have been. Under the crust of regressive tendencies, for which a dogmatic Lutheran theology was responsible, one can still detect critical and even rebellious tendencies. This made Faust so popular.

Whereas the intention of the *Faust* book is clearly outlined on its title page as a warning not to meddle with the Devil, the underlying Faust myth contains questions for which the established institutions of learning and theology had no answers, while its unheard-of stories responded, more importantly, to the anxieties, doubts, and hopes of the times. The stories crystallized around a modern mythical character who dared go beyond the limits of mankind: his name, for times to come, was to be Faust.

The Faust myth soon became firmly established in England. An English translation of Spies's chapbook inspired a "Ballad of the Life and Death of Doctor Faustus the Great Conjurer" (1588); one year thereafter, Marlowe wrote his famous play *Tragical History of D. Faustus*. English theater troupes then brought the play to the Continent where it became tattered, ending up as a puppet play in the 18th century. The same happened to the original chapbook, which underwent numerous editions and revisions until it reached the 18th century in two different versions: one by Pfitzer, which is still fairly close to the original; the other by the "Christlich Meinender" which is basically a plot summary. It was in these distorted or trivialized forms that the serious writers of the 18th century rediscovered the poetic and philosophical qualities of the Faust myth. Faust seemed to be the ideal character for the Age of Enlightenment, during which the attitudes toward faith and knowledge changed radically, and intellectual curiosity became the noblest of human characteristics. "A desire for knowledge is the natural feeling of mankind," states Dr. Johnson, "and every human being, whose mind is not debauched, will be willing to give all he has, to get knowledge."[9] This, from now on, is Faust's case. For a secularized age that measures everything against the yardstick of reason, even the Devil loses his sting: he becomes "part of that force which would do ever evil, and does ever good," as Goethe later put it.[10]

By the time Lessing became aware of the Faust theme and began working on it, many writers seemed to be busy with it, which made Gottsched, the archenemy of popular literature, rather nervous.[11] Lessing wanted to wait to publish his *Faust* until all the other versions including Goethe's had appeared—this in order to make their authors waste paper. He waited too long—although it may be true that a finished manuscript was lost in the mail between Dresden and Wolfenbüttel in 1775, as an often-repeated story has it. What came down to us are only fragments of Lessing's work: one scene which he published in his famous 17th *Literaturbrief* in 1759, and the so-called "Berlin Scenario," a summary of an opening sequence consisting of a prologue and four scenes published posthumously by his brother Karl in 1786. In addition to these five pages and many letters that mention Lessing's work on Faust over a period of twenty years, we have two reliable accounts (by Lessing's friends C. F. von Blanckenburg and J. J. Engel) of the tragedy's outline and its ending, Faust's redemption.[12] There is not much to work with, and interpretation here seems to become an art of overcoming absence. Nothing loftier than to speculate about a text that hardly exists, one might say. Not quite! For Lessing's labor with the Faust myth is clearly reconstructible.

It is quite obvious why Lessing is fascinated by Faust, who represents the modern myth of the human quest for knowledge and truth—a symbol with which he himself could easily identify. That Lessing's conception of his *Faust* tragedy is closely, if not exclusively, connected with the modern drive for knowledge becomes clear when we look at the "Berlin Scenario." Its prologue shows an assembly of devils in an old cathedral where various demons report on their day's work to Beelzebub. At the end, they also talk about Faust, who seems to be indifferent to any temptation, whereupon one devil promises to make him the prey of hell within twenty-four hours.

> Itzt, sagt der eine Teufel, sitzt er noch bey der nächtlichen Lampe und forschet in den Tiefen der Wahrheit.
> Zu viel Wißbegierde ist ein Fehler; und aus einem Fehler können alle Laster entspringen, wenn man ihm zu sehr nachhänget.[13]

Faust's desire for knowledge, which is his only flaw, will bring him down. It seems that Lessing wanted to develop Faust's tragic fate entirely out of this passion for truth. Faust achieves his goal with the help of the Devil which at the same time guarantees his downfall. In contrast to the traditional myth where Faust seeks every pleasure of the world—lust, power, and wealth—and pays for it after twenty-four years, Lessing's Faust is only consumed by one pure desire which is not a vice. In accordance with Aristotle's and his own concepts of tragedy, ἁμαρτία should lead to the tragic ending. But this Lessing could not do. He could not sacrifice Faust for the noblest of all human qualities. Faust must be saved at any price. In Blanckenburg's outline of the play, the ending is quoted as follows:

> "Triumphiert nicht," ruft der Engel [den Teufeln] zu, "ihr habt nicht über Menschheit und Wissenschaft gesiegt; die Gottheit hat dem Menschen nicht den edelsten der Triebe gegeben, um ihn auf ewig unglücklich zu machen."

In the best of all worlds, which is ruled by reason, the passion for knowledge had to be vindicated. Here, exposition and ending clearly conflict with each other; the result of Faust's sole flaw, which, of necessity, must lead to his tragic downfall, can be eliminated only by a trick: Faust merely dreamt his excesses (of the missing middle part) and the Devil is cheated out of his work. What the devils carry away is just a "phantom" of Faust.[14]

This is a clear break with the damnation of Faust. The modern playwright working with the old myth could not follow through on the premise that Faust's thirst for knowledge should end in hell. Faust must be saved even if only a *deus ex machina* can save him, and even if the concept of tragedy suffers. Here, Lessing's philosophy triumphs over his dramatic art. He must have felt this contradiction but did not know how to solve the problem. The Faust myth was no longer suitable for a modern tragedy, or else it had to be altered drastically, in order to fit the anthropology of Enlightenment. Faust's damnation had to be revoked even if the tragedy came dangerously close to becoming a morality play. This is precisely the solution which Engel's outline offers us. Faust has received and understood the "warning": "Er ist jetzt fester in Wahrheit und Tugend, als jemals."[15] A very heavy-handed and didactic ending, unlike Lessing's dramatic art; and we wonder whether Faust has renounced even his desire for knowledge and become a pious philistine. Lessing's break with the tradition is clearly visible, but the fragments and endings as reported by his friends leave too many questions unanswered.

There is one more observation which could explain why Lessing was unable to finish his *Faust*. Granted, he felt congenial and sympathetic to Faust's desire for truth. But, unlike Faust who wanted the whole truth at once—or, at least, in twenty-four hours—Lessing followed the principle of gradualism, as we know from his famous *Duplik* of 1778:

> Wenn Gott in seiner Rechten alle Wahrheit, und in seiner Linken den
> einzigen immer regen Trieb nach Wahrheit, obschon mit dem Zusatze, mich
> immer und ewig zu irren, verschlossen hielte und spräche zu mir: 'Wähle!'
> ich fiele ihm mit Demut in seine Linke und sagte: 'Vater, gib! die reine
> Wahrheit ist ja doch nur für dich allein!'[16]

Faust would never have said this. In Lessing's fragment published in his
17th *Literaturbrief,* he therefore chooses from among the seven devils the
fastest one, who is as fast as the change from good to evil. Faust has not
only "too much desire for knowledge," he also wants to have it in the
shortest time. For Lessing, in contrast, the process of *Bildung* is slow and
includes detours. Or as he informs us in his *Erziehung des Menschen-
geschlechts:* "Es ist nicht wahr, daß die kürzeste Linie immer die gerade
ist."[17] Faust is impatient; he wants to accelerate time and cannot reach
the future fast enough. He is unlike Lessing who knows that the "education of mankind" is a gradual process which cannot be finished in one
generation, and certainly not by one man—even if his name is Faust. It
seems, in the end, that Faust could not be the ideal character or myth for
Lessing, whose understanding of time was not limited to one life, as he
states at the very end of his *Education of Mankind:* "Und was habe ich
denn zu versäumen? Ist nicht die ganze Ewigkeit mein?"[18]

Maybe it is a blessing for German literature that Lessing finished his
Nathan der Weise instead of his *Faust,* and that he left the Faust myth for
Goethe to work with. To do justice to Goethe's *Faust,* on which he
labored—off and on—for almost sixty years, a complete interpretation
has to include two perspectives. First, all major and minor changes of the
old myth must be taken into consideration, and, second, they must be
interpreted in view of the changing circumstances of Goethe's life. His
work on and with this myth is a constant searching for, and selecting of,
images to understand and create his own world, to find answers to the
changing times and to social or political developments; it is an instrument of world orientation. To analyze Goethe's reinterpretation of the
Faust myth would mean nothing less than a reconstruction of his literary
life between 1772 and 1832, as it unfolds within the interrelation of myth
and history.

Goethe worked so freely with the old myth, and integrated it so
completely into his world view, that his *Faust* replaced the old myth.
Even passages which are largely taken from, or inspired by, the chapbook
were transformed into a new symbolic meaning. A case in point, which I
can mention only in passing, is the Helena subplot. The episode as a
whole, as well as Goethe's use of mythology, can be summed up by an
ironic commentary of Chiron. When Faust asks him about the meaning
of Helena, he answers:

> Ganz eigen ist's mit mythologischer Frau,
> Der Dichter bringt sie, wie er's braucht, zur Schau.[19]

Goethe was well aware of his indebtedness to the old legend, as he called it. He considered the Helena episodes "a significant motif," which he used for *Faust II.* The material similarities between Spies's chapbook and Goethe's *Faust* are striking indeed. In both texts, Helena appears twice: first, she is brought back to life in order to satisfy the curiosity of Faust's students, or to entertain the guests at the emperor's palace; then she appears a second time, in order to stay with Faust, become his mistress, and have a son by him. What for Spies are but examples of Faust's trickery and lust becomes in Goethe's adaptation the "Classical Walpurgis Night." For Goethe, Helena symbolizes the reincarnation of classical antiquity: first, as a shadow, a memory of the past; then, in her real appearance, as an appropriation of the past for the present. She is, in short, the embodiment of Goethe's poetic philosophy of history. For Faust, the whole Helena episode is just one important moment in his development: he experiences beauty in its highest and most sensuous form, and at the same time recognizes that he cannot possess and hold her, that beauty is merely an illusion. In the end, he holds only Helena's veil in his hands.

To come back to our original question: How does Goethe use the Faust myth and what does its transformation mean? Of the numerous changes he made, I have to limit myself to the three most important ones: the beginning, the Gretchen tragedy, and the ending.

We enter Goethe's *Faust* through three prologues. These are: the "Dedication" (a personal reflection on his work when Goethe returned to it in 1797), the "Prelude in the Theater" (an improvisational scene between a theater director, a poet, and a "merry person," or harlequin figure, which puts the play into the social context of the literary life of the time), and the "Prologue in Heaven." Of these three, the "Prologue in Heaven" is, from our perspective, the most important one since it provides a transcendental frame for the *Faust* tragedy. It is that of the theater as the whole world, *theatrum mundi,* where man stands between God and the Devil and where the sequence of acts will show what choices he has and how he chooses; it is history presented as salvation history, and man's passage through the world embedded in a morality play. From God's perspective, the world is a stage and Faust is merely a player. This rather traditional theatrical device, with all its metaphysical implications, already prepares the audience for the solution: Faust shall not fall prey to the Devil. There is no question that God is the superior character who knows Faust and is confident that he will win his wager with Mephistopheles—if it is a bet at all. God in his providence knows: "Ein guter

Mensch in seinem dunklen Drange / Ist sich des rechten Weges wohl bewußt" (328f.), while Mephisto wrongly anticipates his triumph: "Staub soll er fressen, und mit Lust" (334). The stage is set; enter Faust.

Faust's famous opening monologue is a desperate negation of human intelligence and science, which leads him to skepticism and even cynicism. Wherever he restlessly searches he faces nothing but limitations. Or as Goethe himself characterized the situation of his hero in 1826:

> The character of Faust, at the exalted level to which our new version has raised him out of the rough old folktale, represents a man who [feels] impatient and uncomfortable within the general limits of earthly life, . . . a mind which, turning in every direction, always returns in a more unhappy state. Such a disposition is similar to the modern one.[20]

Goethe's characterization is, as his usually are, rather general, but it bridges the gap between Renaissance and Enlightenment. Faust becomes a symbol of modern man. His thirst for knowledge is not only frustrated by the limits of scholastic sciences but also by the narrow confines of his life. His "narrow Gothic chamber" is the most powerful image of Faust's limitations. If we look at this scene from the perspective of its origin, it bespeaks the spirit of Goethe's *Prometheus* fragment of 1772, the protest of the self that wants to be God. From a modern perspective, and in the context of the drama as a whole, it seems that Faust suffers from lack of knowledge and of self-fulfillment. Therefore, *Faust* is not just the tragedy of a modern scientist but that of modern man at large, who suffers from want of wholeness, of totality. If this inner conflict is not to end in despair or suicide, Faust needs some help. That's where Mephisto comes in.

He offers Faust his services, yet not in the form of the well-known pact, but as a wager—the second one in the play, which, like the first, underscores its central motif: Faust's striving for total understanding and his longing for self-perfection. It is, however, Faust who proposes the wager:

> Werd' ich beruhigt je mich auf ein Faulbett legen,
> So sei es gleich um mich getan!
> Kannst du mich schmeichelnd je belügen,
> Daß ich mir selbst gefallen mag,
> Kannst du mich mit Genuß betrügen,
> Das sei für mich der letzte Tag!
> Die Wette biet' ich!

And after Mephisto has accepted the bet, Faust continues with the most important lines:

> Werd' ich zum Augenblicke sagen:
> Verweile doch! du bist so schön!

Dann magst du mich in Fesseln schlagen,
Dann will ich gern zugrunde gehn!
(1692ff.)

This is the central point of Faust's wager: the fulfilled moment. It keeps his relation to Mephisto a mystery, making his life an experiment. Already here, the misunderstanding between them begins, for Faust seeks knowledge, understanding of the world, development of all his potentials, and aims for a utopian moment of self-perfection, whereas Mephisto wants only to satisfy Faust's lust for life and to drag him "through shallow insignificance." What Faust desires, Mephisto cannot understand or satisfy. Goethe's important changes of the old myth, the "Prologue in Heaven" with its wager and Faust's bet with Mephisto, anticipate the ending: Faust, the modern man, will be saved, and the Devil will be betrayed twice. Goethe knew what he was doing when he changed the beginning.

The second and most radical change of the Faust myth is more difficult to deal with. How is one to explain that the tragedy of an infanticide constitutes part of the Faust drama? Strictly speaking, the Faust myth and the Gretchen tragedy do not fit together. And yet, when we speak of Faust, common knowledge has it that Gretchen's tragedy comes to mind as well. Goethe made it possible. The old chapbook, of course, mentions nothing of this sort. When Faust, once his dusty academic career and his monastic life-style are behind him, becomes aware of his sexual desires, he wants to marry. The Devil has a hard time convincing Faust that this isn't necessary. He will provide him each night with a new mistress. Faust accepts, and the episode ends with Faust trembling in anticipation. There is only one hint in Pfitzer's *Faust* book of 1674 of Faust falling in love with a beautiful yet poor maiden. But nothing more—no seduction, no infanticide, and, least of all, no tragedy that leads to heaven. No, the old myth did not inspire Goethe's Gretchen tragedy. It has other roots, roots which are closer to his own literary and existential experiences.[21]

The Gretchen tragedy is the central part of the oldest formation of *Faust,* the so-called *Urfaust* which Goethe brought to Weimar in 1775, read to small circles, but never published. It is a bourgeois tragedy in typical Storm-and-Stress fashion. As we know from Goethe's *Dichtung und Wahrheit,* Lessing's tragedy *Emilia Galotti* (1772) had a tremendous impact on the younger generation of writers. The Storm-and-Stress playwrights radicalized the new genre by making the plot contemporary and by presenting the tragic conflict as a class conflict: a young maiden of the middle, or lower-middle, class is seduced by a nobleman; when she is pregnant he deserts her; in despair, and under social pressure, she kills the newborn, and as the law dictates, she is condemned and executed. That is Gretchen's case even though Faust only appears to her as an aristocrat—but he certainly acts like one. Biographical evidence from the years 1771 to 1772 allows us to speculate about Goethe's model in real life: Susanna Margaretha Brandt, who was tried for the murder of her newborn and executed in Frankfurt. She claimed that her seduction was the work of the Devil, who even spoke to her. All of this, and more, explains Goethe's interest in the Gretchen tragedy; it fails, however, to explain why he connected this tragedy, which could easily stand on its own, with the Faust complex. Goethe felt the discrepancy, and for a long time was unable to finish the first part. In 1790, as part of the first edition of his collected works, he published *Faust* as a fragment. Only in 1806 did he finish *Faust I,* which gives us an idea of how he integrated the tragedy of Gretchen.

Structurally, the two segments are connected by the actions of the protagonist, who experiences the "enjoyment of life" in the "small world" of Gretchen before taking off into the higher regions of the "great world."[22] In the finished version of *Faust I,* the new scene "Witch's Kitchen" bridges the gap between the Faust and the Gretchen episodes. Faust, rejuvenated by the witch's potion—let's say, made younger by thirty years—will soon "see Helena in every woman" (2604), as Mephisto remarks. And the first woman who crosses Faust's path in the following "Street" scene is precisely Gretchen. Faust acts accordingly and exclaims to the Devil's delight: "Hör, du mußt mir die Dirne schaffen!" (2619). Mephisto, who obliges, cannot foresee that Faust will fall in love with Gretchen. What on Mephisto's part was meant to be a stepping-stone to the "enjoyment of life" becomes for Faust personal love, and thus complicates their relationship. To make this unmistakably clear, Goethe injected another new scene, "Forest and Cave," where Faust contemplates his ecstasy of love and its contradictions, while at the same time, in a parallel scene, Gretchen at the spinning wheel sings of her love, which transforms during her song into desire. But Faust's restlessness and Mephisto's cynical commentaries on Faust's love already anticipate Gretchen's tragedy. When she is finally ruined, Mephisto wants to distract the guilt-ridden Faust with the spectacle of the Walpurgis Night. This third new scene ends with Faust's vision of Gretchen, a moment of ἀναγνώρισις, which brings back both his love and the recognition of her fate. In a rage, Faust tries to rescue Gretchen from the dungeon, but she, in the twilight of despair and madness, refuses to follow him and Mephisto, whom she senses to be the Devil. Gretchen surrenders herself to the judgment of God while Mephisto drags Faust off to what seems to be his damnation. Here, the last important change occurs. When Mephisto proclaims: "She is condemned," a voice from above answers:

"She is redeemed" (4611). Gretchen's salvation anticipates Faust's, who follows Mephisto on a journey through the "great world." Thus, the Gretchen episode is now fully integrated into the *Faust* drama. What Mephisto intended as sexual enjoyment of life and the first step down to hell has been transformed into personal love and the first step toward heaven. Faust's love for Gretchen, which is inscribed on his body and mind, becomes part of his life experience and of his self-development. The Gretchen tragedy foreshadows, as do the other changes of the original myth, Faust's redemption.

Looking at the grandiose and enigmatic finale, one could sigh with Faust: "Die Botschaft hör' ich wohl, allein mir fehlt der Glaube" (765). What a miraculous ending for him who had moved from one extreme to another, this man of action responsible for outrageous acts! And the list is long: Faust is responsible for the deaths of Gretchen's mother, of her brother, of Gretchen herself; for a paper money fraud, the annihilation of an army, piracy, exploitation, slave labor; and, finally, for the murder of Philemon and Baucis—this Faust is to be redeemed? He is not the Faust whom Lessing would have saved. Goethe's Faust would rightly deserve the verdict: *In aeternum damnatus est!* Instead, we are told by God's angels: "Wer immer strebend sich bemüht, / Den können wir erlösen" (11935f.). Truly, a *salto mortale* into the operatic world which also smells of too much Catholic incense. Maria in person appears as *dea ex machina,* and Faust's sinful acts are covered with the veil of love and grace. There is much room for metaphysical speculation and cheerful misunderstanding. And yet, there seems to be more than meets the skeptic's eye; otherwise, the quarrel about the conclusion of *Faust* would not have attracted the attention of so many illustrious spirits. And let us not forget that the finale of *Faust* is Goethe's poetic testament. These are his sacred last words—piety seems to be in order.

Since my interpretation of Goethe's *Faust* rests on the premise that the two wagers in the beginning and the Gretchen tragedy prefigure the ending, I have to make my final interpretative move. Clearly, Faust's end is a radical break with the myth. As Goethe already knew from Lessing's fragments, Faust could no longer be condemned in a secular age like that of Enlightenment, when hell had lost its chill and the Devil his sting. In a letter to K. E. Schubarth of 1820, Goethe states his intention: "You felt correctly about the ending of the play. Mephistopheles is only permitted to win half of the wager, and when the other half of the guilt rests with Faust, then the Old Man can use his right of grace to the merriest of endings."[23] Judging from Goethe's intention, the wager in heaven—half won, half lost—decides Faust's fate: mercy comes before justice. The natural order of things vanishes and is replaced by a new order we do not yet know. These are the metaphysics of *Faust* as Adorno sees them.[24]

The outcome of the second wager, the one between Faust and Mephisto, is more hotly debated. The theme of this wager is the moment of fulfillment, which Faust seems to have reached when he utters the words:

> Zum Augenblicke dürft' ich sagen:
> Verweile doch, du bist so schön!
> Im Vorgefühl von solchem hohen Glück
> Genieß' ich jetzt den höchsten Augenblick.
> (11581ff.)

Mephisto triumphs. But is this really the moment he has been waiting for? Mephisto takes for real what Faust is only anticipating. Goethe's language is quite precise here: Faust speaks of "foretasting," and he uses the optative. Faust's moment of fulfillment is merely a vision; what he foresees has not yet been experienced.

Even more important seems to be the content of his vision:

> Eröffn' ich Räume vielen Millionen,
> Nicht sicher zwar, doch tätig-frei zu wohnen. . . .
> Solch ein Gewimmel möcht ich sehn,
> Auf freiem Grund mit freiem Volke stehn.
> (11563f., 11579.)

Faust's absolute striving, which could not be satisfied even by the presence of Helena, comes to rest when he envisions his utopia: a free people on free land. As with any vision of a promised land, the content, or even the contours, of Faust's utopia are undetermined; and yet, freedom is the magic word that gives imagination latitude. That Goethe had a socialist utopia in mind is rather doubtful.[25] Bloch, who is the legitimate father of this interpretation, concentrates on the utopian moment when the "not-yet" becomes visible on the horizon, while he calls the content of Faust's vision "capitalistic."[26] One should not overburden Goethe's famous line, and certainly not try to reconstruct a blueprint for Goethe's utopia from it. One should, however, not overlook Goethe's irony, either: the old Faust is already blind, and his blindness does not make him a prophet—on the contrary. When he gives his final speech, he imagines that his workers are tilling the land, while actually they are digging his grave. Faust's illusion of his highest moment is also his last illusion. And one should certainly not forget that this is not yet the ending of *Faust.* The drama does not end with Faust's utopian moment, nor with his death, but with his ascension to heaven.

Therefore, Heinz Schlaffer seems to be right when he stresses once more the importance of Gretchen or, better still, of love, in the final scenes.[27] In this metaphysical "liturgy of love" (Schlaffer), it is Gretchen, as a penitent, who leads Faust to higher spheres, and it is she who educates him now (12090). Gretchen completes Faust's educational journey in heaven. So much for Goethe's apotheosis of woman eternal.

Or is it not even that? Is there underneath all the metaphysical symbolism yet another message, a final myth? Let us once more recall what Faust stands for. He is a man who defies natural limits and restlessly strives for the absolute. He wants to experience the cumulative experience of mankind, in order to enrich and expand his own self. Or to use Faust's motto: "Zum höchsten Dasein immerfort zu streben" (4685). For a restless character like this, who longs for self-fulfillment, one life is far too short. Even Mephisto, viewing Faust's corpse, seems to feel that: "Vorbei! ein dummes Wort. / Warum vorbei? . . . Was ist daran zu lesen?" (11595f.). Indeed! Since only Faust's earthly path ends there, does his continued existence in heaven not suggest more than just redemption, does it not also imply immortality as a means of self-perfection? Lessing's eternal optimism, in the last sentence of his *Education of Mankind,* comes to mind again: "Und was habe ich denn zu versäumen? Ist nicht die ganze Ewigkeit mein?" Perhaps Faust's end is just another variation on the same theme contemplated by Kant, Schopenhauer, and many other contemporaries, too. Goethe, confronted with his own demise, gives Faust this chance. Faust's immortality is Goethe's final myth.

The Faust myth reached its most artistic and symbolic form in Goethe's *opus magnum.* Goethe's work on this myth is comparable only to what Hesiod and Homer did for Greek mythology. His classical form of the Faust myth has inspired many creative minds in literature, art, and music to work with it and transform it again. However, this new work on the Faust myth does not, and cannot, continue *ad infinitum.* As we know from Jolles and Blumenberg, a myth can also be brought to an end. For the Faust myth, that has certainly happened in this century. I think of Paul Valéry's *Mon Faust* and Thomas Mann's *Doktor Faustus,* of Hanns Eisler's *Faust* libretto and Volker Braun's *Hinze und Kunze.* When Günther Anders states categorically that Faust is dead, he implies that the Faust myth, certainly as a German myth, has outlived its usefulness as a symbol for Germany's highest and darkest period. And yet—what if there were still something to say?

Notes

1 Hans Schwerte, *Faust und das Faustische: Ein Kapitel deutscher Ideologie* (Stuttgart, 1962).

2 Thomas Mann, *Die Entstehung des Doktor Faustus* (Stockholm, 1949), 52f.

3 Ernst Bloch, *Erbschaft dieser Zeit* (Zürich, 1935); see especially the second part, "Ungleichzeitigkeit und Berauschung."

4 Karl Heinz Bohrer, ed., *Mythos und Moderne* (Frankfurt, 1983).

5 André Jolles, *Einfache Formen* (Tübingen, 1929). See especially the chapter on "Mythe," 91–125.

6 Hans Blumenberg, *Arbeit am Mythos* (Frankfurt, 1979), 134.

7 Franz Kafka, *Die Erzählungen* (Frankfurt, 1961), 303.

8 Hans Henning, "Das Faust-Buch von 1587: Seine Entstehung, seine Quellen, seine Wirkung," *Weimarer Beiträge* 6 (1960): 26–57.

9 Quoted from J. W. Smeed, *Faust in Literature* (Oxford, 1975), 18.

10 Erich Trunz, ed., *Goethes Faust*, 5th ed. (Hamburg, 1959), v. 1336.

11 Robert Petsch, *Lessings Faustdichtung* (Heidelberg, 1911), 51ff.

12 Ibid., 32–39 ("Texte"), 40–50 ("Die wichtigsten Zeugnisse").

13 Ibid., 37.

14 Ibid., 47.

15 Ibid., 50.

16 Gotthold Ephraim Lessing, *Gesammelte Werke*, ed. by Paul Rilla, 2d ed. (Berlin, 1968) 8:27.

17 Ibid., 614.

18 Ibid., 615.

19 Trunz, *Goethes Faust*, v. 7428f. (All references are to this edition and will be cited in parentheses.)

20 Zweiter Entwurf zu einer Ankündigung der "Helena," Dezember 1826; in Trunz, *Goethes Faust*, 438.

21 Valters Nollendorfs, *Der Streit um den Urfaust* (The Hague, 1967).

22 Schema zu "Faust" (1797–1799?), in *Goethes Faust*, 427.

23 Goethe to Karl Ernst Schubarth, 3 November 1820, in Trunz, *Goethes Faust*, 433.

24 Theodor W. Adorno, "Zur Schlußszene des Faust," in his *Noten zur Literatur II* (Frankfurt, 1961), 7–18.

25 Thomas Metscher, "Faust und die Ökonomie," in *Vom Faustus bis Karl Valentin* (Berlin, 1976 [*Das Argument*, AS 3]), 28–155.

26 Ernst Bloch, "Faust, Makrokosmos, Verweile doch, du bist so schön," in his *Das Prinzip Hoffnung* (Frankfurt, 1973), 1188–1194.

27 Heinz Schlaffer, "Fausts Ende," *Das Argument* 99 (1976): 772–779.

Faust's End:
On the Present Significance of Goethe's Text

THOMAS METSCHER

I will begin with a few opening remarks concerning my aim and method. "Faust," in the title of my essay, refers to Goethe's text. I am not talking about the present-day significance of the Faust theme or figure as such (interesting as this might be) but specifically about Goethe's *Faust.*

My concern is with a literary text, and most of what I have to say is in terms of textual interpretation. This in no sense implies, or openly suggests, a return to Formalism or New Criticism. The position from which I speak is a different one: it is that of a *materialist hermeneutics.* From this position, the literary text is at the center of critical attention (in that respect, there is a link with traditional views of close reading); the text, however, is not seen as a mere formal structure but as a specific, aesthetically organized, ideological form—a specific mode, shall I say, of world reflection, world exploration, and world interpretation undertaken from a particular social stance, inspired and motivated by a specific social interest.[1] In the perspective of materialist hermeneutics, the aesthetic form is regarded not as void of, but as charged with, history: in fact, as inherently historical. The central concern of this approach is to see history *in* the literary text and as a problem of textual interpretation.

Any kind of interpretation (and any act of understanding) presupposes or implies political, ideological, cultural, aesthetic predecisions; it is never undertaken "free of interest." The claim of traditional interpretation to be "impartial" and "nonideological" is not only self-deceptive, it is ideological in itself: it is based on very definite (and, in my opinion, highly problematical) views of literature, criticism, and the function of both. A materialist hermeneutics openly admits, and systematically explains, its implied predecisions; it does not conceal its interest and partiality. It is undertaken from a definite stance in the present, in the here and now of a given historical situation.

There is one other point which I would like to clarify before I begin—a clarification which seems necessary in order to avoid possible misunderstandings. It is one of my methodological premises that an aesthetic text, as a specific form of social consciousness, is *semantically irreducible.* This is to say that its total meaning cannot be reduced to an instance (or instances) outside the text, though its genesis is explicable in terms of history of society, social psychology, etc. The total meaning of Goethe's *Faust,* for example, is with certainty not identical with the views Goethe held otherwise (though the knowledge of these views assists in understanding the text). Each artistic text is a specific mode of ideological articulation, unique in that it is distinct from that of any other given text (though, of course, always related to other texts): it opens up a world view of its own, i.e., a particular view (implying acts of interpretation and evaluation) of that section of reality which is its mimetic object. "Interpretation," therefore, always implies the decoding of the specific and unique world view articulated in an artistic text, the decoding of what I term its *ideological profile.* Inevitably, interpretation is an act of appropriation: the appropriation of a text from a point of view in the present which, at the same time, has to take into account the text's historicity, its genesis in a concrete point in the past. It therefore has to encompass both: the text's *pastness* as well as its *presentness,* its "contemporaneity" (T. S. Eliot); its past significance as a historical-aesthetic document; and its present meaning as a living, contemporary cultural force, as the text received in the here and now of our historical situation.

The problem implicit in my title is, therefore, primarily concerned with the question of what *Goethe's text* means to us today. Its hermeneutic status *for us*—its possible topicality—can only be ascertained by a precise textual reading; a reading with the purpose of establishing its present-day significance; a reading, however, which has to take into account the possibility that, as a result, we might conclude this text is outdated and has little or nothing to say to us, that it is "of value" only as a document of past history and is significant, perhaps, merely as a paradigm of ideological formation within a repressive power structure, fulfilling the function of "containment" and integration.

The following remarks are concerned mainly with a particular section of Goethe's text—with Faust's end: the end of Faust as dramatic persona and protagonist (his death in part 2, act 5, scene "Großer Vorhof des Palasts") and the end of the text (the final scene of *Faust,* "Bergschluchten," i.e., the ending of the whole play).[2]

Faust's end in "Großer Vorhof des Palasts," and, in particular, his "final monologue" (11559–86) offer one of the most challenging problems of the entire text and have with good reason been at the center of a controversy in which I myself was in some way involved.[3] It is certainly one of those sections in the play on which the question of its present significance depends in a very decisive sense. The reason for this shall, I hope, become clear in the course of my investigation.

The death scene can hardly be understood adequately if looked at as an isolated unit. It is closely connected with the previous scene, "Mitternacht," where Faust has overcome the challenge of Sorge (read as a figure of consciousness): the temptation to see human life as permanent worry and mere "being towards death" (Heidegger), a temptation presenting a deep threat to the core and substance of Faust's "striving," attacking the very center of meaningful existence. Faust's rejection of this is founded on the awareness that magic and humanity are incompatible (11404–7), and the decision to act on this awareness (11423). Faust, *erblindet,* conceives of a new stage in his act of "colonization," the action of transforming "nature" into a habitable, human, man-made world: the *größtes Werk* (11509). He sees himself as the mastermind behind the project— the *logos* as *Tat* (to use the terminology of his own translation of the New Testament in part 1, 1224–37)—as *logos creator:* the intellect creating the "greatest work" by means of the *tausend Hände* of his workers' army, the *Knechte, Mann für Mann* (11499–510), the material producers, the "hands" and tools of the great conceiving mind. The *größtes Werk* is quite clearly the aim of Faust's colonization project. It is the construction of a new society, a "new world," the visionary outline of which is given in the great monologue in "Großer Vorhof des Palasts." The monologue at the end of "Mitternacht" (11499–510) and Faust's final monologue are directly related, they are linked to each other in a dramatic and semantic sense: the second responds to the first. The final monologue in fact *explains* what the *größtes Werk* is about; it elaborates, as we shall see, Faust's promise of the *allerschönster Preis* for the lemures workers.

Faust's work is to be brought about by two factors: intellectual and manual labor—*ein Geist* and *tausend Hände* (11510), the intellect of *one* man (note the italicized *ein* in Goethe's text)) and the hands of the many, *tausend* undoubtedly referring to the masses needed for the manual, material construction of this work. It depends—the text is unequivocal in this point—on the existence of what Marx comes to term a "frei disponibles Arbeiterheer," as it depends on the planning mind of the individual bourgeois subject—entrepreneur, engineer, politician, philosopher. The text explicitly states that a division of labor exists and that this division of labor is based on antagonistic social relations: the relationship of *Herr* (singular) and *Knechte* (plural). Both the division of labor and the antagonistic class relationship are in fact the social preconditions of Faust's *größtes Werk.* In addition, it is assumed as unquestionable that the *Herr* is undisputed master (11502), the *Knechte* functioning as mere instruments, as living labor power. They are part of the material means of production. Their being consists of a mere material function: to use *Werkzeug, Schaufel, Spaten* (the terms should be read as symbols referring to the whole complex of "means of production").

A direct link clearly exists between Faust's monologue at the end of "Mitternacht" and the beginning of "Großer Vorhof." One may argue that Faust's monologue should be more aptly rephrased "pseudo-monologue." It has in fact an addressee, and it contains a command: "Vom Lager auf, ihr Knechte! Mann für Mann!" (11503). The addressee of Faust's imperative order is his workers' army, though at the same time his speech is addressed to Mephistopheles, the *Aufseher* (stage directions between 11510–11), in which role he appears immediately afterwards, at the beginning of "Großer Vorhof"; he is the foreman who has the function of organizing and disciplining the anonymous working masses, forming them into a manageable living labor power, living tools.

Let us look at the text closely. The stage directions play a considerable part in the articulation of its meaning: *Großer Vorhof des Palasts. / Fackeln. / Mephistopheles als Aufseher voran.* The term *Fackeln* indicates that the time is still *midnight* (cf. also the chorus of the lemures in 11593–94), midnight being a symbol of high complexity, denoting the end of one time sequence and the beginning of, one might even say, the break toward, another; it incorporates end, climax, and break of *time* as *history*. On the level of the dramatic process, the unity of time in the relationship of the two scenes is thus established, in addition to unity of action and place (while "Mitternacht" plays *inside* Faust's "Palast," "Großer Vorhof" takes place immediately before it). One can therefore speak of the unity of the dramatic structure of these two scenes.

Mephistopheles als Aufseher voran: he obviously obeys (or, at least, appears to obey) Faust's order given in the preceding speech. Faust's "Vom Lager auf, ihr Knechte!" is echoed by his "Herbei, herbei! Herein, herein!" (11511) addressed to the lemures who in their turn reply *im Chor* (i.e., as a group, mass, multitude—as the voice belonging to the *tausend Hände*): "Wir treten dir sogleich zur Hand" (11515).

The suggestion to see the lemures as the *Knechte* to whom the blind Faust addresses his speech is anything but farfetched.[4] It is clearly borne out by the movement of the text. On the immediate textual level at least, the lemures are with certainty Faust's work force, his hands, his proletarian workers' army—though probably quite different in shape from what he imagined them to be. The lemures are, as Gerhard Scholz has termed them, Faust's "heidnisch-griechische Dammbauproleten: die Erben der Leiber von Generationen bislang vergeblich kämpfender Proletariate . . . , über die ganze Erde verteilte Arbeitssklaven."[5] They are in fact close to Marx's description of the alienated laborer in *Ökonomisch-Philosophische Manuskripte*.[6] In Mephisto's opening speech, they are characterized with ironic accuracy as *schlotternd, aus Bändern, Sehnen und Gebein geflickt, Halbnaturen:* only half-developed (or reduced by half), without identity as social beings. They are without memory, not even knowing why they have been called up (11521f.). All they seem to remember is a vague promise of a wide land that is to be their own in an indefinite future (11516–18). They are merely *zur Hand* (11515), at hand as workers, and what they know is that they have been called up to do their work, to act as workers: "Gespitzte Pfähle, die sind da, / Die Kette lang zum Messen" (11519f.), *Pfähle* and *Kette* being their instruments of work, rudimentary means of production. *Die Kette* might even imply that they are in chains, and that the chains they are in serve as an instrument of measurement at the same time. But they have vaguely heard of a "wide land" promised them—the *halb vernommen* of verse 11516 suggesting the imprecise, indefinite, only vaguely understood (or inadequately communicated) character of this promise. The half-heard promise is apparently identical with *der allerschönste Preis* which Faust had offered his workers in the final speech of the previous scene. As it appears, the speech of the lemures should as a whole be read as response to Faust's speech: they explicitly refer to a *Ruf* they have received, which in fact "happened" to them (11521) though they have forgotten the reason why—obviously Faust's "Vom Lager auf, ihr Knechte!"

The lemures are, with certainty, Faust's workers on the immediate level of the theatrical-textual action. On a second level, however, they are grave-digging specters and grotesque dancers, dancing a dance of death.[7] (The coexistence of such levels of heterogenous meaning within one set of metaphors or theatrical personae constitutes the high complexity of Goethe's symbolism.)[8] What in fact happens is a transformation of the lemures figures representing the alienated *Dammbauproletariat* (their direct or "primary" meaning) into the grotesquely dancing specters digging Faust's grave (their "secondary" meaning). This transformation occurs *on stage,* as it were, at the moment when Mephistopheles ironically informs them that "kein künstlerisch Bemühn" (no special working skill) is needed in the particular work they have to perform, merely the simple art of digging a grave for which the "natural" size of their own bodies will do (11523–30).

When the blind Faust enters *(aus dem Palast tretend, tastet an den Türpfosten)* the lemures have in fact undergone this transformation. Faust therefore appears to be grotesquely deceived—and Mephistopheles rightly triumphant—when he takes, indeed "interprets," the sound of their spades as *das Geklirr der Spaten* of *die Menge, die mir frönet, / Die Erde mit sich selbst versöhnet* (11539–42), i.e., the work of his obedient, enslaved proletariat engaged on *das größte Werk* of reconciling the earth with itself, the work of *cultural formation,* of constructing the new world of *tätig-freies Wohnen* (11564). In this new world (and this is built up as the content of the promised utopia) those who are now enslaved will be free, and the order of subordination and compulsion will be replaced by an order of real freedom, communal life, and equality.

Faust, it appears, is grotesquely deceived when he mistakes the sound of the spades digging his grave for that of the workers engaged in working on his utopian project. But he is deceived only in what might be termed the level of the immediacy of the theatrical-textual situation. The text contains a second dimension (as it contains a plurality of semantic dimensions throughout).

The proletarian workers' army—in textual and in real historical terms—is certainly more than a mere figment of Faust's imagination. It exists in social reality, just as it exists as implicit persona in the text throughout the fifth act, and Faust clearly does not turn to a figure of illusion when he orders his foreman Mephistopheles to increase his work force by fair means or foul (11552–54).

The key to the problem of why, in this point first of all, there has been a vast difference of opinion in *Faust* criticism on what the scene means, is to be found in the particular form of the text itself. Goethe's text is no longer a closed semantic unit—certainly not in the traditional sense of an "organic" text. The text does not contain a closed totality. It is, on the contrary, the conscious articulation of *open, unsolved problems.* It is constructed with the reader/spectator (the recipient) as implicit persona in mind. The text "organizes" a specific set of contradictory, ambivalent, and ironic meanings, and the function of this organization is to confront the reader/spectator with these problems in a manner that challenges the recipient, breaks up self-satisfied and prejudicial attitudes, and organizes a problematizing, productive response—a response that directs the recipient toward the solution of the problems with which he/she has been confronted.

Let us now, with this strategy of Goethe's text in mind, turn to the final monologue. In this monologue, Faust explains the aim and purpose of all his activity and striving; he gives the essence of what he considers to be his *größtes Werk.* What the text contains, in precision and complexity of symbolic language—not, of course, in terms of a direct programmatic speech—is in no sense the "vage und fieberhafte Vision eines Sterbenden,"[9] nor is it an imperialist vision of world domination, a "Gigantomachie des Ich."[10]

The final monologue is textually prepared. Long before it (at the beginning of act 4), Faust has articulated what his aims are and what his work is about—in general though, conceptually, no uncertain terms: the control of "chaotic" elemental forces with the purpose of winning "new land" (10198–233). The term *paradiesisch Land* for this newly won world is first used in Philemon's speech in "Offene Gegend" (11083–106), a speech which contains much of the metaphorical material of the final monologue (1105f., 11103–6). Faust's idea of opening up spaces for the many millions to dwell *tätig-frei* (11563f.)—the very core and conceptual substance of his utopian project—is prefigured in the word of *der Völker breiter Wohngewinn* as *des Menschengeistes Meisterstück* (11248–50) in Faust's dialogue with Mephisto in "Palast," preceding, and leading up to, the Philemon and Baucis tragedy. There is even an indication—ironically, in Mephisto's speech—that the "crown" of Faust's *erhaben Glück* is more than mere domination: namely, it is *reconciliation* (11222). This idea is echoed in one of the central metaphors of the death scene, that of reconciling the earth with itself (11541), which is a poetic reformulation of a classical idea of humanist thinking taken up by Marx in his concept of a communist society.[11]

Faust's final monologue is textually prepared in that it is related to the textual-theatrical context by a network of themes, motifs, and images; it does not occur as a lightning flash in the darkness. It is in fact of a structure very similar to that of Faust's final speech in the previous scene, for, in a sense, it is a pseudomonologue. It has an implicit addressee. It can be seen as an address to those who work for Faust, an explanation of what their work is for, an elaboration of what the land of promise is like—the land of which the lemures workers have vaguely heard. First of all, however, Faust's "monologue" is an address to the reader or audience (the implicit instance of the recipient) and operates on the level of *implicit recipient orientation*. It is part of Goethe's strategy of deconstructing the "closed" text and its semantic limitations.

The suggested reading sees the text as a highly complex structure that is no longer a "closed whole" though it is (as any work of art, ancient or modern, that deserves this name) a *functional totality,* as all parts functionally cohere and fulfill a specific, artistically "necessary" aesthetic-semantic purpose. The classicist idea of formal harmony and organic totality of the art work, however, is left behind in the far historic distance. Goethe's text is *highly discursive;* it is a synthesis of mimesis and reflection and comes in some essential way close to Friedrich Schlegel's program of *progressive Universalpoesie* as a synthesis of all genres of poetry, of poetry and rhetoric, of art and life, but above all of *Kunst und Wissenschaft,* art and science, poetry and philosophy.[12]

Goethe's *Faust* continuously breaks up closed textual units and works on the level of aesthetic complexity, of a multiplicity of meaning, of ironic distancing and alienation, with the explicit purpose of organizing a highly complex literary-theatrical effect, of arranging the response of a rhythmic interchange of emotional identification and reflective reasoning, a total response in the sense of a truly "dialectical theater." It is this textual strategy which establishes—on the aesthetic-formal level—

the high *modernity* of Goethe's text, making it our contemporary in terms of a modern aesthetics.

The *present significance* of *Faust* is, however, not merely a question of formal procedure, aesthetic-semantic organization, and textual strategy. The high topicality which I claim for Goethe's text is primarily a *question of content.* Goethe's textual strategy has to be seen in the sense of the dialectics of content and form: as aesthetic-formal articulation of a specific social and historical problem, as an aesthetic formation of reality.

At the center of *Faust* lies a problem of immense and immediate historical importance, a problem the significance of which has *increased* rather than *decreased* since the production of Goethe's text; a problem which in fact has never before possessed the same existential urgency as today. It is the question of, and quest for, the future of the human race in a historical situation in which we are faced with a fundamental alternative: the grim reality of a very particular *either–or.* For *either* we manage to build a society of real freedom, peace, and meaningful living, a world of "tätig-freies Wohnen" for all generations and races of humankind, even though all the odds appear to be against this—*or* we relapse into a suicidal reign of barbarism and terror and turn this globe into an uninhabitable world, with the eventual annihilation of all human life as the most likely historical result: the triumph of "nothingness" will be the outcome of human history, the triumph of the Mephistophelian "Vorbei und reines Nicht, vollkommnes Einerlei" (11597). This comment might still be the final "verdict" on the course of history, though nobody will be there to articulate it.

Placed within its highly complex, dialectical poetic-theatrical context, Faust's final monologue (I retain the term for the sake of clarity) can neither be read as the unproblematical visionary dream of a better world—the blueprint of an unquestioned utopia—nor as deceiving or self-deceiving ideology and empty rhetoric.[13] Viewing it in the context of a history of consciousness, one can easily establish a link between Faust's vision and what Marx termed the heroic illusions of the bourgeoisie—the firm belief, proclaimed in a great number of literary, artistic, and philosophical articulations, that the "work of capital," the progress and ultimate triumph of the bourgeois class, has the happiness of all humans as its ultimate objective; the conviction that the greatest happiness of the greatest number is the hidden goal and implicit aim of bourgeois emancipation and world domination—what I term the teleology of bourgeois consciousness.

Examined closely, however, Faust's vision goes beyond the bourgeois ideology and illusion of happiness for all—it definitely transcends the teleology of bourgeois consciousness. In Faust's anticipation, first of all, the future is in no way seen as a static utopia of fulfillment; it is anything but the myth of a bourgeois Land of Cockaigne. Indeed it is a world of a continuous life-and-death struggle, of a life that is *tätig-frei* (free through everyday activity and strife), a life of *liberated human productivity;* of an activity on a qualitatively higher level of cultural and social accomplishment than that achieved in all hitherto existing societies. It is a world, to use Goethe's own symbolic key term, free of *Magie* (the central symbol of false, prehuman relations of subject and object, and subject and subject in Goethe's text): i.e., free of all those relations between man and nature, as well as between humans, which are based on force, compulsion, exploitation, and repression of the other. The life envisaged in the final monologue is a very real, concrete praxis of freely associated men and women, an active life in which *Gemeindrang* has replaced magic as the primary means of controlling the destructive elemental natural forces,[14] a control that is the precondition of any form of human civilization, a precondition, in fact, of the survival of the human species.

As Faust's monologue has been analyzed competently and in great detail in a number of recent commentaries,[15] I restrict myself, by way of a summary, to those points which I consider to be the most essential for the present purpose:

(1) The *tätig-freies Wohnen* of liberated mankind is a dynamic process: the continuous (one might say, eternal) struggle of all generations of mankind with elemental natural forces, a struggle that forms the *material basis* of all human existence, of all societal and cultural life.

(2) Mankind is thus always *umrungen von Gefahr:* the elemental forces can be controlled, but they can never be fully overcome. They exist as a perennial potential of disruption and destruction (the image of the *draußen rasende Flut*). Their release (the image of the breach of the dike), possible at any given moment in history, threatens the very existence of human civilization, the life and survival of the species. It is for this reason that *freedom* (the concrete cultural and social content of the new, advanced form of living) as well as *life* (the immediate material existence) have to be *daily won,* literally "conquered."

(3) The elemental forces, upon the control of which all civilization depends, are not just forces of destruction or a power of external hostility. They are more than mere chaos (cf. above all 10198–233). They constitute a natural and necessary basis of human civilization. *Das herrische Meer vom Ufer auszuschließen* (10229) implies that the one would not exist without the other. Faust's new world is possible only on the basis of those "elements" the control of which is the material precondition of its existence. *Das Ufer ist dem Meer versöhnt* (11222) even suggests a balance or "reconciliation" of the two. Goethe's poetic idea, as expressed here, is

with certainty a deep and lasting philosophical contribution to a *dialectics of nature.*

(4) The relationship of man and nature in Faust's vision exists on two levels: as control of potentially dangerous elemental forces and in the form of a harmonious relation between these two. *Inside* the world of free and active life, there exists a harmony of nature and man: the *Gefilde* is *grün* and *fruchtbar; Mensch und Herde* and *behaglich auf der neusten Erde.* The conceptual core of this vision is that of a dynamic *idyll,* in some ways close to Schiller's conception of the term,[16] though the nearest affinity is to Engels's notion of freedom as "Existenz in Harmonie mit den erkannten Naturgesetzen."[17]

(5) The *sea/flood* symbolism as the key metaphor representing the elemental forces which have to be controlled as a precondition of freedom and life (this, at least, is a possible connotation of Goethe's symbolism) is not restricted to external natural forces, but it includes forces inside the human psyche: elemental or "basic" forces within humans which present a potential danger of disruption on an individual as well as social level.

(6) The means of controlling these (external and internal) elemental forces are the unified, collective efforts of real men, women, and children—all generations of mankind, the *free people:* the *Gemeindrang* of *viele Millionen, kühn-emsige Völkerschaft, Kindheit, Mann und Greis, freies Volk.*

(7) It is possible, at least in the sense of an interpretative hypothesis, to see a connection between the *kühn-emsige Völkerschaft* in Faust's utopia and the exploited lemures workers of the preceding textual setting: that is, to recognize the many millions living *tätig-frei* as the descendants of Faust's exploited and dehumanized workers' army, as the children, in fact, of the "Generationen bislang vergeblich kämpfender Proletariate."

(8) Freedom is not an abstract ideal but a matter of everyday activity and social fulfillment, a communal effort of the common people.

(9) In his anticipation, Faust wishes to participate in the collective life of the free people: the *I* is transformed to the *we.* The individual *(ein Geist)* sees himself as one of those whom he had previously only perceived as an anonymous mass of *tausend Hände;* he envisages himself as standing *auf freiem Grund mit freiem Volk* (11580), i.e., as one of the many, equal among equals. It is at this moment that Faust anticipates fulfillment and utters the fatal words of the bet, "Verweile doch, du bist so schön."

(10) Though Faust wishes to merge with the common people at the high moment of anticipated fulfillment, he regards the making of this new world as *his work,* he in fact sees himself immortalized in this his *größtes Werk—des Menschengeistes Meisterstück.* Both, the achievement of the

utopia of a free people on a free earth and his immortalization in it and by it, make up the *highest moment* which Faust *enjoys now.*

It is particularly this latter point—the fact that Faust regards the making of utopia as his own work—which has been the stumbling block of some recent criticism. Cases and Schlaffer take it as proof of the inherent bourgeois individualism, or even the totalitarianism, of Faust's vision (for Schlaffer, the monologue is Faust's herostratic conception of himself as imperial maker and master),[18] contaminating anything Faust has to say. Both ignore the fact that his view of himself as the maker of the intellectually anticipated brave new world is fully consistent with the inner semantic development of the text and the implicit social psychology of the Faust figure (Faust as *bourgeois* and *citoyen*). Moreover, in Faust's view, the new world, if once achieved, will have no individual self at its center but the collective self of *all.* The world thus anticipated clearly transcends that of the bourgeois subject. Faust's position makes sense also in the context of a social history of modern consciousness. The final monologue, like all of Faust's utterances, is an articulation of bourgeois self-consciousness, with all its illusions and self-deceptions—bourgeois consciousness, however, at the point, or in the process, of transcending itself. Faust's monologue is an act of *Grenzüberschreitung* (Ernst Bloch): the crossing of a historic frontier, that between capitalism and socialism. The direction taken is the new social thinking and moral awareness of which Marx and Engels are the outstanding representatives in the 19th century. Though it would be nonsense, of course, to classify the world view expressed in Faust's monologue as "socialist"—socialism, to begin with, is a political ideology and Faust's vision is in no direct sense political—it corresponds historically, in its cultural essence and implicit philosophy, to utopian socialism as an ideological and philosophical historical position.[19]

The conditional and optative sense in which the "highest moment" is experienced implies, unambiguously, that the envisaged fulfillment is one of anticipation: the anticipation of a possible future world. All that is possible in the *now,* the present moment—*jetzt*—is a *Vorgefühl:* the *Vorgefühl von solchem hohen Glück* (11585). It alone can be consumed in the present. In this essential sense, Faust does *not* deceive himself. Much as he is mistaken about the true nature of those who are working for him, and about the character of the work they are engaged in, he is not mistaken in the character of his vision and of his present happiness as being a kind of anticipation only. Thus the metaphor of his blindness contains the inherent paradox that the latter signifies a state of ignorance and knowledge at the same time—of *ignorantia* and *gnosis.* Faust is blind in one respect and truly seeing in the other.

This point is totally missed by Mephistopheles (as it is missed,

ironically, by Cases and Schlaffer). For him, Faust's *kairos,* the happy
moment of anticipation, is merely "der letzte, schlechte, leere Augen-
blick" (11589): *leer,* because it has no reality in the present; *der letzte,*
because it is the moment of death. For Mephistopheles, it is in fact the
worst possible moment. Mephisto's viewpoint is that of the immediate
present, without future and past. He is the positivist *par excellence,* we
may say. His stance is the here and now of the immediately given. From
this point of view, Faust is the grotesquely tragic victim of his own self-
deception; his striving, a mere illusion subjected to time—*die Zeit wird
Herr* (11592). Mephistopheles' résumé of Faust's life is an articulation of
the nothingness of existence, of the total meaninglessness of human life
and history vis-à-vis the inevitable physical end. Being, for him, is a mere
"Sein zum Tode" (Heidegger). He articulates, as the result of the dramatic action, what Sorge had implied in her attack on the center of Faust's
self-confidence. In terms of a history of consciousness, Mephisto's view
signifies a position of nihilism.[20] This nihilism is explained in the figure
of the circularity of existence—in the metaphor of the circle.

Of decisive importance for an adequate interpretation of what is
going on in the text is Mephisto's inability to understand what Faust is
saying. He completely fails to grasp the meaning of Faust's words, a
disjunction in the semantic relationship between the key figures of the
text, which essentially contributes to its open, ironic structure. The text,
we discover, establishes an ensemble of contradictions, ironies, even
apparent paradoxes which are interrelated, but are not solved on the level
of textual articulation—their solution is transferred to the implicit instance of the recipient who is directed to recognize the problems posed as
his/her own, and to participate in their solution.

The most fundamental level within this set of ironies and contradictions is the juxtaposition of the positive vision of Faust's monologue
and the factual negativity of the real situation (Faust's death and the
presence of the lemures) which forms the basis of—and, to a degree,
justifies—Mephisto's point of view. *Both sides,* Faust *and* Mephistopheles, *are posited as opposites within an unsolved contradiction.*
Through this juxtaposition, a problem of highest order is presented: the
quest for meaning in individual life and in history; the question, in fact,
of the intrinsic value of human activity without theological sanctioning
and religious hope or justification.

It is clear beyond doubt, in my view, that the positive content of
Faust's vision, though it might be relativized, is in no sense discredited in
its essence by Mephistopheles' insistence on the here and now (which
forms the basis of his theoretical nihilism)—Mephisto, as has been
pointed out, is not even able to understand what Faust means. On the
other hand, however, and in view of the realities of the given, dramat-

ically presented, situation; in view of what has been happening in acts 4
and 5; in view of Faust's whole "story" (which represents a *history* ruled
by force and compulsion, "Blut und Feuer");[21] in view, not least, of the
empirical reality of those whom he calls up to construct his utopia
materially—in view of all this, it is equally certain that the present is a
situation of negation, and that Mephistopheles has some good points in
favor of his opinion. We are indeed faced with a problem of far-reaching
dimensions. The visionary meaning is juxtaposed with the "nothingness"
of the immediately given: a society governed by violence in which
progress is possible only at an enormous expense of suffering and depra-
vation. In this sense, but in this sense alone, the Mephistophelian viewpoint of the meaninglessness of Faust's end is to a certain degree justified.

As I have argued elsewhere, the ideas of history and progress in *Faust*
transcend by far the teleological views of classical bourgeois ideology as
incorporated, for instance, in the Hegelian notion of history as "Fort-
schritt im Bewußtsein der Freiheit."[22] Faust's thirst for world appropriation, in many sections of the text, resembles what Marx termed the
"Vampirdurst des Kapitals nach lebendigem Arbeitsblut."[23] It plays on a
world-historical scene of human sacrifice. The idea of progress in
Goethe's *Faust* is indeed a dialectical one. Its physiognomy is fright-
eningly similar to Marx's metaphor of the "scheußlicher heidnischer
Götze, der den Nektar nur aus den Schädeln Erschlagener trinken
wollte."[24]

The Mephistophelian stance, as I have suggested, is that of the
immediacy of the present, his world view is that of nihilism as a metaphysics of the given. The inherent falseness of Faust's point of view lies in
that side of it which is illusion and dream, in its ignorance of the facticity
of the given: Faust's inability, if you like, to recognize the requirements of
the present. Faust's limitations, in short, are those of utopian consciousness. In opposition to this consciousness, there stands the claim to
immediate desire and interest, the justified demand that human life
should be lived in the present: the demand for immediate fulfillment. The
element of truth in Faust's point of view lies in the fact that his vision
contains more than a mere promise or empty dream: it incorporates a
deep and complex idea of human life, of culture, social progress, and
historical possibility. It articulates, written less than twenty years before
the *Communist Manifesto,* what at this particular moment in history
began to become recognizable as a concrete historical possibility. The
truth of Faust's vision, therefore, is not that of the idea alone, but resides
in the fact that his new world is actually more than a mere utopia—that it
presents a material possibility. It indicates a possible direction human
history might take—a possibility that might be achieved or might be
missed. It articulates one of the alternatives at the crossroads of present-

day history. In this sense, it can be said to formulate the "non-teleological telos" of human development. The alternative to Faust's vision is always present. In Goethe's text, it is represented by Mephistopheles—"Vorbei und reines Nicht, vollkommnes Einerlei!"

The death scene cannot be understood in isolation. It is part of a wide textual strategy which extends over the whole of part 2 and, in a wider sense, over the whole of the dramatic process, including part 1. The death scene, therefore, must be seen in relationship to what follows in the remaining section of the play, as it must be read as a result of what has gone on before: i.e., as the outcome of a highly complex theatrical process.

The essential caesura in Faust's development, indeed the turning point of the inner action of *Faust II,* occurs in the opening scene of act 4, the "Versuchungsdebatte" between Faust and Mephistopheles.[25] The contrast between the dream reality of the third act and this opening of act 4 could not be sharper, although Faust's decision to act, his new practical orientation, is in fact the result of the aesthetics of the Helena act. "Schönheit," according to Wolfgang Heise, is seen as giving birth to "Tätigkeit und Tat," in accordance with the emancipatory aesthetic idea of the classical period.[26]

Faust's decision to act coincides with his rejection of the "old world" of traditional society, both the courtly-aristocratic world and that of the petit bourgeois small town. He explicitly rejects Mephistopheles' offers which center on the idea of unproductive, parasitic, merely consumptive enjoyment. The split between the two protagonists of the play becomes fully apparent for the first time. Mephistopheles here is unable even to guess what Faust means—an anticipation of the communicative gap between them which plays such an essential role in the death scene. When Faust rejects Mephisto's offer to live "von Hunderttausenden verehrt" in the bourgeois town, or to enjoy, in an aristocratic environment, the pleasures of the senses with "die Schönen im Plural," Mephistopheles can, as an alternative, only think of fantasy and longing, the desire for the romantically sublime (10177–80). All this, by the way, contains a high element of comedy; it is one of Goethe's *sehr ernste Scherze.* Even when Faust gives him the clue and quite explicitly declares, "Mit nichten! dieser Erdenkreis / Gewährt noch Raum zu großen Taten" (10181), Mephistopheles is only able to understand the statement in terms of a traditional (here, the knightly-aristocratic) code of *Ruhm* (10185), to which Faust replies, "Herrschaft gewinn' ich, Eigentum! / Die Tat ist alles, nichts der Ruhm" (10187f.), only to be again misunderstood by Mephistopheles. At the end, Faust gives up and rightly concludes: "Was weißt du, was der Mensch begehrt? / Dein widrig Wesen, bitter, scharf, /

Was weiß es, was der Mensch bedarf?" (10192–95). This comment remains true up to the very end. For whatever Faust's "false consciousness," whatever the character of his illusions, in his final vision he articulates "was der Mensch begehrt" and "was der Mensch bedarf," and this is what Mephistopheles (like all metaphysics of the immediately given) is unable to understand.

Herrschaft, Eigentum, Tat: it is the new world of capitalist civilization—progress through the action of the individual self, the continuously revolutionary process of bourgeois development—which is introduced at this moment into the dramatic action.[27] Faust enters the modern world, we may say—that world which is still ours.

Faust, at the end of the conversation with Mephistopheles, explains in considerable detail what his plans and intentions are—the primary addressee of this explanation, however, can no longer be Mephistopheles, who has proved that he is unable to understand what Faust means. It is, rather, the implicit recipient. (In a sense, this speech possesses the same explanatory character as the final monologue, to which it is dramatically and semantically related.) Faust says: "Mein Auge war aufs hohe Meer gezogen. / . . . / Da faßt' ich schnell im Geiste Plan auf Plan: / Erlange dir das köstliche Genießen, / Das herrische Meer vom Ufer auszuschließen . . ." (10198–233). *Genießen* here lies in the rational control and domination of elemental natural forces—*rational*, because this control is based on observation and on the recognition of natural laws.

It is at this point of the play, and in connection with the theme of practical activity, that the central sea metaphor is introduced (in the "Klassische Walpurgisnacht," it had an entirely different meaning)[28] as key metaphor in the context of Faust's "colonizing" activities, "colonizing" being another multidimensional symbol. The sea serves as an "object" in the process of the transformation of nature and the formation of the human world—what I term *process of cultural formation*—an object, however, which is an agent of its own (the sea is *active*) and which follows a definite pattern of movement that can be studied and formulated in terms of "natural laws." The sea represents a "zwecklose Kraft unbändiger Elemente" (10219) which Faust plans to utilize for a specific human purpose, that of *winning new land* (signifying the central act of cultural formation).

It represents elemental natural forces[29] which can be used productively for a human purpose, though at the same time containing a perennial potential for disruption, disorganization, and destruction. The control of these forces becomes a precondition of human survival—a precondition, in fact, of human existence on all levels, that of material reproduction and that of productive social fulfillment: of *Leben* and *Freiheit*. Evidently, the central ideas and key concepts of the final vision are present, at least implicitly, at the beginning of the particular part of the theatrical action which leads directly up to the final scenes.

Faust, however, has not yet reached the level of consciousness at which he is able to conceive of, and articulate, the utopian vision of the free and active life of the free people as the ultimate aim of his striving and the purpose of his work. This implies a further development of action and reflection. By the beginning of act 4, he can only conceive of his activity in terms of *Herrschaft* and *Eigentum, Kämpfen* and *Besiegen*, i.e., in terms of property and domination. Heise is right, though, in stressing that, at this moment, Faust's insistence on *Tat*—activity, sensuous praxis—marks a tremendous step forward, both historically and in the play.[30] Faust's alternative to the mere consumptive enjoyment of the "sardanapalische Daseinsweise"—as well as to the theoretical nihilism of Mephistopheles—is "Sinngebung geschichtlichen Handelns aus menschlicher Produktivität." Das Sinngebende ist menschliches Schöpfertum."[31] Faust's way, however—or, more precisely speaking, the historical course which he signifies as a poetic figure—is "Verwirklichung produktiven Tuns unter den Bedingungen von Eigentum und Herrschaft."[32] This is the real basis underlying the contradictions and ironies at the end of the play. In this sense, one may say that the contradictions determining Faust's end are inherent in the whole dramatic process, and explicitly so in acts 4 and 5. They certainly inhere in those sections of the text which symbolically portray the development of the modern social formation—capitalism as a historical social form rising out of the dying, decaying world of feudalism.

The dialectics of Faust's end, one might conclude, are implicit in the whole dramatic action. Faust's progress which is positive insofar as it is a process of the development of the human potential, of productivity, of the formation of subjective and objective culture, is based on compulsion and force (*Gewalt* being a key word in the two final acts). Faust's progress is achieved at the price of *Menschenopfer* (11127–30). The brutal dialectics of this progress is accompanied by the increasing awareness—an awareness on the part of Faust himself—that the historical realization of full human potential, both of the individual and of the species, is possible only in a world without magic (11404), magic signifying, at its core, a prehumane form of control of objectivity (of natural and social relations) by force, compulsion, and repression of the other. Full human development is possible only in a world without Mephistopheles, the representative of the magic control of the world.

It is an awareness anticipated by Faust himself in "Wald und Höhle" of part 1, fully realized and acted on with bitter consequences by Gretchen at the end of the "Kerker" scene. There, she rejects rescue and escape with the assistance of Mephistopheles (4601–12). In the context of part 2, this awareness reaches its first climax in "Mitternacht," when Faust reflects, shortly before his confrontation with Sorge: "Noch hab' ich mich ins Freie nicht gekämpft. / Könnt' ich Magie von meinem Pfad entfernen, / Die Zaubersprüche ganz und gar verlernen, / Stünd' ich, Natur, vor dir ein Mann allein, / Da wär's der Mühe wert, ein Mensch zu sein" (11403–7)—an echo, incidentally, of Mozart's *Zauberflöte. Das Freie* is related here to a world free of magic, beyond a merely repressive relationship in natural and social conditions. In addition, it alludes to "open spaces" of future development, symbolized by the open spaces beyond the *Bergschluchten*. It is also echoed in the *tätig-freies Wohnen* of the many millions in Faust's final monologue, where the collective subject does indeed stand *alone* vis-à-vis nature (that is, without Mephistopheles), *Gemeindrang* having replaced magic as force of control, and is for this reason *free—freies Volk auf freiem Grund.* The decisive transformation taking place between Faust's monologue at the beginning of "Mitternacht" and the final monologue in "Großer Vorhof" is that from the solipsistic (socio-historically speaking, bourgeois) *ein Mann* to the ensemble of collective mankind: *Kindheit, Mann und Greis, kühn-emsige Völkerschaft, Gewimmel.*

The final scenes of *Faust II* articulate the poetic as well as philosophical sum of the whole theatrical process in both parts of the play. What remains to be done, in our attempt at reconstructing, in terms of a materialist hermeneutics, the complex meaning of the final section of the text, is to look at the "Epilogszene,"[33] "Bergschluchten."

This operatic-symphonic finale is one of the major riddles of the text. It presents an obstacle to any materialist reading. For this reason, I presume, it has been mostly ignored, or only dealt with casually, by Marxist critics. In the following, I am therefore entering untrodden ground in more than one way.

Let us begin with one of the few points of certainty. There can be little doubt that the key word of the final scene is *love,* the place of action being, as Chor and Echo inform us, a *geweihter Ort,* a *heiliger Liebeshort* (11852f.). The term *love* indicates, among other things, that in the world here evoked domination by force has been replaced by the rule of love—reconciliation. It is a world, therefore, beyond magic and Mephistopheles, *die Erde, mit sich selbst versöhnt* (to use the text's own wording). *Waldung, Felsen, Wurzeln, Stamm, Woge, Höhle, Löwen* all are active participants in the process of reconciliation. They are no longer mere objects (cf. 11844–53). Even the lions have become *stumm-freundlich,* silent and kind, honoring the *geweihter Ort*—the utopian *topos* of the reality of love. In Pater Ecstaticus, the core of love is revealed as the essence within all existence: *ewiger Liebe Kern.*

Though the terminology of the text is primarily of Christian origin—

particularly of the Catholic, medieval-baroque tradition—its content can hardly be equated with any form of established religious metaphysics. One should rather call it an articulation of a new, highly individual form of "humanistic metaphysics," a very personal Goethean type of a *Third Testament* drawing, conceptually and metaphorically, on traditional Christian-Catholic material.[34] To read it merely as "skeptisch-ironischer Abgesang"[35] underestimates the philosophical weight of the concluding scene.

The love articulated in the epilogue clearly retains the Christian *agape* even though it is radically transformed by this reformulation. *Agape* is transfigured—"changed utterly"—by its symbiosis with the pagan *eros:* the eros celebrated in the sea festival of the "Klassische Walpurgisnacht," "So herrsche denn Eros, der alles begonnen!" (8479).[36] The rule of love in the epilogue, one might say, is the envisaged rule of *eros* transformed by Christian *agape*—and, in this sense, *humanized.* A clear echo of the asserted rule of love can be found in the lines, "So ist es die allmächtige Liebe, / Die alles bildet, alles hegt" (11872f.): Love here functions as *formative cultural power:* it is *bildend* (i.e., forming, creating; love as *forma,* inherent form) and *hegend* (which includes the senses of nursing, protecting and preserving, fostering and tending)—it embodies a manifold of meaning which goes back to the idea of *eros creator* as celebrated in the "Klassische Walpurgisnacht."

To return to *eros:* the *heilige Liebeslust* of Doctor Marianus is certainly not only of mystical origin, but again expresses a union of the sacred and the erotic; and the ecstatic language of Pater Ecstaticus is mystical as well as sexually orgastic in its connotation (11854–61). Love in the epilogue is, as textually prepared in the "Klassische Walpurgis-nacht," *eros/agape* transformed into *prime mover* of all being, a basic ontological force, source of all productivity, having replaced the Aristotelean-scholastic *first principle,* the *nous theos* of Greek metaphysics as well as the personal God of the Christians and the Jews. The traditional metaphysical principles are dethroned and placed *inside nature,* in the sense of primary creative forces—a transformation and rearticulation inspired by Spinoza's idea of *natura naturans,* eternally creating nature, incorporated in the figure of the Erdgeist in part 1 of Goethe's play.

In *Faust,* in the course of its transformation of meanings which occurs in the process of its poetic-theatrical action, the "natural" *eros* itself undergoes a series of transformations. It becomes *agape,* and both inhere in the highest form of love as celebrated at the very end: *human love* embodied in the figure of Gretchen, metaphorized in the *Himmels-königin, höchste Herrscherin der Welt, Jungfrau, Mutter, Königin* (11994–12011), and conceptualized in *das Ewig-Weibliche* (12110). This love is *Herrscherin der Welt* in the *Himmel* extending above and beyond

the *Bergschluchten.* Though it appears to be "just" a metaphysical principle, it finds its incorporation, indeed the place of its concrete transfiguration, in the personal human love of Gretchen. It is Gretchen's love in
the name of which *das frische Leben* and *der neue Tag* are born (12084–
93). Gretchen's love is the place of the concrete transfiguration of *eros*
and *agape,* of the *humanization* of the two. And it is essentially her love
that is metaphorized in *Jungfrau, Mutter, Königin* (in fact, she was
Jungfrau and *Mutter,* and now becomes *Königin*), and conceptualized in
das Ewig-Weibliche—a love that she had experienced, found, and preserved in her "real" history. It found its first expression in the unforget-
table poetry of "König in Thule" and proved its reality in the rejection of
Mephistophelian assistance in the "Kerker" scene. Her ultimate transfiguration is indicated in the lines with which the first part ends: the
response of a Stimme von oben—"Ist gerettet!"—to Mephistopheles'
"Sie ist gerichtet!" and her own, *von innen, verhallend,* "Heinrich! Heinrich!" (4611–14).

   There are many echoes of figures, metaphors, and events from the
entire play in this final scene. They are reflected in the imagery of the text
as in a kind of mirror (an application of Goethe's poetic principle of
Spiegelung). The epilogue clearly responds to "Wald und Höhle" (a key
scene of part 1), as it is related to "Anmutige Gegend" (which in itself is
an indication of the semantic unity of the text). In "Wald und Höhle,"
tragedy was implicit. Though Faust was aware that the potential of a
world beyond magic exits—man as part of *herrliche Natur,* fulfilling
himself inside it (3220–39), a prefiguration of the key theme in Faust's
final monologue—he saw no possibility ever to achieve the freedom of
this status (3240–50). He regarded himself as *Flüchtling, der Unbehauste,
Unmensch ohne Zweck und Ruh,* and saw his life in the image of the
Wassersturz, begierig wütend nach dem Abgrund zu, Gretchen being a
tragic victim of hell, the end, utter destruction. *Zusammenstürzen* and
zugrunde gehn are the key terms in the final lines (3348–65). "Anmutige
Gegend" enacts a process of healing, regeneration, and reconstruction
after the consummation of tragedy and the experience of intense suffering, again with the recognition of a potential of freedom, of a life of
human fulfillment inside nature (note the semantic transformation of the
key image of *Wassersturz*), a recognition clearly on a widened, deepened
plain: the appearing cosmos as the realm of productive self-realization.
The symbols of *Wassersturz/Abgrund* are echoed in Pater Profundus'
Felsenabgrund/tiefer Abgrund: "Wie tausend Bäche strahlend fließen /
Zum grausen Sturz des Schaums der Flut" (11866–69), which now serves
as a paradigm of "allmächtige Liebe / Die alles bildet, alles hegt"
(11872f.). The image of *stürzende Wasserfülle,* which in *Wald und Höhle*
served as symbol of tragic destruction, has been utterly transformed. It

has become *liebevoll im Sausen, berufen, gleich das Tal zu wässern* (11876–78); it fulfills a purpose, a productive function as force of cultural formation. *Der Blitz, der flammend niederschlug,* another image of tragic potential (signifying a threat of destruction) equally fulfills a positive purpose: that of "die Atmosphäre zu verbessern, / Die Gift und Dunst im Busen trug" (11880f.). *Gift und Dunst* can, without difficulty, be related to the world of Mephistopheles. Both *Wassersturz* and *Blitz* are now experienced as *Liebesboten:* "sie verkünden, / Was ewig schaffend uns umwallt" (11882f.): they announce the eternally productive power in us and around us—in the whole of being. This is another poetic reformulation and philosophical transformation of the notion of *natura naturans* of Spinozistic origin, the idea of productivity and creativity which Goethe had identified in the Greek *eros* within the pagan environment of the "Klassische Walpurgisnacht," and which he rediscovered in the Christian notion of *agape* inside the specific surroundings of this final scene. Goethe's poetic procedure is that of an amalgamation of ideas and images from very different cultural and theoretical sources, with the specific purpose of articulating his own, highly individual and utterly unique, philosophical point of view.

The philosophy implicit in the text has metaphysical (perhaps we should say, ontological) as well as philosophical-historical and anthropological dimensions. At its center is a notion of creativity (an idea of cultural productive formation) to which the concept and the imagery of *Liebe—eros, agape,* and, above all, *humanized love* embodied in the personal love of Gretchen—are the key. *Das Ewig-Weibliche* is, as I have indicated, the conceptualized formulation of this idea, its conceptual epitome. It is clearly a principle beyond Mephistopheles and all he stands for, as it points to a world beyond patriarchal domination. It finds reality and fulfillment in the symbolic union of Faust and Gretchen: in the creation of *frisches Leben* and the beginning of *der neue Tag.* The very end of the play signifies a new beginning—in this sense, too, Goethe's text has an "open" structure—the beginning of a new life and a new world the principles of which are formulated in the highly complex concept of love. In a sense, this final scene responds to, and extends, Faust's final monologue, pointing beyond the vision of *tätig-freies Wohnen* to an even more distant future of human development. It is an addition and extension also insofar as it presents the Epimethean viewpoint of *vita contemplativa,* similar to the way that Faust's final monologue can be said to represent the idea of *vita activa,* which is closely connected with the Prometheus figure. The existence pointed to in the unending movement of the final scene (close in spirit, I feel, to Titian's famous *Assumption of Mary* in Venice) is certainly one based on human relations entirely different from those in a world controlled by *Magie*—subordination, repression, and exploitation—different, with certainty, from the world in which we live and which we empirically "know."

The most significant "mirroring" to be found in the final scene is that of the "Prolog im Himmel." The final scene presents a movement upwards from *Wald, Fels, Einöde* at the beginning of "Bergschluchten" to *höchste Gipfel* (Chor seliger Knaben), *höhere Atmosphäre* (Engel . . ., *Faustens Unsterbliches tragend*), and *Himmel,* in the appearance of *Himmelskönigin im Sternenkranze* (11994f.), as a final stage of textual articulation—though the suggestion is transmitted that the movement continues beyond that level; that it is, in a way, infinite, unending. It must be evident, even without the terminological level (*Himmel* does not appear in all editions of the text), that the operatic-symphonic finale of *Faust* articulates a response to the "Prolog im Himmel." In this sense, it explicitly has the character of an *epilogue.*[37]

The function of the "Prolog im Himmel" was, above all, to establish the philosophical-historical and, in a specific sense, the metaphysical level of the text: *Faust* as "universalpoetische Weltdichtung,"[38] as a poetic-dramatic quest for meaning in the history of the human race. Each of the three prologues—"Zueignung," "Vorspiel auf dem Theater," and "Prolog im Himmel"—has the function of establishing fundamental relations in which Goethe's text stands: that of individual experience and articulation ("Zueignung"), that of social communication and theatrical action ("Vorspiel"), and the thematic relation of a philosophy of the history of humanity. The three prologues might be termed poetological commentaries to Goethe's text. The "Prolog im Himmel" establishes the level of highest philosophical generalization: *Faust* as "Drama der Menschengattung."[39]

What is truly significant in the relationship of the "Prolog im Himmel" and the epilogue of the "Bergschluchten" is the fact that the two—though clearly related in the structural sense suggested by the very terms *prologue* and *epilogue,* as well as in the specific Goethean sense of *Spiegelung*—are not identical in terms of philosophical content. They do in fact contain essential elements of thematic nonidentity and contradiction, of what I term a semantic rupture, a break of conceptual identity. This break signifies a radical change of viewpoint and perspective, between the beginning and the end of the play. It is evident, to start with, that the whole "story" of Faust—the protagonist's own "history," his actions, his activity, his fate, the *real praxis* of his "striving"—is anything but an illustration, let alone a vindication, of the Leibnizian optimism of the Lord, though it is not one of mere contradiction, either. The central ideas of productivity and love (the thematic core of the dramatic process) are mentioned in the Lord's speech (346f.); yet they are hardly at its center. The relationship of prologue and central action is one of questioning, relativization, change of viewpoint and perspective.

The most essential difference between prologue and epilogue can be said to lie in the fact that, at the end, the figure of the *Herr*—the male God of traditional Christian theology—is replaced by a female one, the *Jungfrau, Mutter, Königin, Göttin* (12102f.), *höchste Herrscherin der Welt*, who, in her turn, is much less an isolated figure than one in the midst of an ensemble. In a sense, she is a *prima inter pares,* an incarnation of the essential love of *all.* God as master—*Gott der Herr,* a key figure of domination (*male* domination, if you like) in the history of European civilizations—has given way to a principle of love embodied in *Jungfrau, Mutter, Königin, höchste Herrscherin der Welt,* conceptualized in *das Ewig-Weibliche* as the principle of *a new life* ("frisches Leben" / "neuer Tag"), and envisaged dramatically in the configuration of female figures which dominate the text at the end—with *una poenitentium, sonst Gretchen genannt,* at the center. Though *Gott* (11888, 11921) and *Götter* (12011) are still mentioned, they play only marginal roles, even on the level of terminology; they sound like echoes of a past and half-forgotten world.

There can be no doubt that the end of *Faust* is a truly dark and, let us face it, almost *unknown* text. Any interpretation, therefore, has to proceed cautiously and can hardly be more than tentative. It would be tempting, of course, and close to the heart of some feminist criticism, to read the end as a replacement of the patriarchal principle of male domination and a "logo-centric" culture by a matriarchal principle, the "female" symbol signifying a world of feeling, compassion, and love. Another suggestion worth further discussion might be to argue that the final scene is Goethe's "Epimethean utopia" of *vita activa* as outlined in Faust's final speech.

I would hesitate to give a definitive reading of the text in any of these suggested senses of appropriation, although I consider them to be legitimate responses. It is clear that the epilogue has to be seen in conjunction with Faust's end—this follows from the requirements of the basic dramatic structure—and it is in this connection that the end of the text can be seen as a searching and, in many ways, uncertain attempt on the part of the aging Goethe at giving articulation to what one might term a humanistic principle of hope, akin to Ernst Bloch's *Prinzip Hoffnung,* the articulation of an "anthropological optimism" (Scholz), an optimism, however (to use Romain Rolland's formidable phrase), *which has passed through catastrophes.*

Goethe's *Faust* does not offer an "answer" to the problems of history exposed in the text, and this remains true to the very end. *Das Ewig-*

Weibliche is with certainty no "answer" to these problems, but the very personal, very private articulation of a world-historical principle of hope. Love, for Goethe, was the key word to this principle: *human* love, in which *eros* and *agape* have become one. In this sense, the final scene is more than a "skeptisch-ironischer Abgesang"; it is the enactment of that fundamental principle of hope—though, again, it should not be regarded as a "last word," nor be seen in isolation. It is an element in what I termed the ensemble of ironies and contradictions with which the text confronts us—an essential part of *diese sehr ernsten Scherze,* part and parcel of a poetic and philosophical provocation.

Notes

1 Cf. my "Literature and Art as Ideological Form," *New Literary History: A Journal of Theory and Interpretation* 11 (1979): 21–39. For an exposition of the problem of a materialist hermeneutics, see my "Grundlagen und Probleme einer materialistischen Hermeneutik der Literatur: Ein theoretischer Entwurf," in *Erklären, Verstehen, Begründen,* ed. by G. Pasternak (Bremen, 1985), 196–223.

2 Goethe has dealt with this problem as early as *Pandora* (1807). See my "'Prometheus': Zum Verhältnis von bürgerlicher Literatur und materieller Produktion," in *Literaturwissenschaft und Sozialwissenschaften 3: Deutsches Bürgertum und literarische Intelligenz 1750–1800* (Stuttgart, 1974), 410–416.

3 Cf. my "Faust und die Ökonomie: Ein literarhistorischer Essay," in *Vom Faustus bis Karl Valentin: Der Bürger in Geschichte und Literatur* (Berlin, 1976), 28–155; Gerhard Bauer, Heidegart Schmid Noerr, "Faust, Ökonomie, Revisionismus und Utopie," *Das Argument* 99 (1976): 780–792; Gert Mattenklott, "Literarische Komplexität und der Komplex Ökonomie," ibid., 734–746; Gerhart Pickerodt, "Geschichte und ästhetische Erkenntnis," ibid., 747–771; Heinz Schlaffer, "Fausts Ende," ibid., 772–779; Heinz Hamm, *Goethes "Faust": Werkgeschichte und Textanalyse* (Berlin, 1978; rev. 3d ed., 1985); Thomas Metscher, "Faust und die Kunst zu erben," *Das Argument* 115 (1979): 352–368; Cesare Cases, "Fausts 'Schlußmonolog': eine Diskussion und ihre Folgen," in *Deutsche Klassik und Revolution,* ed. by Paolo Chiarini and Walter Dietze (Rome, 1981), 299–321; Heinz Hamm, "Julirevolution, Saint-Simonismus und Goethes abschließende Arbeit am 'Faust'," *Weimarer Beiträge* 28, no. 11 (1982): 70–91; Bernd Mahl, *Goethes ökonomisches Wissen: Grundlagen zum Verständnis der ökonomischen Passagen im dichterischen Gesamtwerk und in den "Amtlichen Schriften"* (Frankfurt, 1982), 103–111.

4 There has been some controversy on this point. Hamm, for instance, rejects the view of the lemures as material producers (*Goethes "Faust,"* 227f.); in a later essay ("Julirevolution, Saint-Simonismus") and in the third edition of his book, however, he has considerably modified his opinion. Two essential contributions to the problem are Günther Mieth, "Fausts letzter Monolog: Poetische Strukturen einer geschichtlichen Vision," *Goethe Jahrbuch* 97 (1980): 90–102 and Brunhild Neuland, "Faust, die drei Gewaltigen und die Lemuren: Zur Beziehung von Mythos und Geschichte in *Faust II,*" in *Ansichten der deutschen Klassik,* ed. by Helmut Brandt and Manfred Beyer (Berlin and Weimar, 1981), 276–295.

5 Gerhard Scholz, *Faust-Gespräche* (Berlin, 1967), 212f.

6 Karl Marx, Friedrich Engels, *Werke (MEW),* Ergänzungsband I (Berlin, 1968), 512f.

7 Cf. Neuland's excellent analysis of the dancer symbolism (pp. 293f.).
8 This alone shows that Heinz Schlaffer's classification of *Faust II* as *allegory,* in his *Faust Zweiter Teil: Die Allegorie des 19. Jahrhunderts* (Stuttgart, 1981), is one-sided and highly reductive; cf. my review in *Das Argument* 138 (1983): 286–89 and "Geschichte und Natur in Goethes Klassischer Walpurgisnacht," in my *Der Friedensgedanke in der europäischen Literatur: Studien zum Verhältnis von Literatur und Humanität* (Fischer-hude, 1984), 84f.; Wilhelm Emrich's view of the dominance of symbolism in *Faust II* in his *Die Symbolik von Faust II: Sinn und Vorformen,* 2d ed. (Bonn, 1957) can be said, at least in this respect, to be vindicated.
9 Cases, 313.
10 Schlaffer, "Fausts Ende," 774f.
11 Cf. Marx, "Ökonomisch-philosophische Manuskripte," in *MEW* 1:538.
12 In terms of poetic form and structure, *Faust* has strong affinities with the concept of modern art as outlined by Schiller, Hegel, and, above all, the young Friedrich Schlegel (see my "Faust und die Ökonomie," 34–41, a point which is totally missed by Mattenklott and Cases). Dieter Borchmeyer, on the other hand, rightly acknowledges "Goethes Annäherung an die Romantik" in his "Goethes Annäherung an die Romantik: Das Spätwerk. Summe des Schaffens: *Faust,*" in *Geschichte der deutschen Literatur vom 18. Jahrhundert bis zur Gegenwart,* ed. by V. Žmegač, vol. 1/2 (Königstein, 1979), 178–215.
13 This view, as put forward by Cases, can hardly be surpassed in lack of poetic as well as historic imagination.
14 Joachim Müller, "Die tragische Aktion: Zum Geschehen im 5. Akt von 'Faust II' bis zum Tode Fausts," *Goethe Jahrbuch* 94 (1977): 204.
15 Cf. Müller; Mieth; Neuland; Wolfgang Heise, "Die Idee der Entwicklung im Spiegel von Goethes 'Faust II' unter besonderer Berücksichtigung der Versuchungsdebatte, Vers 10128–10195," *Goethe Jahrbuch* 99 (1982): 89–104.
16 Cf. Friedrich Schiller, *Über naive und sentimentalische Dichtung.*
17 *MEW* 20:107.
18 Schlaffer, "Fausts Ende," 774f.
19 The impact of Saint-Simonism on Goethe's final work on *Faust* has now convincingly been established by Heinz Hamm in his "Julirevolution, Saint-Simonismus."
20 Goethe's text appropriates *historical* positions not only in terms of economic, social, and political history but also in terms of *history of consciousness.* In this context, it has to be asserted that Faust's final monologue and Mephisto's commentary represent historically opposed positions: the latter that of nihilism. Nihilism, as a historical-ideological formation, is not an invention of Friedrich Nietzsche. It emerges, as Detlef Kremer has recently shown in his *Wezel: Über die Nachtseite der Aufklärung. Skeptische Lebensphilosophie zwischen Spätaufklärung und Frühromantik* (Munich, 1985), in the period of the break-up of the Enlightenment. It can be said to be an implicit possibility of a text such as Voltaire's *Candide* (Swift, by the way, has been accused—though unjustly—by F. R. Leavis of a position of pure negativity; cf. his "The Irony of Swift," in his *The Common Pursuit* [Harmondsworth, 1962], 73–87). Nihilism, which can be interpreted as an abstract negation of the experience of "the death of God," is reflected, as a deeply-threatening possibility of modern consciousness, in Jean Paul's "Rede des toten Christus vom Weltgebäude herab, daß kein Gott sei" (cf. Walter Rehm, *Experimentum Medietatis* [Munich, 1947]). It casts its shadows over Romanticism and finds a classic articulation in the figure of Dostoevsky's Ivan Karamasov (cf. Heise, 101). The figure of Mephistopheles can be said to be, in many ways, an objective correlative to these historical tendencies, without being equatable to any definite position within them. Faust represents the opposite: the tradition from Spinoza and Enlightenment to early socialism. In many ways, one may argue, the secret (or "implicit") author of the final monologue is Herder as well as Saint-Simon.
21 *Blut und Feuer:* the metaphor is Marx's. For its relevance for *Faust,* see my "Faust und die Ökonomie," 82–93, espec. my interpretation of the Philemon and Baucis tragedy.
22 Cf. my "Geschichte und Natur in Goethes Klassischer Walpurgisnacht," 91–97, 105–107.

23 Karl Marx, *Das Kapital 1, MEW* 23:271.
24 *MEW* 9:226.
25 Cf. Heise, 89f.
26 Ibid., 90f.
27 There is little conviction in Hans Rudolf Vaget's interpretation which sees Faust as a reactionary and representative of feudal restoration because he takes the side of the Kaiser in opposition to the Gegenkaiser; see his "Faust, der Feudalismus und die Restauration," in *Akten des VI. Internationalen Germanisten-Kongresses Basel 1980,* Teil 4, ed. by Heinz Rupp and Hans-Gert Roloff (Bern, Frankfurt, Las Vegas, 1980), 347. The party of the Gegenkaiser can hardly be said to represent a "progressive"—in whatever sense of the term—social or political force (compare the role of the leaders of the Church). Second, and more important, Vaget ignores the fact that Faust represents a new, dynamic principle of world appropriation (identifiable as *bourgeois* in its major characteristics) which stands, as a disruptive force, in opposition to the self-destructive *stasis* of the feudal world (the war between Kaiser and Gegenkaiser is in itself a self-destructive feudal war, motivated by greed and the desire for aggrandisement, not a struggle between opposing historical principles or parties). Faust's life principle of world appropriation and development, as principle of the "new" (i.e., bourgeois) society, stands in fundamental opposition to the merely "consumptive" and parasitic orientation of the Kaiser and the whole feudal world. It has never been argued that Faust as bourgeois represents a position of conscious *political* opposition to the Kaiser.
28 Cf. my "Geschichte und Natur in Goethes Klassischer Walpurgisnacht," 98–105.
29 Cf. Goethe's *Versuch einer Witterungslehre* of 1825, discussed by Neuland, 277.
30 Heise, 99.
31 Ibid., 101.
32 Ibid., 102.
33 Scholz, 219.
34 The religious-metaphysical symbolism of Goethe's final articulation of a world-historical and basically humanistic principle of hope can be seen as his very personal response to the challenge of Saint-Simonism. Saint-Simon conceived of the future socialist social and cultural order, where the earth is transformed into a "paradise," in terms of a new "religion" and a "New Christianity" (cf. Frits Kool and Werner Krause, *Die frühen Sozialisten,* vol. 1 [Munich, 1972], 155), as the coming "Golden Age" of mankind (173). The conception of a "union" of Christianity and socialism was, in Goethe's age, by no means restricted to Saint-Simonism (cf. Michael Vester, *Die Frühsozialisten 1789–1848* [Reinbek, 1970], 238). It is interesting to note that even Heinrich Heine conceives of the future, where the "Jungfer Europa" is married to the genius of freedom, in terms of a *Himmelreich auf Erden* and a *new God,* and refers to the new order of socialism as *Kirche von dem dritten neuen Testament* (cf. his *Deutschland, ein Wintermärchen,* "Auf diesem Felsen," *Neue Gedichte*).
35 Gerhart Pickerodt, "Nachwort," in Goethe, *Faust* (Munich, 1978), 995.
36 For this and the following, see my "Geschichte und Natur in Goethes Klassischer Walpurgisnacht."
37 Cf. Erich Trunz's commentary in *Goethes Faust,* 6th ed. (Hamburg, 1960), 622.
38 Borchmeyer, 214.
39 Georg Lukács, "Faust-Studien," in his *Faust und Faustus* (Reinbek, 1967), 144.

Music in Goethe's *Faust:*
Its First Dramatic Setting

RICHARD D. GREEN

There are in the history of literature a few works of significance in which music figures prominently in the narrative. In most of these, such as in Tolstoy's *Kreutzer Sonata* or James's *The Portrait of a Lady,* music is of secondary importance to the exposition of the plot and the development of its characters and is unusually little more than a prop or an excuse for philosophical reflection. Goethe's *Faust* is virtually a singular exception wherein music contributes in an essential way to the very style of the work, serves as the vehicle of the plot, and is heard as an autonomous sounding medium. Music in *Faust* is as ubiquitous as the sea in novels by Conrad, or the vast landscapes in works of Stifter, and, as such, is an important component of the personalities of the characters and accompanies many of the principal moments of the drama.

A modest number of respectable studies have investigated Goethe's awareness of musical literature, his aesthetic comments on the nature of music and musical experience, his personal association with composers of his day, and the influence of his musical consciousness on his poetic style in general.[1] From this literature, one must conclude that Goethe took an extremely active and discriminating interest in music, that his comments on the nature of this art were generally in accord with those of philosophers of his day, and that for much of his life he sketched one form of musical drama after another. He began early in his career to write libretti for Italian operettas, *Singspiele* and *Lustspiele* with arias and *Lieder.* It was with great reluctance that after the appearances of Mozart's *Die Entführung* and *Die Zauberflöte* Goethe gave up his persistent hope of guiding the emergence of the new singspiel genre. The influence of music on his verses can be traced from at least the time of Goethe's encounter in Strasbourg with Herder's influential work with *Volkslieder,* and throughout his important Weimar residence much of what he wrote was intended for musical accompaniment. The monodrama *Proserpina* was to be spoken to music; *Lila* is a fairy opera, and, of course, such libretti as *Erwin und Elmire* and *Jery und Bätely* are authentic *Singspiele.* To varying degrees, certain of his operatic works seem to demand musical accompaniment, and some, such as *Claudine von Villa Bella,* contain dialogue that is occasionally interrupted by songs, duets, or arias. The Italianate *Scherz, List und Rache* as well as the second versions of *Erwin* and *Claudine,* with their occasionally recitative-like style, appear to have been modeled on the operetta. From his first play, *Die Mitschuldigen,* to part 2 of *Faust,* music was a significant stylistic feature of Goethe's dramaturgy and is mentioned in the stage directions of twenty-eight dramatic productions.

From its conception, *Faust* was closely bound with thoughts of music. In part 1, choruses and songs are interspersed in a manner that seems to have been inspired by singspiel. In fact, the libretto for Goethe's first singspiel dates from 1774, the year of the first authenticated references to work on *Faust.* In both parts of the drama, a large number of musical texts appear, and the stage directions call for an extraordinary variety of musical styles and effects. During the time that Goethe worked on part 1, he simultaneously planned to write a sequel to Mozart's *Zauberflöte* and even defended the value of this work against the criticism of many of his friends. Eventually, a fragment of this "musical poem" (as Goethe referred to it) was published. It has been concluded that on the basis of the independence of the choral parts, and the intermingling of simple prose and rhymed verse, the project served as a preparatory sketch to the second part of *Faust.*[2] Goethe himself recognized the operatic nature of the work when, in 1827, he commented to Eckermann:

> The first part of *Faust* can only be entrusted to the greatest tragedians. Then, in the operatic part, the different characters must be in the hands of the finest singers. The role of Helen cannot be played by one person, but rather must be taken by two great artists; for it is very rare that a singer is at the same time a tragedian of first rank.[3]

Judging from the *Urfaust* of 1775, the initial plans for the musical content of the play involved merely the insertion of song lyrics, such as "König in Thule," in the manner of *Wilhelm Meister.* During the writing of part 1 after 1797, Goethe became acquainted with the Berlin composer Carl Zelter, with whom he was to correspond regularly for the rest of his life. It is tempting to speculate that the specifically musical nature of *Faust* was strongly influenced by this intimate and impelling friendship.

The musical appeal of *Faust* that has provoked a large variety of dramatic responses in music may be found in four of its features: (1) the musical nature of the language itself; (2) the power of its drama, the fullness of its scenes that suggest pantomimic and sensual displays evoking musical accompaniments; (3) direct references to music within the text itself; and (4) indirect references in which the presence of music is suggested. These elements in no way account for all aspects of the work's style, but may in part explain the attraction of the drama to composer's throughout the 19th century.

(1) The musical qualities of Goethe's poetry are well known, and there is sufficient literature to document that much of what he wrote was inspired by the structure and effect of music.[4] In the lines of a love poem, he once enjoined: "Nur nicht lesen: immer singen! / Und ein jedes Blatt ist dein." There are many verses of *Faust* that are as alluring in their suggestive imagery as in their sensual tone. The musical effect of the following lines from part 2, act 2, is obvious and penetrating:

> Rege dich, du Schilfgeflüster!
> Hauche leise, Rohrgeschwister,
> Säuselt, leichte Weidensträuche,
> Lispelt, Pappelzitterzweige,
> Unterbrochnen Träumen zu!

In lines such as these, meaning resides not only in objective connotations, but, as in music, also in sensual appeal and suggestive allusions.

(2) Certain particularly colorful scenes of *Faust* might easily adapt to operatic staging and forceful orchestral accompaniment to vivify their demonic or etherial atmosphere. Because of its ability to suggest the indescribable, music is especially effective in passages of dramatic intensity where it can create moods without depending upon the text. As Goethe himself expressed it: "It is a great and noble advantage of music that it can move the soul without using a common external means."[5] We can imagine the *Walpurgisnacht* as an antecedent to act 2 of Weber's *Der Freischütz,* and much of *Faust II* is comparable in style and mood to E. T. A. Hoffmann's opera *Undine.*

(3) Generally speaking, there are three types of direct musical references in *Faust:* (a) incidental music, including fanfares and instrumental stage effects; (b) stage directions calling for choirs of various sizes and constitutions; and (c) accompanied and unaccompanied solo songs.

(a) *Incidental Music.* In *Faust,* as in many dramas before and afterward, certain scenes, especially those involving important or royal protagonists, are introduced by the sounding of drums, bells, or trumpet fanfares. The trombone *(Posaune),* for example, has been for centuries associated with the Day of Judgment, and in Luther's translation of the Bible the instrument is used by the angels of the Apocalypse. Goethe calls for the trombone only two times in all of his works, and both are in part 2 of *Faust.* In act 1, the Herald at the Emperor's court cries "Let the spirits enter!" as we hear a flourish of trombones. Then again in act 4, as the Emperor's forces seem to be losing the battle with the enemy, Mephistopheles works his supernatural magic to call forth an army of wraithlike knights. There is suddenly a fearful blast of trombones from above, and the hostile army begins to waver. Sounding from above, the trombones connote threatening images recognizable to both the enemy soldiers and to the audience of *Faust,* and they seem convincingly to reinforce Mephistopheles' demonic power.[6]

Toward the end of act 3, in part 2, the scene involving Euphorion, Faust, and Helena is preceded by the following comment: "A charming, purely melodious music of strings rings out from the cavern. All become attentive and soon seem to be deeply touched. From now on to the designated 'pause' there is continuous and full-bodied music." Such indications as these may suggest that Goethe intended *Faust* as a kind of grand melodrama with incidental music, at the very least, or perhaps even a nascent *Gesamtkunstwerk.* The multiple appeal to the senses is suggested, for example, at the end of the *Walpurgisnacht,* where, after Ariel's bid to follow his airy track up the hill of roses, the direction reads: "Orchestra (pianissimo): Train of clouds and misty veil from above are illuminated. Breeze in the leaves and wind in the reeds, and all is dissipated." A few such effects in *Faust* were unquestionably too demanding to have been realized literally before the modern age of audio and cinematographic technologies, as the poet required a very lively imagination of his readers to envision these fantastic scenes. Consider the opening of the "Walpurgis Intermezzo," in which an orchestra is described as consisting of "snout of fly and nose of gnat, along with all their kindred, frog in the leaves and cricket in the grass," to which is soon added a soap bubble as a bagpipe. In all of his works, Goethe's stage directions call for a total of twenty-three different instruments, not including the soap-bubble bagpipe.

(b) *Stage directions requiring various types of choirs.* Many of the passages in *Faust* that call for choirs are, to be sure, too long and complex for musical setting. Certain others, however, may have been intended to be sung or at least were inspired by obvious musical models. At the beginning of the drama, as Faust raises a goblet of poison to his lips, he hears a choir of angels singing the traditional Easter Hymn "Christ ist erstanden," and he is saved from death. This is the first of two moments in the drama in which Faust's life is spared by the sounding of music. Faust has come to view suicide as a dignified means to new adventures, from which neither human nor spiritual reason can dissuade him. Only the heavenly sound of music that transcends all reason, and appeals directly to the soul, can rescue him. This passage is one of a small number of texts found in *Faust* that were traditionally associated with music. Margaret's prayer to the Mater Dolorosa is a textual parody of the *Stabat Mater,* and her visit to the cathedral occurs during a service while an organ is playing, accompanied by a choir singing the 13th-century hymn *Dies irae, dies illa.* One observes also that some of the most sublime verses of the drama, such as the concluding "Alles Vergängliche / Ist nur ein Gleichnis," are to be intoned to music. One might conclude that for Goethe words such as these, so powerfully profound yet so profoundly limited, demanded the support of music to convey their richness and depth.

At one point in the beginning of part 2, the singing of the chorus is precisely orchestrated by Goethe. When the chorus responds to Ariel's song, they do so, according to the directions, "singly, by twos, or in numbers, alternately and collectively." Later, we encounter the Sirens in a bay of the Aegean Sea, "reclining on the cliffs around, fluting and singing." Himself a theater director, Goethe was one of a small number of great German poets who set the full power of their imagination to the writing of libretti, and who generally did so with consideration of the musical-dramatic conventions of the day.

(c) *Accompanied and unaccompanied solo songs.* Certain passages of *Faust,* particularly the soliloquies, have the poetic structure of free-form operatic arias, while others, being shorter and in more regular verse, closely resemble *Lieder* texts. In a few of the solo passages, Goethe specified the instrument of accompaniment, always a solo instrument capable of being played by the singer himself, and always chosen specifically to support the atmosphere of the lyrics. At the beginning of part 2, Faust is revived—here, for the second time in the drama—by Ariel's singing accompanied by an Aeolian harp. It is, of course, humanly impossible to accompany oneself with the Aeolian harp, an instrument of six or more gut strings set in vibration by the force of the wind. Its unpredictable and etherial tone could only be controlled by a spirit such as Ariel.

Two scenes later, the flower girls sing to mandolin accompaniment, and the gardeners are accompanied by a theorbo, or large double-necked lute. Such moments of song are of course common among some of Goethe's works. When *Wilhelm Meisters Lehrjahre* appeared in 1795, it included eight musical settings of the *Lieder* texts by Goethe's acquaintance, the Berlin composer Johann Reichardt. With this edition, readers could retire to the *Hammerflügel* to realize exactly the melodies of the *Lieder* as they might have been sung by the protagonists of the drama. No such music was ever included in the authorized editions of *Faust.*

For many of the more famous songs of *Faust,* accompaniment was not specified in the directions, and one must assume that none was required. Mephistopheles is given no opportunity to fetch a lute before singing the song of the flea in Auerbach's Cellar, nor can Margaret be expected to undress and play the harp simultaneously while singing "Der König in Thule." Her soliloquy "Meine Ruh ist hin" is accompanied only by the sound of her spinning wheel.

In addition to the direct musical references within the text of *Faust,* there are, I suggest, numerous passages of the play which, by virtue of their dramatic structure, resemble specific operatic conventions common at the beginning of the 19th century. Virtually all the types of scenes found in the traditional singspiel and German opera of the time are represented in certain sections of *Faust,* including arias and recitatives, *Lieder,* duets, trios, choruses, and love scenes. For example, in the evening following the first meeting of Faust and Margaret, Faust, left alone on stage, reflects: "Welcome, sweet twilight, as you permeate this sanctuary! Seize on my heart, sweet pain of love." Just beyond the middle of this soliloquy, his mood changes abruptly when he questions: "And you, Faust? What brought you here? How deeply stirred I feel!" In structure as well as in content, the passage might easily have served as an aria libretto (in fact, it has), for it corresponds neatly to the popular binary aria form of the *Cavatina,* that is, a lyrical, reflective song followed by a livelier virtuosic *Allegro.* Elsewhere in *Faust,* passages can be found that resemble the recitative-aria structure, such as the meeting of Faust and Margaret, and the traditional binary duet form, as in the scene with Faust and Mephistopheles in the dark gallery, part 2, act 1. These observations should not be understood as implying that Goethe consciously followed common operatic devices, but they rather serve to demonstrate the basic adaptability of the drama to existing operatic formulae with which most poets and composers were familiar.

Since the 17th century, the Faust theme has been the subject of numerous musical settings in large dramatic genres, incidental music, programmatic instrumental forms, ballets, and smaller genres as well. Despite the significance that Goethe's version of the story has assumed in more recent times, and the frequency with which the legend was set to music during the 19th century, remarkably few of these settings were based directly upon Goethe's play. For, while the play was studied among learned circles after the publication of part 2, and certainly inspired a variety of musical responses directly (some of them quite enduring), in the fifty years after Goethe's death his reputation declined and his works, including *Faust,* became at times even the subject of ridicule.[7] While the most popular settings of the theme, including those by Berlioz, Gounod, Boito, and Busoni, were no doubt inspired by Goethe's model, their libretti generally follow only loosely some of the principal scenes of the story as narrated in the folk legend or in any of the other literary versions. For example, Louis Spohr's opera *Faust,* premiered in Berlin in 1813, was based on a text prepared by J. K. Bernhard which, although inspired by part 1 of Goethe's *Faust,* borrowed more directly from the old folk play and occasionally from F. M. Klinger's *Fausts Leben, Thaten und Höllenfahrt* (1791). The dynamic instrumental settings by Wagner and Liszt are programmatic character sketches of the principal figures of the play inspired by the strongly atmospheric style of Goethe's poem, but not based directly upon its text.

Two reasons might be advanced in explanation of this observation. First, the proprietary attitude toward Goethe's text felt outside Germany was not so dominant within German-speaking states where poets, librettists, and composers were more often prevented by a sense of decency from altering the text to conform to conventional musical dramaturgy. Second, the style of much of the poem is itself alien to those conventional operatic forms and may have been considered even "undramatic" for musical purposes. It may have been argued that for traditional dramatic genres Goethe's *Faust* contains too many secondary characters, too frequent changes of scene, and too complicated a narrative to serve successfully as a musical libretto without substantial alterations.

The first musical response to Goethe's *Faust* came as a result of the publication of the *Faust* fragment in 1790. The *Neues Journal für Theater und andere schöne Künste* announced in 1796 that a four-act "Original Oper" entitled *Doktor Faust* had been completed. The premiere of the opera was evidently given the following year in Bremen. It has been determined that the text of this work, written by Heinrich Schmieder, was virtually plagiarized from the fragment, from which scenes and text were freely taken and woven into a popular pastiche.[8] The music for this opera, which was never published and is unobtainable, was composed by Ignaz Walter. Sometimes shortly after 1802, Walter's music was used again in a setting with a new libretto, also drawn from Goethe's fragment, by C. A. Maeninger. This second production, likewise never published, may have been known by Carl Zelter, Goethe's musical confidant, who spoke respectfully of Walter in his correspondence with Goethe.[9]

In 1807, the year before part 1 of *Faust* was published, Goethe wrote to Zelter referring to his progress on the drama: "I am anticipating with joy your diversion over the continuation of my *Faust;* it contains, too, things which will interest you from a musical point of view."[10] Three years later, he took the first active step toward arranging for a musical setting of the drama when he wrote again to Zelter, whose *Lieder* from *Faust* were finding acceptance among academic circles, and asked him to compose music to selected scenes. For two months, Zelter pondered the idea of writing music to *Faust,* but, following a few unsuccessful attempts, he wrote to Goethe in February of 1811 claiming that he was occupied with other responsibilities, and suggested that Goethe turn to another. In response, Goethe wrote: "I cannot quarrel with you for declining to compose the music to *Faust*. My proposal was rather frivolous, like the undertaking itself. So this, too, may be set aside for yet another year."[11] Nonetheless, this brief exchange between Zelter and Goethe may have indirectly stimulated the creation of the first dramatic setting of the play. For it is likely that Zelter mentioned Goethe's plan of a musical setting of *Faust* to a Berlin acquaintance, Prince Anton Heinrich Radziwill (1775–1833) whose home Zelter occasionally visited, and who sang in Zelter's *Liedertafel*. Radziwill, evidently already at work on a score to *Faust,* may have been encouraged by Goethe's query to Zelter which he took as tacit approval to continue composing a more extended setting.

Radziwill was related to the Prussian throne through his marriage in 1796 to Princess Louise, daughter of Prince Ferdinand of Prussia, and afterward he held minor positions in Posen and at the Berlin court. Before pursuing a career in political service he studied mathematics and music; he was said to have had an outstanding tenor voice and to have been quite proficient in playing the violoncello. His compositions, mostly *Hausmusik,* include *Romanzen,* polonaises, solo *Lieder* and duets, most of which remain in manuscript except for his grand opus, the incidental music to *Faust*, part 1, published in 1835 by the Berlin Singakademie.[12]

By December of 1810, Radziwill had completed at least three sections of the score—those that were eventually included as Numbers 5, 7, and 8, and may have had the Easter Chorus performed by the Singakademie before meeting with Goethe in Weimar in 1814.[13] It is probable that during the visit Goethe gave Radziwill specific suggestions concerning the musical numbers of the scenes, as two years earlier he had made an outline of the play for a planned staging in Weimar in which he had included his musical intentions. In the *Tag- und Jahreshefte,* Goethe confided: "The visit of Prince Radziwill excited a virtually insatiable desire. His ingenious composition to *Faust* swept us away, and gave us remote hope of seeing this peculiar piece on stage."[14] Ten days after Radziwill's visit, Goethe wrote to the Prince in Berlin to say that he felt the scene of the *Gartenhäuschen* was too short in its original form for musical setting, and he included in the letter a new version that was eventually set in the score as Number 19.

Radziwill's *Faust*

ACT 1

Overture
No. 1. Melodrama: "Flieh! Auf! Hinaus in's weite Land!"
      2. Chorus of Angels: "Christ ist erstanden"

 3. Beggar's Song: "Ihr guten Herrn"
 4. Soldiers' Chorus: "Burgen mit hohen Mauern und Zinnen"
 5. Peasants *Unter der Linde:* "Der Schäfer putzte sich zum Tanz"
 6. Melodrama: "Was stehst du so und blickst erstarrt hinaus?"
 7. Melodrama: "Ach wenn in unsrer engen Zelle"
    Melodrama: "Im Anfang war das Wort"
    Chorus of Spirits: "Drinnen gefangen ist einer"
    Melodrama: "Salamander soll glühn"
 8. Chorus of Spirits: "Schwindet, ihr dunkeln Wölbungen"
 9. Evocation: "Der Herr der Ratten und der Mäuse"
10. Chorus of Spirits: "Weh! Du hast sie zerstört, die schöne Welt"
11a. Chorus of Spirits: "Wird er schreiben?"
11b. Chorus of Spirits: "Hinauf, hinaus, kühn und munter"

ACT 2

No. 12. Overture and scene in Auerbach's Cellar: "Das liebe heil'ge röm'sche Reich"
13. Brander's Song: "Es war eine Ratt' im Kellernest"
14. Mephistopheles' Song: "Es war einmal ein König"
15. Quartet: "Trauben trägt der Weinstock"
16. Scene in Gretchen's Room: Melodrama
    Gretchen: "Ich gäb was drum, wenn ich nur wüßt'"
    Faust: "Willkommen süßer Dämmerschein"
    Faust: "Was faßt mich für ein Wonnegraus!"
    Gretchen: "Es war ein König in Thule"
    Gretchen: "Was hilft euch Schönheit"
17. Recitative and Aria of Faust: "Wenn ich empfinde"
18. Scene in the Garden, Melodrama: "Ich fühl' es wohl"
    Duet: "Allein gewiß, ich war recht bös' auf mich"
19. Quartet: "Die Nacht bricht an"
20. Gretchen: "Meine Ruh' ist hin"
21. Gretchen: "Ach neige, du Schmerzenreiche"
22. Mephistopheles' Song: "Was machst du mir vor Liebchens Thür"
23. Requiem in the Cathedral: "Wie anders Gretchen war dir's"
24. Scene in Prison: "Meine Mutter die Hex'"
25. Witch's Scene: "Supplement"

In February of 1816, Zelter announced to Goethe that the Crown Prince in Berlin had decided to allow a performance of *Faust* with Radziwill's music. Prince Karl von Mecklenburg was to read the part of Mephistopheles, while Faust and Gretchen were to be taken by distinguished members of the court theater. At the end of the following month, Zelter reported that after several rehearsals with the orchestra and chorus (which were conducted by Zelter himself) there had been a reading rehearsal with music at the home of the Radziwills, with the family circle in attendance. The parts had been delivered rather convincingly, and the poem itself had had a very remarkable effect upon the youthful audience. It is doubtful that on this occasion, or for any performances of the score, the actors sang their own parts, as several of the numbers are technically quite challenging in range and bravura, and would have been beyond the capabilities of most amateur singers. Zelter added: "The composer has hit off much to admire; the defect consists in this that he, like all artists at the outset of their career, makes main points of what should be secondary." In Zelter's opinion, Radziwill was little more than a gifted dilettante. During the next three years, rehearsals sporadically continued in Berlin, and were occasionally attended even by members of the court, including once by the King of Prussia himself, Friedrich Wilhelm III. Then on 24 May 1820, Radziwill's birthday, *Faust* was, in Zelter's words, "smoothly and fairly launched." The king, entirely pleased with the production, praised Goethe and Zelter both, and, at supper, a hundred voices shouted, "Long live Goethe!" Concerning the music, Zelter could say only that "even if Radziwill's music had no merit at all, he is entitled to great praise for having brought to light a poem hitherto concealed in darkest shadow."[15] One wonders whether the complete text of Goethe's play was given in this performance, for had it been, this production would have preceded Klingemann's acclaimed premiere of part 1 of *Faust* by nine years. The preface of Radziwill's score laments only that a complete performance of the *music* had, by 1835, not yet been arranged.

Between 1820 and 1830, Radziwill completed three new scenes to his score: Faust's walk with Wagner before the gate, the walk in the garden, and the scene in the church. Zelter wrote to Goethe, this time in praise of Radziwill's attention to detail and sensitivity to prosody: "Yesterday, Prince Radziwill let me hear three new scenes from his *Faust*. I cannot sufficiently praise the care with which everything is thought out, even to the smallest details . . . Here [in the garden scene] the music is quite nice, now and then charming, even ironic, and is tastefully unified. Verse and rhyme are so sensitively and metrically interwoven into the style of the music that I consider it the best that can be done in this genre."[16]

In the anonymous preface to the published score, Radziwill is commended as an immortal composer who tirelessly pursued the task of setting *Faust* to music throughout his life, and who completed this masterpiece of unusually high caliber only three years before his death. In his music, the preface claims, he infused the mundane and the artful with heavenly power, and in a manner corresponding to the spirit of the modern age. "In the novelty and occasional uninhibitedness of his style, he consistently remained within the realm of the beautiful, and remote from the purely sensual appeal that was unfortunately too often the only goal of the new, misguided style."

Radziwill's score to *Faust,* part 1, is in two acts of twenty-five numbers. Eleven numbers and an overture comprise act 1; act 2, which begins with the scene in Auerbach's Cellar, contains the remaining four-teen. A number of general comments can be made concerning the style of this work. One unsettling section of the score is found, alas, in the overture, the second part of which is an orchestration of Mozart's Fugue in C Minor for two pianos, K. 426. Radziwill may have known the work either in its original form, or even in the orchestrated arrangement by Mozart himself. The inappropriateness of the fugue to the opening of *Faust* was noted by the critic of the *Allgemeine Musikalische Zeitung,* and later even by Robert Schumann.[17] Perhaps aware of the fact that Goethe was extremely fond of Mozart's music, Radziwill may have inserted the fugue in the hope of gaining the poet's favor.[18]

The orchestration of the score itself is quite rich, and calls for harmonium, then a popular domestic instrument (used here in Number 1 only), piccolo, other woodwinds in pairs, four horns, two trumpets, three trombones, harp, guitar (used in Number 22 only), strings, and percussion (tympani, triangle). Several prominent violoncello solos throughout the work were no doubt composed by Radziwill for his own amusement. In its variety, the score is more demanding than even Weber's *Freischütz,* which saw its premiere in Berlin in the year after the first performance of Radziwill's *Faust,* so that it could only have been given with the complete cooperation of Gasparo Spontini, General Music Director to the Court. According to Zelter, it was primarily because of the popularity of Rad-ziwill's setting of the play that Goethe's *Faust* became popular in broader circles in Berlin; indeed, judging from the list of subscribers to the score, which included the Queen of England, the Philharmonic Society of London and the Duke of Cambridge, several royal princes in Prussia, and publishing houses in Prague, Warsaw, and Vienna—the work may have contributed in a significant way to the acceptance of the play before 1850 throughout much of Europe.

All but one of the passages in part 1 that Goethe indicated as requiring music were scored by Radziwill. The exception was the trio in the *Walpurgisnacht,* with Faust, Mephistopheles, and the Will-o'-the-wisp "singing in turn," a scene certainly too unimaginably fantastic to have been realized literally on any stage in Berlin. In the first act, arranged by Radziwill as alternating scenes of solo and choral singing, numbers 2, 3, and 5 are settings of passages Goethe intended to be sung. The longer and more diverse second act contains the remaining musical scenes of the play, set as numbers 12, 13, and 14; Gretchen's "Es war ein König" of Number 16; and Numbers 20, 22, and 24.

In his score, Radziwill ventured beyond the simple expectations of incidental music by attempting the difficult task of molding the play to more elaborate musical requirements, for he composed music to many passages that did not originally demand musical setting. His challenge lay in dealing with the multiplicity of musical scenes suggested by Goethe, in selecting other appropriately musical texts within the play compatible with these, and in integrating all these passages into an extended musical score that must be both varied and cohesive. In all musical settings of plays, there is a certain irreducible number of dramatic and psychological moments of the plot that must be dealt with if the score is to suggest that spiritual depth and intensity of the original libretto. The twenty-five numbers in Radziwill's *Faust* include most of the crucial episodes of the plot, although certainly not all. The memorable scenes of the Walpurgis Night and the following Walpurgis Night's Dream are not represented in the score, nor is the dialogue between Mephistopheles and the student in Faust's study. The composer has excluded minor figures from the musical numbers, and has chosen the scenes so as to present the protagonists in solo as well as in ensembles with each other. Dramatic libretti demand a variety of forms—e.g., recitatives, arias, strophic *Lieder*; diversity in genres—e.g., solos, trios, quartets; and numbers alternating in vocal types—e.g., first the tenor, then the soprano and the chorus. In this sense, the musical dramaturgy of the second act is more successful in its variety than is that of the first, in which the chorus dominates. Those dramatically cogent sections of the drama alien to the spirit of music, or to its traditional forms, were set as melodrama, that is, as spoken text accompanied by music.

Radziwill accepted not uncritically a *fait accompli,* without the advantage of collaborating with a librettist aware of the musical conventions of his day, whose text was intended for dramatic scoring and which could be altered at will. Throughout most of the score, Goethe's text is set entirely faithfully, with but few line repetitions. Only occasionally does the composer adopt a more proprietary position on his libretto. One of these passages is the famous scene of "Gretchen am Spinnrad," in which Radziwill's through-composed setting clearly contradicts Goethe's strophic text. This version does not support the repetitions of strophes 4 and 8, beclouds the autonomy of the other strophes, and repeats strophes 3 and 4 in altered form as a coda.[19] A more serious revision of Goethe's text is found in the scene of the Witch's Kitchen. The composition of this number was completed after Radziwill's death according to his sketches, and was included as a supplement to the score, Number 25, rather than being placed between Numbers 15 and 16, as in the play. We must

wonder whether this scene of sorcery, calling for singing glasses and
humming kettles, was ever staged in Berlin. But if it had been, this
arrangement offers intriguing evidence of the performance history of
Faust, for much of the original text was omitted, and what remains was
significantly altered and compressed. The scene begins and ends in the
middle of passages for Mephistopheles and intersperses Faust's remarks
before the magical mirror with those of the monkeys.

For the scene within the cathedral, Radziwill altered Goethe's original text in a manner different from what we have just observed, for here
he added several lines of the *Requiem* text to the service. The chorus now
sings in homophony from the opening lines, *Requiem aeternam*, through
the *Dies irae*, including parts of the *Tuba mirum*, and ends appropriately
with *Quid sum miser* as Gretchen faints. This is sung simultaneously with
monophonic chantlike incantation by the evil spirits, creating an effect of
ominous piety throughout the scene.

Immediately after Radziwill's visit in 1814, Goethe began rewriting
portions of his play to provide the composer with a fresh libretto. There
are two scenes of Radziwill's score for which the text was altered by the
poet expressly for the Berlin production. In the first of these, Number 11
a/b, the new text is sung by a double chorus immediately before and after
Mephistopheles' words "Blut ist ein ganz besond'rer Saft." Pausing
before singing the fateful oath, Faust says, "If this gives you complete
satisfaction, then let's abide by the old farce." The number then begins
antiphonally:

Chorus I: Wird er schreiben?
Chorus II: Er wird nicht schreiben.
both: Blut ist ein ganz besond'rer Saft,
            wirkend im Innern Kraft aus Kraft.
            Reißt ihn die Wunde rasch nach außen,
            draußen wird er wilder hausen.

Mephistopheles then recites the words already given to him by the spirits,
"Blut ist ein ganz besond'rer Saft," and the chorus continues with more
new material, this time in homophony:

            Hinauf, hinaus, kühn und munter,
            sind wir einmal oben auf,
            geht's wieder herunter.

Following these lines, Faust extends the image with the original text: "I
had inflated myself too high, and it is only to your level that I belong."

The most substantial addition to the play is the quartet set as
Number 19 of the score. The number begins with the concluding lines of
the Garden Scene, starting with Martha's "Die Nacht bricht an," and

continues uninterruptedly into the following dialogue in the Gartenhäuschen. The thirty-four new lines that Goethe provided for this scene
replace the first half of the existing text, and involve longer exchanges
between Faust and Margaret. The new text begins as Margaret whispers:

> Er kommt! Er kommt so schnell,
> Er wird mich fragen.
> Da draußen ist's so hell—
> Ich kann's nicht sagen.

It is then Faust, not Margaret as in the former text, who first confesses his
love, and ends the dialogue:

> O welchen süßen Schatz
> Hab ich genommen!
> So sey denn Herz an Herz
> Sich hoch willkommen.

Then, according to traditional operatic formulae, Faust and Margaret
sing lines in duet drawn from the previous text:

> Komm an mein Herz! du bist,
> Du bist willkommen!

The scene turns into a double duet as Martha and Mephistopheles comment on the passion of love. Finally, again according to convention, the
double duet becomes a quartet in which the last lines of the new text are
intermingled with those from the second half of the original text. In the
last two strophes of the insertion, the lines of the four characters are so
well intertwined that it appears Goethe must have had just this musical
form in mind:

> Mephistopheles and Martha: Wer Gelegenheit gegeben,
>   Der soll leben;
>   Wer Gelegenheit benommen,
>   Schlecht willkommen!
> Margaret and Faust: Sag, wer hat es uns gegeben,
>   Dieses Leben?
>   Niemals wird es uns genommen,
>   Dies Willkommen.

The number of passages of this score that revise Goethe's text is
small, however, compared to those that set it faithfully. In fact, several of
the very dramatic scenes of the play have been scored by Radziwill as
melodrama in which Goethe's text is included verbatim. The genre was
by no means original with Radziwill but was used here with unusual
frequency and variety. Two large sections of both acts are devoted to this
style, and these deal with particularly theatrical moments of the drama:
Faust's encounter with Mephistopheles, and the Evening Scene with

Gretchen, Faust, and Mephistopheles. Throughout the work, five styles of melodrama can be identified. The first calls for nonrhythmical speech accompanied by sustained, slowly progressing chords in the strings, as in Number 1 of the score. Though this was certainly the most common variety of melodramatic declamation during the first third of the 19th century, its use here did not please Goethe. While in Berlin in 1821, Goethe commented to Förster that the monologues of Faust ought not to be accompanied by music, since the instrumental accompaniment gave the work an undesirable hybrid character and made the proper coordination of music and drama impossible. When it was pointed out that Beethoven had written accompaniment to Egmont's monologues in prison, Goethe defended his having done so, stating that here he had explicitly directed that music should accompany this scene during the appearance of the dream vision: "In this instance, musical accompaniment is appropriate, and Beethoven has followed my intentions ingeniously."[20]

The second form of melodrama used in the *Faust* score alternates recitation, either unaccompanied or accompanied by static chords, with orchestral or vocal interjections. This is employed in Number 7 of act 1 during Faust's attempts to translate the New Testament. Here the Biblical quotations, "In the beginning was the word / . . . the sense / . . . the force," and Faust's unsuccessful efforts to render each in German, are spoken without accompaniment but are separated by brief orchestral gestures.

One of the significant problems in writing incidental music to a drama such as *Faust* involves the organic integration of the musical numbers (e.g., the songs, trios, and choruses) into the context of the play. Radziwill has accomplished this skillfully throughout the score by the frequent use of melodrama, and the flexible employment of standard musical forms. Mephistopheles' song of the flea, set by the composer as Number 14, is an example of the alternation of song and speech. In Goethe's text, the Devil begins his song "Es war einmal ein König," but is abruptly interrupted by Frosch's laughter at the mention of a flea. Mephistopheles then begins the first strophe anew and sings it to the end, when he is again interrupted by the jesting Brander warning the tailor to measure the pants precisely. Mephistopheles is allowed to complete the second and third strophes, the last two lines of which are repeated by the chorus: "Wir knicken und ersticken / Doch gleich, wenn einer sticht." Radziwill's setting of this scene follows exactly the alternation of song and speech according to Goethe's text, but adds the choral refrain to the end of both the second and third strophes.

In the third variety of melodrama, the recitation is accompanied by the orchestra in a style that carries modest melodic interest of its own. This can be found in Number 7. The fourth type is scored for unmea-

sured speech with accompaniment in the orchestra that is rhythmically
derived from the meter of the poetry; this is heard in Number 6 as part of
the dialogue between Faust and Wagner during their walk. The fifth style
of melodrama, the most effective, might be referred to as "measured
melodrama," in which the recitation and orchestra move in the same
rhythm, as in a "song without melody." It is used by Radziwill with
particular dramatic force in Number 9, the *Beschwörungsszene* with
Mephistopheles. There it is written as follows:

Der Herr der Rat- ten und der Mäu- se /   Der   Flie-gen, Frö-sche, Wan-zen, Läu- se

Despite this apparent wealth of dramatic variety, the score as a
whole is weakened severely by its preponderance of choruses and melodramatic scenes. Many of the solos, especially those for Gretchen, are
imaginative and sensitively arranged, but there is insufficient variety
among the ensembles of both acts. As incidental music to a play, Radziwill's score is successful in its adherence to the poet's dramatic intentions; as singspiel, however, it fails for its absence of significant secondary
voices and dominance of Faust and Gretchen in act 2.

In a review of Radziwill's *Faust* that appeared in the Leipzig *Allgemeine Musikalische Zeitung* of 1835, it was predicted that the song
"Meine Ruh ist hin" would become popular especially among women
"who are sensitive not only to fashionable tunes and meaningless passage
work and virtuosity, but who still value the tender German *Lied* in
expanded form (as in the songs of Schubert)."[21] Carl Loewe, a prodigious
composer of ballads, wrote upon hearing Radziwill's *Faust* in Berlin in
1831:

> I heard here something new, original, powerful; an original genius of my art.
> My interest grew more intense with each number. A bold, daring and extra-
> ordinary comprehension of this immortal poem mingled with musical forms
> and enchanting melodies, such as only a thoroughly cultured spirit, deep and
> genuine understanding, a bold leap of the imagination are capable of com-
> prehending. One can truthfully say, we have now a Faust in musical
> literature.[22]

Although performed frequently in Berlin during the twenty years
following its premiere, Radziwill's score has not endured as have the
songs of Schubert. It survives, rather, as the first of many musical works
to enhance this enigmatic masterpiece, and represents the only setting
known and generally approved by the poet, and the only one in which he
himself collaborated.

Notes

1 Cf. Hans Pyritz, *Goethe-Bibliographie,* ed. by Heinz Nicolai and Gerhard Burkhardt, 2 vols. (Heidelberg, 1965–68). An authoritative work on the subject is that of Wilhelm Bode, *Die Tonkunst in Goethe's Leben,* 2 vols. (Berlin, 1912). See also Friedrich Blume, "Goethe und die Musik," in *Syntagma musicologicum: Gesammelte Reden und Schriften,* ed. by Martin Ruhnk (Kassel, 1963), 757–813. Studies in English are less numerous and generally less exhaustive, although two are recommended: Romain Rolland, "Goethe's Interest in Music," *The Musical Quarterly* 17 (1931): 157–94; Annemarie M. Sauerlander, "Goethe's Relation to Music," *The University of Buffalo Studies* 20 (1952): 39–55.

2 Cf. Friedrich Blume, *Goethe und die Musik* (Kassel, 1948), 52; Hermann Abert, *Goethe und die Musik* (Stuttgart, 1922), 98.

3 *Gespräche mit Eckermann* (Leipzig, 1925), 177 (January 29, 1827).

4 Cf. Frederick W. Sternfeld, *Goethe and Music* (New York, 1979).

5 Letter to Adalbert Schöpke, 16 February 1818; cf. *Briefe der Jahre 1814–1832,* in *Gedenkausgabe der Werke, Briefe und Gespräche,* ed. by Ernst Beutler (Zürich, 1965), 21:275. Goethe felt that there was something "rather demonic" in the appeal of poetry to the subconscious, and that "the same is true in the highest degree for music which, being so lofty, no reason can appreciate"; *Gespräche mit Eckermann,* 375 (March 8, 1831).

6 Cf. Bayard Quincy Morgan, "Goethe's Dramatic Use of Music," *PMLA* 72 (1957): 104–12.

7 Cf. Wolfgang Leppmann, *The German Image of Goethe* (Oxford, 1961).

8 Philipp Spitta, "Die älteste Faust-Oper und Goethe's Stellung zur Musik," *Deutsche Rundschau* 58 (1889): 376–97. See also James Davies, "The Earliest Musical Settings to Goethe's *Faust,*" *Journal of English and Germanic Philology* 25 (1926): 517–30.

9 The speculation is tempting that Goethe's friendship with Zelter, whose musical insights he greatly respected, may have influenced the specifically musical content of *Faust.* During the time that Goethe worked to reshape the *Urfaust* into part 1, he continued an active correspondence with his friend in Berlin and often discussed matters of musical concern. Compared with that of the *Urfaust,* the musical component of parts 1 and 2 of the final version is far more prominent and pervasive.

10 *Briefwechsel zwischen Goethe und Zelter in den Jahren 1796 bis 1832,* ed. by Friedrich Wilhelm Riemer (Berlin, 1833f.), 1:261.

11 Ibid., 429.

12 Robert Eitner, "Anton Heinrich Radziwill," *Allgemeine Deutsche Biographie* (Leipzig, 1888), 27:154–55.

13 Bettina Brentano, writing to Goethe during Advent of 1810, stated that she had heard the three numbers performed, and said: "It chills one to the marrow to think that a person could have such a penetrating imagination." See *Briefe an Goethe* (Hamburg, 1969), 2:75.

14 *Goethe's Werke* (Weimar, 1893), 36:88.

15 *Briefwechsel,* 3:98–99.

16 *Briefwechsel,* 6:67–68.

17 J. P. Schmidt, "Über die erste Aufführung des 'Faust' von Goethe, mit Musik vom Fürsten Radziwill . . .," *Allgemeine Musikalische Zeitung* 37 (1835): 800–811; Robert Schumann, *Die Neue Zeitschrift für Musik* 6 (1837): 144. Schumann wrote: "The truly very unsuccessfully orchestrated overture must immediately open the eyes of musicians, if not, then the choice of a Mozart fugue will open those of the critic. If the composer were not up to the task of writing the overture himself, and could not realize the idea—an idea which should not be dismissed—of beginning the Faust drama with a fugue, the profoundest form of music, then certainly there are themes more Faust-like in character than that by Mozart, which no one who knows those by Bach and Handel can call a masterpiece.

18 In 1829, during a conversation with Eckermann, Goethe lamented his difficulty in finding suitable music for *Faust:* "It is quite impossible. It would have to be in parts repulsive, disagreeable and terrible, which are all contrary to our times. The music would have to be in the character of *Don Giovanni.* Mozart should have composed it." Cf. *Gespräche mit Eckermann,* 249 (February 12, 1829).

19 Goethe's opinion of the through-composed form was recorded in the *Tag- und Jahreshefte* of 1801: "How objectionable are all the so-called through-composed *Lieder,* in which the general lyrical character is abandoned and a false emphasis on details is demanded and provoked." Cf. *Goethes Werke,* 35:90–91.

20 *Goethes Gespräche,* ed. by Ernst Beutler (Zurich, 1949), 2:140–41.

21 Schmidt, "Über die erste Aufführung," 808.

22 *Carl Loewes Selbstbiographie,* bearbeitet von Carl Hermann Bitter (Berlin, 1870; reprint, Hildesheim, 1976), 134.

Faust/Faustine in the 19th Century: Man's Myth, Women's Places

NANCY A. KAISER

In Karl Gutzkow's *Wally, die Zweiflerin* (1835), the title figure wonders at one point why women are not supposed to read *Faust*.[1] In Irmtraud Morgner's *Amanda* (1983), Laura Salman recalls her choice of the opening monologue from Goethe's *Faust* for the declamatory portion of a school examination. She is informed by her teacher that it is an inappropriate text for a girl.[2] We might conclude that there is a cultural injunction which discourages women's appropriation of Faust. At the same time, women and "the feminine" are integral elements of the Faust legend. The conjuration of Helen is a traditional episode in the early Faust books and in the puppet plays. In Marlowe's version, the lovely lady from antiquity begins to take on a metaphorical dimension. And we are all too familiar with the tragedy and ultimate redemptive qualities of Gretchen, the function of Helena, and the transcendence of the "eternal feminine" in Goethe's *Faust*. Women, therefore, have their places in Faust.

Regarding the history of the Faust legend, it is in the final decades of the 18th century that the participation of women in versions of *Faust* increases markedly, and the beginnings of an ontologized "feminine" presence become evident. The places of women and the function of woman then become more clearly defined in the first half of the 19th century, where there are also attempts at establishing new roles for women in the old story: Mephistophela and Faustine. The woman as devil in Heine's ballet scenario is not entirely innovative, but Ida Hahn-Hahn's Faustine is an interesting and problematic development. Although not a strict version of the Faust legend as the other works which I am considering, her novel of 1840 was written both within and against the system of cultural meanings typified by the Faust myth.

That system of cultural meanings is directly implicated in the tangled history of subjectivity, in the constitution of a dominant masculine subject, with its claim to universality, and the subjugation of nature, of the feminine, and of women in the process. Since issues of knowledge, power, and desire form the essence of the Faust myth, the problems inherent in women's appropriation of Faust have a broader resonance. Having long been excluded from powerful knowledge in patriarchal culture, kept unknowledgeable about power, and held as objects of desire, women must struggle against their cultural definitions in order to assert themselves as subjects with knowledge, power, and desires of their own. The bourgeois formulation of those cultural definitions is at stake in versions of *Faust* from the late 18th century through the first half of the 19th century. It is the era marked by the restriction of middle-class women to the privatized family, but also by the large-scale entrance of women into the sphere of cultural production and by initial impulses toward what will later become the German women's movement. It is my purpose to trace the representation of women and the underlying meanings accorded "woman" as a cultural construct in the literary versions of *Faust* from this period. The story I hope to reveal exposes contradictions in the humanistic tradition which claims the cultural myth of Faust as, in the words of one critic referring to Goethe, "das Drama der Menschengattung."[3]

The entrance of women as individualized characters into the Faust legend coincides roughly with the routine portrayal of women as heroines in middle-class drama.[4] It is in the literary versions of Faust in the 1770s and in those influenced by them, that female roles are developed. E. M. Butler entitles the section of her book on *Faust* which deals with the period 1772–1778, "Womanizing Fausts." She finds it difficult to specify "that the Gretchen *motiv* entered the Faust legend in the 1770s or that the Faust *motiv* entered domestic tragedy. They gravitated together naturally."[5] I am of course suspicious of "natural gravitation" as an explanation for cultural phenomena. The entrance of Faust into middle-class drama juxtaposes Faust with the female characters which Butler subsumes under "the Gretchen motiv." The Faust figures acquire families and domestic worries but remain characterized by restless activity and by the power one acquires through a daring, or despairing, pact with the Devil. The roles accorded women in these literary versions of *Faust* portray them as domestic and devoted. The main individualized female figures are loving, faithful, and other-oriented, i.e, Faust-oriented. While not passive in the manner of many heroines of middle-class tragedy since *Miss Sara Sampson,* their activity is restricted to the private sphere and its defense. They are excluded from the struggle and change marking the Faust figures.

Such contrasting representations of male and female spheres and types of activity correspond to the cultural definitions of allegedly inborn male and female character differences in the final decades of the 18th century. A conceptual polarization of male and female nature is evident in philosophy, practical handbooks, and literature of the period. Gender characteristics are attributed to innate, unalterable differences rather than to social status or function.[6] A familiar example of such a cultural codification is found in the following lines by Schiller:

> Der Mann muß hinaus
> Ins feindliche Leben,
> Muß wirken und streben . . .
>
> Und drinnen waltet
> die züchtige Hausfrau,
> Die Mutter der Kinder,
> Und herrschet weise
> Im häuslichen Kreise.[7]

Further examples include the concepts of feminine "Anmut" and masculine "Würde," or the corresponding Kantian exclusion of women from the independent moral activity necessary for "erhabene Tugend."[8] Women are simultaneously idealized and denied a self-identity, as in Fichte's "Deduktion der Ehe" from the *Grundlage des Naturrechts: "Liebe* ist also die Gestalt, unter welcher der Geschlechtstrieb im Weibe sich zeigt. *Liebe* aber ist es, wenn man um des Anderen willen, nicht zufolge eines Begriffs, sondern zufolge eines Naturtriebs, sich aufopfert."[9] Ideologically, such definitions of an essentially passive and subordinate female nature reinforced the restriction of women to the home with the structural changes in the family brought by preindustrial capitalism. They also served to relegitimate patriarchal structures that had been challenged by emancipatory expectations raised as a result of the Enlightenment and the French Revolution. The cultural definitions of the nature of woman as selflessly loving, innately virtuous, and situated in static tranquility in the private, domestic sphere are manifest in the literary versions of *Faust* from the 1770s into the 19th century. In the earliest works, the individualized female characters exhibit a certain ambivalence. Subsequent renditions heighten the idealization of women, with a concomitant castigation of deviant female behavior, of the manifestation of the "Geschlechtstrieb im Weibe" in a form other than selfless love.

The first version of *Faust* to combine the legend with the genre of domestic tragedy is Paul Weidmann's *Johann Faust: Ein allegorisches Drama von fünf Aufzügen.* Performed in Prague in 1775, it was published anonymously that same year.[10] The drama takes place entirely during the last day of Faust's life, with a cast of characters including Faust's aging parents, his son, and his lover/companion Helena. In later versions, Faust is often a married man, in clear departure from the prohibition of marriage in the legend. Throughout Weidmann's drama, Helena is a "Geliebte," although in a role close to that of a spouse. Apart from her name, there is no real connection to the Helen of classical legend. As a family drama, *Johann Faust* is typical of the emerging middle-class morality characteristic of other plays of the period. Yet Helena would make a poor Luise Millerin. When Faust insists they must separate, her response would only partially satisfy Fichte's concept of female nature:

> Mein gutes Herz spricht noch für dich. . . . Um dich hab ich Eltern, Freunde, Anverwandte verlassen. Dir hab ich mein Herz, meine Liebe, geweiht, und du willst mich verlassen?—Geh, eil, flieg, wirf dich in die Arme meiner Nebenbuhlerin, aber zittre!—Fürchte ein beleidigtes Weib! Ich werde Himmel und Erde und Hölle wider dich waffnen und mich rächen![11]

Goethe's Gretchen would never utter the second half of this speech. Helena is a mixture of devoted "spouse" and assertive woman, although her self-assertion is aimed solely at retaining her man. She is a mixture of the passive, suffering woman and the raging woman, character types which are usually split in dramas of the period, most often along class lines.[12]

Helena is mistaken in her assumption of a rival for Faust's affection. He has simply decided to make a last-minute bid for salvation and follow the good spirit Ithuriel. In Weidmann's *Faust,* woman is not yet connected with redemption, as salvation apparently involves abandoning both lover and child. Helena's role is a confusing one, ranging from pulling a dagger on her son and accepting her own pact with the Devil to meekly pledging to serve Faust as a maid and be content "wenn oft ein mitleidiger Blick meine Zärtlichkeit belohnet."[13] Her behavior is a curious blend of loving submission and determined action. In the end, Ithuriel and his angels appear, and the entire family is saved through divine grace. The salvation is unconvincing, and Weidmann's *Johann Faust* is by no means remarkable. It warrants attention because of the introduction of an individualized female character, and because of her ambivalence. She is both passive and active, loving and violent, domestic and associated with the Devil.

A related, although much less pronounced, ambiguity characterizes the figure of Minchen in the fragment *Fausts Leben dramatisiert* (1778) by the *Sturm und Drang* author Friedrich "Maler" Müller. Minchen is suspected by some as having willingly joined her father in betraying Faust in financial matters. Wagner, however, defends her as "die tugendhafte Seele," the "Engel," the "reinste Unschuld," and the action supports his assessment. Minchen takes money to Faust's aging, infirm parents and is instrumental in bringing Faust's father to Ingolstadt to plead with his son.[14] A related domestication of women is found as well in the drama *Doktor Faust* (1797) by Julius Freiherr von Soden.[15] Lieschen, a "holdes, naives Bauernmädchen," is Faust's fiancée and the mother of his son Gürgel. Helena, conjured up in the traditional manner to distract and seduce Faust, has only one line ("Ich liebe dich"). Faust returns to marry Lieschen, but she cannot save him from his fate.

The first author to make the explicit connection of Faust's salvation to woman's intervention is Johann Friedrich Schink, who wrote several versions of *Faust* between 1778 and 1804.[16] The main work is *Johann Faust: Dramatische Phantasie nach einer Sage des 16. Jahrhunderts,* published in two volumes in 1804. In the Pandemonium prologue, Faust's guardian angel Ithuriel proclaims:

> ... da Tugend nie siegender,
> Überzeugender nie spricht zu den Sterblichen,
> Als durch edeler Frau'n sanfte Beredsamkeit,
> Soll ein tugendlich Weib,
> Seiner Jugend Gefährtin, sich
> Leis' ihm nah'n und ihn retten!
> Denn du schmücktest mit Schönheit
> Und mit Anmuth das Weib aus;
> Schufest weich ihm das Herz, gabst ihm den sanften Geist,
> Daß es zähme den Mann, trotzig und unbeschränkt,
> Ihm sein sichtbarer Engel sei![17]

These words are a variation on the meaning of woman as virtuous, devoted, and other-oriented. Schink's innovation is the redemptive quality. Faust's "verlassene Geliebte" follows him in male disguise, warning and assisting him. Since he had entered upon a wager with the Devil, Faust can be, and is, eventually saved. Mathilde, who is joined after initial hesitation by Faust's "Famulus" Eckhard, is characterized as an angel, as Faust's "Genius," as the spirit of love and purity. As she herself states: "Des Weibes Herz, des Weibes Geist ist Liebe, / Und seine Stärke feste Treue nur."[18]

It was not only love and fidelity which formed the cultural definition of female nature from the end of the 18th century onward. The function of woman was to mediate man's self-development. Women were credited with a heightened sense of humanity or an intensity which served men's growth and progress. Their deeds, as in Goethe's *Iphigenie,* or their very being, as in Schlegel's *Lucinde,* were seen in the service of man's becoming. The redemptive female figures in versions of *Faust* from Schink onward reinforced this meaning of woman as the subordinate term in a process which privileges the development of the dominant (masculine) entity. Defined through the opposition of male and female nature as the "Other," the cultural construct "woman" is instrumentalized and serves the advance of the masculine subject. Schink's Faust tells Mathilde: "Dein Herz bedarf ich mehr, als Deine Dienste; / Dies Herz bürgt mir das meine. .... / Bleibst du mir nah, / So werd' ich nie mir selbst verloren gehen."[19] His words prove true, as Mathilde's vigilance precludes his succumbing to Mephistopheles' temptations, and Ithuriel's appearance at the end indicates, as in Weidmann, the defeat of the Devil. Only in Schink's *Johann Faust* is the instrument of salvation woman's repeated intercession.

Schink's Mathilde displays none of the ambivalences of Weidmann's Helena, and in many 19th-century versions of *Faust* the idealization of the female figures seems complete. At the same time, a secondary role develops for women. The ideal of woman as loving, virtuous, and re-demptive is seemingly powerful but, in actuality, is restrictive and subor-dinating. Its embodiment as "the eternal feminine" in the Faust myth in the 19th century is accompanied by a second set of female figures. Often undefined and mysterious, they are connected with disorder and chaos, characterized at times by independent action, often by collusion with the Devil. Surely they may be viewed as an extension of the chapbook versions of woman as a tool of the Devil. Their erotic character corre-sponds to the archetype of woman as temptress, woman as succubus. Yet these female figures also clearly represent the nether side of the feminine ideal. In analyzing the literary development of the Faust myth as a struggle over the meanings of "woman" and the establishment of an identity for "man," I read those figures as the ominous yet alluring presence of such aspects as are repressed in the definition of the "eternal feminine." Women like Schink's Mathilde can be subsumed as media-tion, as subordinate term, contributing to the development and salvation of "man," of Faust. Women who elude the definition as ideal are marked as destructive and treacherous, and obsessed by their own insatiable desires. Their sexuality connects them to the realm of untamed nature and assures both man's attraction to them and his fear of their revenge. As examples, I would like to regard briefly works by Voss, Klingemann, Holtei, and Heine.

Julius von Voss borrowed extensively from Schink for his 1823 drama, *Faust*. Distinctly reminiscent of Schink's Mathilde, the figure of Seraphina sings at critical moments throughout the play, in order to warn and sustain Faust. She assures him: "Mein ganzes Leben sei nur ein Gebet für Euch——."[20] However, in contrast to Schink, her efforts are in vain, and Faust is damned. In a subplot which is concerned with Faust's intervention in the peasant uprisings and the figure of the popular hero Robertus, a second female figure is introduced.[21] Aurelia is Robertus' companion, and she clearly subverts the idealized definition of woman. When Robertus reminds her: "O, Lieb' und Häuslichkeit nur ziemen Frauen," she places public action first: "Ruft die gemeine Sache, / Muß Liebe schweigen."[22] Her figure recalls such women of the French Revo-lution as Olympe de Gouges, and she is judged negatively within the play.

Her opposition to Robertus' attempts at channeling the uprising back to "die Treue [zu] einem Fürsten" aligns her, within Voss's conservative drama, with the forces of chaos, disorder, and destruction. Robertus is killed, and she takes her own life.

Aurelia is connected with independent action and resultant violence, but she is only marginally connected with Faust. Although her figure creates a contrast to the virtuous Seraphina, the two women are not directly linked within the text. A clearer example of the duality of the disempowered woman-as-ideal and the mysterious, threatening adversary is found in August Klingemann's *Faust*. Published in 1815, this work remained a popular drama throughout the 19th century. In Klingemann's play, the female figures of Käthe and Helene are juxtaposed. The character of Faust's wife Käthe is summed up in the words of his old, blind father: "Du treues Kind."[23] Faust explicitly recognizes her role of devoted mediator when he states: "Du könntest mit mir selber mich versöhnen."[24] Unfortunately, Faust abuses his opportunity, as he poisons his faithful Käthe. He does so at the request of Helene, the mysterious "other" woman. An enigmatic figure, Helene is presented twice as an image before appearing on stage. Such an introduction is in keeping with the Faust legend, as Faust is often tantalized by observing a woman in a mirror. In Klingemann's *Faust,* however, the image is first seen by Käthe, thus juxtaposing very clearly the idealized woman and her unseemly counterpart. Käthe's reaction upon perceiving Helene's image exemplifies the threat to her as idealized woman. At first attracted by the portrait which appears in her home, she is then repelled and finally terrified by the eyes: "Sie wollen mich ermorden!"[25] She can only "save" herself by covering the painting, a fairly transparent representation of repression. The woman-as-ideal can continue to exist only by the denial of the possible existence of a powerful woman with desires and strategies of her own.

Faust is predictably captivated when he returns home and unveils the painting. He then glimpses the image a second time in a locket worn by Der Fremde, and his desire for Helene is manipulated carefully to accomplish his doom. The aspects of "woman" which elude the idealized definition are clearly lethal for the stable identity of "man." In the final act of Klingemann's drama, Helene appears masked. When Faust removes the mask for what he assumes to be the bridal kiss, the barren skull of death returns his gaze. This final telling image in the play embodies an additional aspect of many of the enigmatic "other" women. Representing what is idealized out of woman as subordinate mediation of the male self, they repeat the gesture of attempted subjugation. To this extent, they are not to be viewed as positive images of female power, but as reflections of male fears and desires.

Karl von Holtei's *Dr. Johannes Faust* (1829) does not really add any new themes to the set of secondary, sinister female roles in the 19th century, although his Helena achieves independence from the Devil. The play opposes Helena and Margarethe, the latter being so thoroughly domesticated that act 1 opens with her sweeping out Faust's study in Wittenberg. In act 2, which takes place at the court in Parma, Helena is a foreign countess who wants Faust to go to Greece with her. When Faust and the devil figure, Voland, are forced to flee, Helena and Voland fight for possession of Faust. Helena confounds the Devil and appears in the final act to threaten Margarethe, indeed to attempt to steal her child. Powerfully insistent upon asserting her own desires, she is only defeated when Faust expressly rejects her advances for his Margarethe, whose intercession in the last scene appears to secure his salvation.

It must be left to Heine to draw the most vivid conclusions from the dynamics of the cultural conceptions of woman in the Faust myth, and his version accentuates the independence of Holtei's Helena. Before regarding his ballet scenario, however, it is time to turn to the master. Holtei, Klingemann, Voss, Schink, Soden, Müller, and Weidmann presented plays relatively transparent to analyze, although it is often the "lesser" works of art which supply clues to the construction of cultural definitions. The definitive version of Faustian striving, of man's restless struggle and change, is Goethe's *Faust.* His drama also provides the most remarkable individualized female figures and the most abstractly conceptualized rendition of the function and meaning of woman. In both parts of *Faust,* there is a perceptible tension between the individual and the abstract, between women and "woman." The tendency is consistently to absorb the personal identity of the women figures into a broader concept which serves the development of man's (Faust's) identity. It is the same process of positioning woman as the subordinate term, and privileging the dominant term, which operates less elegantly in other Faust texts from Schink onward. The lack of any accompanying embodiment, in Goethe's *Faust,* of the repressed elements of the definition of woman is hardly surprising. The "Prolog im Himmel" incorporates, and thereby defuses, any manifestation of negation or radical difference. It is not within Goethe's conception of Faust to allow for independent self-assertion of the "Other," be it woman or Devil.

In *Faust I,* the tension between woman in the abstract and women as individuals begins in the scene "Hexenküche." Faust originally desires woman as image; even in the ensuing encounter with Gretchen, it is still the abstract which he desires in the particular. In the scene "Abend," a visit to Gretchen's room elicits a rapturous patriarchal vision. The chair upon which he sits is apostrophized as "Väterthron," and he is infatuated with the spirit of abundant maternal order which he views as guiding every action of the "Mädchen" he desires. What he terms "Liebestraum" in this scene is an abstract enchantment with his own projected images. In similar fashion, the scene "Wald und Höhle" subjects the concrete figure of Gretchen to conceptualization and also shows most clearly the adherence to the cultural definitions of innate male and female nature. Faust's final speech in this scene begins with concrete references to "her" embrace and "her" needs but rapidly switches to a more abstract juxtaposition of the nature of his character as a raging waterfall and hers as "Häusliches Beginnen / Umfangen in der kleinen Welt."[26] Faust evades responsibility here by projecting a clash of male and female nature, and his abstract imagery is entirely self-serving.[27]

The scene "Wald und Höhle" is followed by the concrete emotion expressed by Gretchen at the spinning wheel. For her, Faust has become the focus of all thoughts, activity, and unconscious desires. Everything that she does and suffers originates in her love for him. Her individual character and fate are movingly depicted, and the social criticism of the plight of such unwed mothers in the 18th century is admirable. But we must not forget that, within *Faust,* Gretchen and her tragedy are presented as a necessary stage in the development of Faust. Her individuality is subordinated to the process of his becoming—a process which ultimately, with feminine intercession, will bring redemption for Faust and leave Gretchen doing penance. Margaret Guenther has written that this inequity is perhaps the true tragedy of Goethe's drama.[28] The female penitents at the end of *Faust II* atone for their sexual transgressions, for their desires. The *magna peccatrix* and the *Mulier Samaritana* from the New Testament, as well as Maria Aegyptiaca, are noted for their open sexuality and for their fervent contrition. In Goethe's *Faust,* women's desires require atonement. Man's desire, even when causing tragedy, is inherent to his striving and warrants fulfillment and final redemption.

If the encounter with Gretchen mediates for Faust the realm of human existence and emotion, the Helena phantasmagoria in *Faust II* represents Faust's experience of beauty and classical antiquity. A female character much different from Gretchen, Helena is Faust's equal. Their union is ephemeral, but the encounter sustains and uplifts Faust. Within the skillful blend of highly abstract meaning and strikingly concrete action of the third act of *Faust II,* Helena functions both as the shade, or image—mediating art, antiquity, and beauty for Faust—and as an individual woman. As an individual, her person is made uncertain and insecure by the meanings attributed to her. In the Helena scenes, the tension is between the individual identity of the female figure and her cultural meanings. Her initial words of self-introduction already convey this complexity: "Bewundert viel und viel gescholten, Helena" (8488). Referring both to her representation in antiquity and to the mixed reactions to Faust's conjuration in the "Rittersaal" scene, the passive and ambivalent introduction indicates a self-alienation. The sharp interchange between Phorkyas (Mephistopheles) and the chorus later deepens her confusion:

> Ist's wohl Gedächtnis? War es Wahn, der mich ergreift?
> War ich das alles? Bin ich's ? Werd' ich's künftig sein,
> Das Traum- und Schreckbild jener Städteverwüstenden?
>   (8838–8840)

When Phorkyas reminds her of elements of her meaning as Helena in poetry and myth, she denies knowing which Helena she really is (8875). The addition of the legend of her union with Achilles causes her to fear a total loss of self:

> Ich als Idol, ihm dem Idol verband ich mich.
> Es war ein Traum, so sagen ja die Worte selbst.
> Ich schwinde hin und werde selbst mir ein Idol.
>   (8879–8881)

Phorkyas' purpose had of course been to unnerve her so that she would seek refuge from Menelaus with Faust. His strategy works, and Helena assumes her place in Faust's development. In the "Innerer Burghof" scene, she is reminded again of her legendary reputation. She pardons Lynkeus for having neglected his duty while lost in contemplation of her beauty and then laments her fate:

> . . . Wehe mir! Welch streng Geschick
> Verfolgt mich, überall der Männer Busen
> So zu betören, daß sie weder sich
> Noch sonst ein Würdiges verschonten.
>   (9247–9250)

Although she turns the lament against herself, its rightful target should be the uses and abuses men have made of her, the meanings which they have imputed to her.

Even in the idyll with Faust, Helena cannot secure her existence. At the end of the "Schattiger Hain" scene, she is reduced to her attributes, as she disappears, leaving only her dress and veil. In her own transformation into the "eternal feminine," they change into clouds which carry Faust upward. The cloud symbolism is clearly linked to the power of woman's love within man's development in the "Hochgebirg" scene, which opens the fourth act. The cloud divides, and Faust's monologue makes it clear that the sections represent Helena and Gretchen. Of the representation of the latter, Faust states in the final lines that it "erhebt sich in den Äther hin / Und zieht das Beste meines Innern mit sich fort"

(10065–10066). This opening monologue in "Hochgebirg" foreshadows the "Ewig-Weibliche" of the final scene of Goethe's *Faust* and is characteristic of the representation of women and the function of woman in the work. In the apotheosis of woman as the "eternal feminine," transcendent to, and yet in the service of, man's nature and development, the concrete individuality of women is lost.

Penetrating the aura of Goethe's *Faust* is not easy, and a full feminist critique of the drama has yet to be written. I would suggest that it must include a careful analysis of the concepts of love and eros and their function within the work, as well as a feminine iconography of the "Klassische Walpurgisnacht." Perhaps the appropriate conclusion to my partial analysis is a brief, iconoclastic reading of the Mothers as a paradigm for the representation of women and the meaning of "woman" in Goethe's complex, definitive version of the Faust myth. Imbued with all possible mystical, mythical meanings both by Faust in his exposition in the "Rittersaal" scene, and by generations of critics ever since, the Mothers are in actuality relegated to the remotest regions of "Einsamkeit," effectively excluded from the sphere of social action. Such is also the position of women as embodiment of the "eternal feminine." Designating Goethe's *Faust* as "das Drama der Menschengattung" or as establishing "The Meaning of Human Identity" conceals the manner in which "human" is equated with "man," and woman is abstracted to a functional ideal.[29]

To return to Heine: his version of Faust was conceived in conscious opposition to Goethe's—as he put it: "rivalisierend mit dem großen Wolfgang Goethe."[30] His ballet scenario *Der Doktor Faust: Ein Tanzpoem* was written in 1847 for the director of Her Majesty's Theater in London. First published in German in 1851, it was not performed until the 20th century. The work has been read within the context of Heine's conceptual dualism of sensualism and spiritualism, although scholars have also noted that its complexity tends to elude such an opposition.[31] His female Devil Mephistophela has been designated as the great-grandmother of Wedekind's Lulu and as evidence for Heine's personal ambivalence toward women.[32] At least two critics have pointed out that in Heine's *Faust* the "eternal feminine" exhibits a decidedly downward pull.[33] It is perhaps an antidote to Goethe's *Faust*.

The action of the *Tanzpoem* and the entire constellation of female figures illustrate the tensions already analyzed in Klingemann and Holtei. But Heine's version conveys a clearer awareness of what is at stake. In the first act, Faust conjures a variety of beasts which do not frighten him; then, finally, a female Mephistophela appears as a ballet dancer. Overcoming his initial astonishment, Faust lets himself be entertained and is eventually attracted by the image of a duchess in a mirror. In order to win her favor, he must take dancing lessons and change his attire after signing a pact with the female Devil. In the second act, Faust meets both the duchess and the duke. Discovering that the duchess is really a prominent bride of Satan, Faust makes a date with her for the Witches' Sabbath. This festival, described in appropriately lascivious detail, forms the third act. During the course of it, Faust and the duchess absent themselves. When they return, Faust shows obvious signs of disgust and attempts to avoid her lustful caresses. He yearns to escape from her demands to the realm of Greek harmony where the characters are "uneigennützig." Mephistophela complies, and the fourth act is one of perfect harmony on an island with Helen of Sparta. But the arrival of the duchess destroys both the landscape and the beauty of the figures. Faust kills the duchess and flees with Mephistophela, whose attitude during the second half of the act had been "Schadenfreude." The final act takes place in a picturesque 16th-century Dutch village. Faust, as a traveling quacksalver, falls in love with the "Natürlichkeit, Zucht und Schöne" of the blond daughter of the mayor. As they are entering the cathedral for their wedding, Mephistophela appears. A large black hand grabs Faust, and he is carried off to hell.

The final two acts are related to the Helena and Gretchen episodes of Goethe's *Faust*. It has been suggested that Faust's shy courting of the mayor's daughter is practically a parody of the inability of Goethe's Faust to woo Gretchen without assistance from the Devil.[34] And Goethe's Helena scenes were the only sections of *Faust II* of which Heine approved. In a certain sense, the Hellenistic episode in Heine's text clearly embodies his own ideals as well. In the final two acts, however, any establishment of a patriarchal vision of woman as ideal is thwarted. Both the domesticated daughter of the local mayor and the figure which Heine describes in his notes as "jenes ewig blühende Ideal von Anmut und Schönheit" are destroyed by the "other" women, by the duchess and Mephistophela. As with the character of Helene in Holtei and Klingemann, Faust is both attracted to, and ultimately opposed by, these figures. His repulsion in the face of the active assertion by the duchess of *her* desires is the fear of those aspects of woman which cannot be defined and controlled. And in Heine's ballet scenario, man has very little control. His *Tanzpoem* exposes the contingency of the cultural definition of "woman" which is central to the other Faust texts.

The literary versions of Faust from the 1770s through the first half of the 19th century tell the story of the cultural definition of woman as well as that of the constitution of the male subject. Women play the supporting role, whether antagonistic or redemptive. They are praised as angelic, or damned as alluringly destructive; and I have indicated the dynamics connecting the roles. Two additional texts by well-known authors would warrant an analysis. Grabbe's *Don Juan und Faust* (1829) enacts the subjugation of "woman" as consumption (Don Juan) or as possession (Faust). Lenau's *Faust: Ein Gedicht* (1836/1840) explicitly connects woman and nature. Faust's longing for unity with nature, and her ultimate indifference or treachery, would support my initial connection of women with subjugated nature in the Faust myth.

But the other questions with which I began remain to be answered. How are women to read Faust? And what happens when women appropriate the central role? As I suggested at the outset, Ida Hahn-Hahn's female Faust is an interesting and problematic development, one which must be read both within and against the system of cultural meanings typified by the Faust myth. Her novel *Gräfin Faustine* (1840) is not a true version of the Faust story but rather an appropriation of Faust through the life of the protagonist. With its autobiographical undertones, the book connects the myth of Faust with the dilemmas of the first generation of female authors in the *Vormärz,* with the "Ausbruchs- und Aufbruchsfrauen."[35] Hahn-Hahn's novel combines the Faust legend, 19th-century Faustian ideology, and the historical reality of women. Despite the aristocratic background of both the author and the protagonist, Hahn-Hahn's appropriation of Faust has implications of a broader nature for the development of women's identity and subjectivity.

Gräfin Faustine was the best known of Hahn-Hahn's novels, receiving comparison with work by George Sand as well as a parody by Fanny Lewald (*Diogena,* 1847). Partially popular because it revealed in a brief episode the story of the author's own early, miserable marriage, it is clearly a *Salonroman* and an example of what Friedrich Sengle calls the "Weltschmerzexpansion."[36] In the title figure's explicit rejection of the second part of Goethe's *Faust,* and in the reduction of Faust to the concept of "striving," the novel is also definitely a product of its literary-historical period. Faustine's second husband says of her: "Streben war ihr einziges Glück," and she herself explains her attraction to her "Taufpate Faust" as follows: "Ich wollte immer mein eigenes Schicksal in diesem rastlosen Fortstreben, in diesem Dursten und Schmachten nach Befriedigung finden."[37] But in acting out the Faustian ideology as a woman, a central conflict arises between striving, "sich zur möglichsten Vollendung durchzuarbeiten," and the definitions and boundaries set for women.[38] The problematic aspect is the (impossible) reconciliation of the Faustian character with the cultural meanings established for woman. Faustine discards all the traditional categories—mother, wife, socialite, temptress, muse, nun—but she is continually forced back into them. When Renate Möhrmann regards Faustine as a female Faust only in a qualified sense because she is restricted to a "Skepsis des Herzens," she is actually describing the very problem.[39] Hahn-Hahn's protagonist is limited in her restless search for self-fulfillment by the boundaries of the roles and spheres of action to which women are culturally consigned.

Briefly, the novel begins with Faustine widowed after an inhuman first marriage from which she had fled. She is living in a mutually satisfying relationship with Baron Andlau. While he is away on a trip, she develops a passionate love for Mario Mengen, who insists on marriage. She writes a farewell note to Andlau, effectively ruining his life. After several years of marriage, motherhood, and success as a painter, she enters a convent. Life as a nun is also not satisfying, and she dies shortly thereafter. In a subplot, she struggles against the adoration of her brother-in-law, Clemens Walldorf, who eventually shoots himself in despair in her sitting room. During the course of her life, she lives out all of the identities available for women but can find self-fulfillment in none of them.

In *Faustine,* Ida Hahn-Hahn tells the story of a woman who is not fulfilled by women's roles but can find no alternatives. Her "Streben" is perceived within the novel, by contemporaneous readers and by many modern critics, as characteristic of an "Unweib," as "demonic."[40] Even her author designated her as a "Vampyrnatur."[41] Hahn-Hahn had to write a special preface to the third edition, as so many readers had protested Faustine's infidelity to Andlau, her desertion of her husband Mengen to enter the convent, or her abandonment of her son. In attempting to assert herself as an independent subject, Faustine is judged by the system of cultural definitions typified by the myth of her namesake. "Wer immer strebend sich bemüht" is not a gender-free assertion, as the fate of Faustine indicates.

Hahn-Hahn's novel is not a faithful rendition of the Faust legend. But it is a dialogue with the system of cultural meanings associated with the Faust myth in the 19th century. The definitions of "woman" which I have traced through the literary versions of *Faust* preclude women's attainment of their *own* subjectivity, of their *own* identity. I would conclude by returning to our title: "*Our* 'Faust'?" I can only emphasize the question mark.

Notes

1 Karl Gutzkow, *Wally, die Zweiflerin* (Stuttgart, 1983), 42.
2 Irmtraud Morgner, *Amanda: Ein Hexenroman* (Berlin/GDR, 1983), 126–127.
3 Georg Lukács, "Faust-Studien," in his *Faust und Faustus* (Reinbek, 1967), 144.

4 The young peasant woman in Pfitzer's 1674 version deserves mention as a precursor. Faust loves her, but she resists his advances when he will not marry her. This figure and the reintroduction of Helen as a concubine are Pfitzer's main deviations from Widmann's 1599 version of the chapbook.

5 E. M. Butler, *The Fortunes of Faust* (Cambridge, 1952), 132.

6 Detailed analyses of the process of the production of cultural meanings which define the ostensibly inborn nature of woman in this period are provided by the following studies: Karin Hausen, "Die Polarisierung der 'Geschlechtscharaktere': Eine Spiegelung der Dissoziation von Erwerbs- und Familienleben," in *Sozialgeschichte der Familie in der Neuzeit Europas,* ed. by Werner Conze (Stuttgart, 1976), 363–393; Barbara Duden, "Das schöne Eigentum: Zur Herausbildung des bürgerlichen Frauenbildes an der Wende vom 18. zum 19. Jahrhundert," *Kursbuch* 47 (March, 1977): 125–140; Silvia Bovenschen, *Die imaginierte Weiblichkeit: Exemplarische Untersuchungen zu kulturgeschichtlichen und literarischen Präsentationsformen des Weiblichen* (Frankfurt, 1979); Susan Cocalis, "Der Vormund will Vormund sein: Zur Problematik der weiblichen Unmündigkeit im 18. Jahrhundert," in *Gestaltet und Gestaltend: Frauen in der deutschen Literatur,* ed. by Marianne Burkhardt (Amsterdam, 1980), 33–35; Brigitte Wartmann, "Die Grammatik des Patriarchats: Zur 'Natur' des Weiblichen in der bürgerlichen Gesellschaft," *Ästhetik und Kommunikation* 13, no. 47 (1982): 12–32; Volker Hoffmann, "Elisa und Robert oder das Weib und der Mann, wie sie sein sollten: Anmerkungen zur Geschlechtercharakteristik der Goethezeit," in *Klassik und Moderne: Die Weimarer Klassik als historisches Ereignis und Herausforderung im kulturgeschichtlichen Prozeß,* ed. by Karl Richter and Jörg Schönert (Stuttgart, 1983), 80–90; Sally Winkle, "The Construction of a Bourgeois Ideal of Women as Developed in Sophie von La Roche's *Geschichte des Fräuleins von Sternheim* and Goethe's *Die Leiden des jungen Werthers*" (Ph.D. diss., University of Wisconsin-Madison, 1984).

7 Friedrich Schiller, "Das Lied von der Glocke," in *Schillers Werke,* ed. by Norbert Oellers, 2 vols. (Weimar, 1983), 1:230.

8 Kant's contributions to the opposition of male and female nature are found in his essay "Beobachtungen über das Gefühl des Schönen und Erhabenen" (1764) and in his *Anthropologie in pragmatischer Hinsicht* (1798).

9 Johann Gottlieb Fichte, *Grundlage des Naturrechts nach Prinzipien der Wissenschaftslehre* (Hamburg, 1960), 304.

10 There was speculation that this work, by a Viennese bureaucrat, might be the lost *Faust* by Lessing. Even as conjecture, the idea is ludicrous. It was also later assumed that the anonymous author must have belonged to the *Sturm und Drang,* and there are many parallels with the Faust renditions by Maler Müller and Klinger. Roderich Warkentin, *Nachklänge der Sturm- und Drangperiode in Faustdichtungen des achtzehnten Jahrhunderts* (Munich, 1896), 1–8.

11 Paul Weidmann, "Johann Faust: Ein allegorisches Drama von fünf Aufzügen," in *Faust,* ed. by Margret Dietrich (Diessen, 1970), 255.

12 Ursula Friess characterizes Helena as Lessing's Sara and Marwood combined; cf. her *Buhlerin und Zauberin: Eine Untersuchung zur deutschen Literatur des 18. Jahrhunderts* (Munich, 1970), 59–60. For an analysis of the suffering woman and the raging woman, see Andreas Huyssen, "Das leidende Weib in der dramatischen Literatur von Empfindsamkeit und Sturm und Drang: Eine Studie zur bürgerlichen Emanzipation in Deutschland," *Monatshefte* 69 (1977): 159–173.

13 Weidmann, 279.

14 In 1776, Müller had published the fragmentary scene with Faust and the King and Queen of Aragon, "Situation aus Fausts Leben" (cf. Dietrich, 359–71). According to Butler, he continued to work on the Faust material, and the remaining acts, written after the publication of Goethe's *Faust I,* borrow heavily from Goethe and Schink for the figure of Lenchen, who is a victim but also the agent of Faust's salvation; see Butler, *Fortunes of Faust,* 150–152.

15 Julius Freiherr von Soden, "Doktor Faust: Volks-Schauspiel in fünf Akten," in *Die Faustdichtung vor, neben und nach Goethe,* ed. by Karl G. Wendriner (Berlin, 1913), 3:151–298.

16 The redemptive qualities of woman are already evident in the earliest version, *Doktor Faust: Ein komisches Duodrama* (1778). Rosalinde, disguised first as a student, then as the Devil, finally as Helen of Troy, effectively stages the entire "tragedy" in order to cure Faust and eventually to marry him; see Butler, *Fortunes of Faust*, 139.

17 Johann Friedrich Schink, *Johann Faust: Dramatische Phantasie nach einer Sage des sechzehnten Jahrhunderts* (Berlin, 1804), 1:22–23.

18 Ibid., 172. Even the most serious threat to Mathilde's influence, the character of Raphaele in vol. 2, conforms to the prevailing concept of woman's nature. She is the embodiment of the image of Schirin, with which Mephistopheles tantalizes Faust, but she herself is characterized by innocent virtue.

19 Ibid., 171.

20 Julius von Voss, *Faust, Trauerspiel mit Gesang und Tanz,* ed. by Georg Ellinger (Berlin, 1890), 59.

21 Several motifs are taken from Friedrich Maximilian Klinger's *Sturm und Drang* novel *Fausts Leben, Thaten und Höllenfahrt in fünf Büchern* (1791), among them Faust's intervention in the peasant uprisings and the figure of Robertus.

22 Voss, *Faust,* 61, 63.

23 August Klingemann, "Faust: Trauerspiel in fünf Aufzügen," in *Gestaltungen des Faust,* ed. by Horst Wolfram Geißler (1927; reprint, Hildesheim, 1974), 3:24.

24 Ibid., 45.

25 Ibid., 52.

26 Johann Wolfgang von Goethe, "Faust: Eine Tragödie," in *Goethes Werke,* ed. by Erich Trunz (Hamburg, 1967), 1:107. The passage quoted is taken from lines 3354–3355. Further references to Goethe's *Faust* will be given as line numbers parenthetically within the text.

27 Margaret Guenther observes that Faust equates libido with "natural" phenomena in this scene, in order to avoid the realm of morality in justifying his treatment of Gretchen. See her *"Faust:* The Tragedy Reexamined," in *Beyond the Eternal Feminine: Critical Essays on Women and German Literature,* ed. by Susan L. Cocalis and Kay Goodman (Stuttgart, 1982), 90–91.

28 Guenther, *Faust,* 96, 98. The comment is also made explicitly by the editors on p. 12.

29 As detailed in n. 3, "das Drama der Menschengattung" is Lukács's term. "The Meaning of Human Identity" is a term used by Stuart Atkins in his *Goethe's Faust: A Literary Analysis* (Cambridge, 1958), 192.

30 Heinrich Heine, "Der Doktor Faust," in *Heinrich Heine, Sämtliche Schriften,* ed. by Klaus Briegleb (Munich, 1975), 1:373.

31 Jeffrey L. Sammons, *Heinrich Heine: A Modern Biography* (Princeton, 1979), 289–290.

32 Carl Brinitzer, *Heinrich Heine: Roman seines Lebens* (Hamburg, 1960), 480. See also Sammons, *Heinrich Heine,* 290.

33 Oskar Walzel, *Heines Tanzpoem Der Doktor Faust* (Hildesheim, 1917), 9. Benno von Wiese, "Das tanzende Universum," in his *Signaturen: Zu Heinrich Heine und seinem Werk* (Berlin, 1976), 116.

34 Wiese, "Das tanzende Universum," 125.

35 Renate Möhrmann, "Die lesende Vormärzautorin: Untersuchungen zur weiblichen Sozialisation," in *Literatur und Sprache im historischen Prozeß,* ed. by Thomas Cramer (Tübingen, 1983), 317.

36 Friedrich Sengle, *Biedermeierzeit* (Stuttgart, 1971), 1:235. In volumes 1 and 2 of his Biedermeier study, Sengle is condescendingly critical of Hahn-Hahn.

37 Ida Hahn-Hahn, *Gräfin Faustine* (Berlin, 1845), 229.

38 Hahn-Hahn, *Faustine,* 169.

39 Renate Möhrmann, *Die andere Frau: Emanzipationsansätze deutscher Schriftstellerinnen im Vorfeld der Achtundvierziger Revolution* (Stuttgart, 1977), 107. Möhrmann's perceptive analysis connects the novel with George Sand's *Lélia* and considers the question of the female assumption of a literary role usually reserved for male characters.

40 Hahn-Hahn's contemporary Therese von Bacheracht describes Faustine as an "Unweib" in comparison to the figure of Margarita in Hahn-Hahn's novel *Ulrich* (1841), who is "ein echtes, rechtes Weib, ein Weib, so zart, daß es einem wie Mondstrahl in's

Herz dringt." See Bacheracht's *Menschen und Gegenden* (Braunschweig, 1845), 15 as quoted by Gert Oberembt in his *Ida Gräfin Hahn-Hahn: Weltschmerz und Ultramontanismus* (Bonn, 1980), 116. Oberembt himself (p. 390) refers to Faustine as demonically insatiable.

41 Hahn-Hahn, 320.

Romantic Tragedy or National Symbol?
The Interpretation of Goethe's *Faust*
in 19th-Century German Art

FRANÇOISE FORSTER-HAHN

Illustrations of literary works do not only translate text into image, they also are visual expressions of a specific reading of the text at a particular time. Thus, they simultaneously function on two different levels: on an aesthetic one and a historical one. As pictorial interpretation, illustrations are dependent upon, and limited by, the ideas and the narrative of the text; as images created at a specific time and place in history, they act perhaps as the most tangible record of its critical reception. Therefore, the study of images illustrating a text reveals the subtlest changes of understanding which literary works undergo.

An analysis of 19th-century illustrations of Goethe's *Faust* defines the changes in the critical reception of Goethe's tragedy long before photography and film (as records of the theater) assumed this role in the 20th century. While stage productions became the most visible documents in our century—often signaling the most extreme readings—illustrations in all media served this purpose in the 19th century, especially at a time when the number of theatrical performances of *Faust* remained rather limited. The strong interdependence of these two traditions is reciprocal: at first, the pictorial translation of the text exercised a considerable influence upon stage productions; later, the intellectual and visual power of the theater often inspired artists to create new and original images. Both theatrical productions and artistic images are intricately bound up with the course of German history in their critical appropriation of Goethe's text.

The intimate interaction of these two visual traditions has to be taken into account in any comprehensive study of Goethe's *Faust* and the arts.[1] But rather than focusing on this interrelationship, I propose to concentrate on the effect of German history upon the pictorial interpretation of Goethe's tragedy. Not the changing artistic modes shaped the "visual" reading of Goethe's *Faust,* but the course of German history during the crucial period from the Napoleonic Wars to the Wilhelminian Empire. The profound change in the interpretation of *Faust* as well as in the critical assessment of its author occurred in the 1860s. This new aesthetic and ideological appropriation of the text is clearly linked, first, to the national ideals of German unification and, later, to the outspoken nationalistic fervor of the Empire. When an articulate German ideology increasingly penetrated all realms of the cultural life, images acted as the most tangible medium in shaping and expressing this new national identity. If Menzel's images of Frederick the Great were transformed into icons of a heroic patriotic past,[2] Goethe's *Faust* became the symbol of the determined man of action whom the Empire needed to fulfill its mission. Inherent in both Menzel's depiction of Frederick II and Goethe's *Faust* were all those elements which could effectively be exploited for popular success. Thus, the Prussian king and the medieval scholar became rallying points in the search for a new German national identity.

Before the first public theatrical productions of *Faust* took place in January of 1829 in Braunschweig and in August of that same year in Weimar,[3] a number of artists had either created independent graphic cycles, published without the text, or illustrated the text editions which appeared during Goethe's lifetime. The most pertinent graphic works are those of Peter von Cornelius and Moritz Retzsch in Germany and, of course, Delacroix's illustrations for the French translation by Albert Stapfer of 1828.[4] Goethe's somewhat harsh judgments of those artistic interpretations are well known, as is his belief that, in essence, his work was entirely unsuited for any illustration, much less for more independent visual interpretation. In 1805, Goethe wrote to his publisher, Cotta: "Den Faust dächt ich, geben wir ohne Holzschnitte und Bildwerke. Es ist schwer, daß etwas geleistet werde, was dem Sinne und dem Tone nach zu einem Gedicht paßt. Kupfer und Poesie parodieren sich gewöhnlich wechselweise. Ich denke der Hexenmeister soll sich allein durchhelfen."[5] *Faust, ein Fragment* had been published in 1790 with one engraving by Johann Heinrich Lips (1758–1817) that shows Faust in his study and is a variation on an etching by Rembrandt. Rembrandt's print had been identified as "Faust" since the 18th century, providing the model for many similar representations thereafter.[6] When the first part of *Faust* was finally published in 1808, this edition appeared without any illustration at all.[7] In 1836, Wilhelm von Kaulbach was commissioned to execute twelve steel engravings for an edition of Faust, but this project was never realized, and it is only in 1854 that Cotta published the richly illustrated edition of *Faust I* for which Engelbert Seibertz had been asked to provide the drawings.

Because of Goethe's conviction that no images could adequately represent the metaphysical content and meaning of his tragedy, his assessment of all contemporary illustrations and graphic works was extremely cautious, if not outright negative. Nevertheless, he executed several drawings of scenes for *Faust I* himself, which convey his powerful visualization, especially in the *Appearance of the Earth Spirit* (ill. 1), the poodle episode, and the scene in the Hartz Mountains *(Brockenszene)*. These sketches, however, were never intended as illustrations but as pictorial preparations for a theatrical performance planned in 1812, and the sequence of drawings, especially the first six of them, might therefore be dated between 1810 and 1812. In the three most finished drawings, Goethe translates the magic and otherworldly sphere into images which, most probably, could have served as inspirations for stage decorations. When in May of 1819 Count Brühl reported to Goethe about the private staging of *Faust* by Count Radziwill, he also asked the poet how he would imagine the appearance of the Earth Spirit. Goethe answered: "Es . . . war mein Gedanke, . . . einen kolossalen Kopf und Brustteil transparent vorzustellen, und ich dachte, dabei die bekannte Büste Jupiters zugrunde zu legen."[8] As the drawing shows, he had thought, at the time of its creation, of the features of Apollo. In the episodes of the *Appearance of the Earth Spirit,* the exorcism of the poodle, and the Walpurgis Night, Goethe stresses the confrontation of the magic and spiritual realm with the reality of Faust's existence in the material world by harsh contrasts of lighting. This conflict is also evident in the disturbing discrepancy of proportion between the relatively small figure of Faust and the looming and threatening shapes of the spirit. In their visual conception as well as in their stylistic features, these drawings clearly express the romantic mood of the period.

While Goethe intended his own drawings as "sketched ideas" for a theatrical production, other graphic works began to be published before the first productions reached the stage. Of particular artistic and historical significance is the cycle by Peter von Cornelius, because the artist's intentions and his stylistic treatment focus on the political meaning which he attached to Goethe's *Faust.* Cornelius executed the first seven drawings in the spring of 1811 in Frankfurt, three years after the publication of *Faust I* in 1808. These seven scenes are: *Auerbach's Cellar, Gretchen's First Meeting with Faust, Marthe's Garden, Margaret's Prayer, Margaret in the Cathedral, Faust and Mephistopheles in the Hartz Mountains* (Blocksberg Scene), and *Faust and Mephistopheles Speeding Onward on Black Horses round the Raven Stone.* In the autumn of 1811, Cornelius, then twenty-eight years old, moved to Rome where he completed the *Faust* cycle with the following five episodes: *Before the City Gate, Valentine's Death, Margaret in the Dungeon,* the title page for the entire cycle, and one print illustrating the *Prelude on the Stage.*

The entire sequence of twelve scenes, including the title page, appeared in print in 1816.[9] The most striking feature in this selection is the omission of any image of the old, desperate, brooding, and doubtful

Faust, or of the contemplative scholar in his study. Cornelius interprets Faust as an energetic, taut, virile figure, a German knight whose gestures express an intense determination and a strong inclination for action, making him an equal, if not a superior, counterpart to the almost comical stage figure of Mephistopheles, who appears with the traditional feather on his cap, a horse's foot, and fingernails which extend into long claws. In *Faust's First Meeting with Margaret* on her way home from church (ill. 2), as well as in the scene in *Marthe's Garden* (ill. 3), the setting is medieval German. Faust and Gretchen are clearly the predominant figures characterized as the ideal Northern pair: Faust, the youthful knight, pursuing Gretchen, the shy and then amorously submissive young woman. The sources for Cornelius's pictures are not found in classical idealism—then primarily associated with the classical tradition of French art—but in the art of Dürer and the North. Even though Cornelius focuses on the tragedy of Gretchen, he shows the scenes of love and despair, especially *Gretchen in the Dungeon* (ill. 4), with a cool austerity that is far from the emotionally charged drama of Delacroix's erotic scene (ill. 5), or the theatrical sentimentality of the final composition in Radziwill's series of eight lithographs, a picture portfolio that was published in 1835.[10]

The crucial scene in Cornelius's sequence, in which the artist poignantly defines the relationship between Faust and Mephistopheles, is the seventh print: *Faust and Mephistopheles Speeding Onward on Black Horses round the Raven Stone* (ill. 6). The major role which Cornelius assigns to Faust becomes even more apparent when we compare his interpretation to Delacroix's (ill. 7). Whereas Delacroix shows Mephistopheles as the agile, ever-persuasive representation of evil that is in total control of the action,[11] Cornelius almost reverses the roles: Faust's virile figure and almost imperial gesture do not display any of the horror and fright at the dreadful vision of the diabolical figures who lead the young woman resembling Margaret to the gallows. The stern defiance of Faust's look and the commanding gesture of his arm almost contradict the frightful question in Goethe's text: "Was weben die dort um den Rabenstein?" The stooped figure of Mephistopheles in the background seems to be much more in awe of the gloomy sight than Faust, whose dynamic figure completely dominates the composition, radiating the same force which Delacroix attributes to Mephistopheles. In Delacroix's conception, Mephistopheles represents the powerful force of evil assuming a diabolical role of intrigue and fascination (ill. 8).

An analysis of Cornelius's *Faust* cycle immediately reveals two outstanding features: his selection of scenes focuses almost entirely on the storytelling facts of the tragedy which are bound to the material world, and he largely excludes the spiritual and magic elements which Delacroix and also Goethe himself explored in their drawings. Cornelius concentrates on the tragedy of Gretchen, making her the center of his narrative. His style and setting for the *Faust* tragedy are typical expressions of the Nazarene concept of contemporary German art—what Goethe critically called "altdeutsch"[12] when he referred to Cornelius's drawings was far more than an argument of taste. While Goethe's preference for the classical tradition at this time expresses his more international and cosmopolitan attitude, Cornelius's neomedieval interpretation reveals his patriotic intention: his *Faust* and, even more so, his *Nibelungen* illustrations are deeply rooted in the national revival of the time.[13] It is no historical coincidence that, in 1867, another time of strong national tendencies, Alfred von Wolzogen rediscovered these political underpinnings, stressing the national spirit of Cornelius's *Faust* in his monograph on the artist.[14] In his approach to Goethe's *Faust,* Cornelius was inspired by the national-patriotic mood of the period marked by the aggressive anti-French, anti-Napoleonic political movement. In the letter he wrote to Goethe in 1815, he explained his *Faust* images in these terms: "Wenn auch jede wahre Kunst nie ihre Wirkung auf unverdorbene Gemüther verliert, und die Werke einer großen Vergangenheit uns mächtig in die damalige Denk- und Empfindungsweise hineinziehen, so sind doch die Wirkungen einer gleichzeitigen Kunst noch ungleich größer und lebendiger, und ganze Völker, ja ganze Zeitalter sind oft von den Werken eines einzelnen großen Menschen begeistert worden. Wie Ihre Exzellenz auf Ihre Zeit und besonders auf Ihre Nation gewirkt haben, ist davon der sprechendste Beweis. . . ."[15]

When Cornelius planned his next graphic project, the *Nibelungenlied,* in Rome between 1812 and 1817, he was even more articulate in expressing his patriotic convictions: "Es soll ein Werk werden, worin sich die ganze Herrlichkeit der alten Welt, vorzüglich aber die unseres Vaterlandes spiegeln soll."[16] This was precisely the motivation of his *Faust* illustrations. As an old man meditating on the creative impulses in his early years, he defined this goal in one of the many exchanges with Hermann Riegel: It had been his conscious intention to create something "altdeutsch" with his *Faust* cycle, and he went on to explain that it was above all this national German spirit which aroused violent criticism in the academies.[17] The equation of the so-called "altdeutsch" mode with concrete political aims also applied to other artistic activities. In a letter to his publisher Wenner of May 1814, Cornelius compared the project of a general exhibition of German artists in Rome to the German fight for freedom from Napoleonic domination.[18] The artist's passionate identification with the Faust theme and the political ideals linked to it might have been the reason for including his own self-portrait in the Cathedral Scene (ill. 9).

While Cornelius's political interpretation of Goethe's *Faust* remains unique for its time, the most complete and popular sequence of prints by Moritz Retzsch is as free of political connotations as it is of psychological depth. Retzsch executed twenty-nine plates of *Faust I* for Cotta in 1816, followed by eleven compositions for *Faust II* in 1836. Both parts were published together in one edition as *Umrisse zu Goethe's Faust* in 1837.[19]

In these line engravings, Retzsch followed the style of Flaxman's and the brothers Riepenhausen's classicizing print cycles of Homer's *Iliad* and *Odyssey,* i.e., a pictorial translation of text into image that had developed in England during the latter part of the 18th century. Being entirely in the tradition of this style of pictorial narrative, the images alone translate the literary text into a picture-story accompanied only by subtitles or short explanatory comments in the preface. Therefore, the artist had to select carefully the most telling episodes which mirror the chronological sequence of the narrative, and simultaneously highlight the dramatic turning points of the text. The clarity of the line drawings, and the compositions in their straightforward and uncomplicated design, make the figures appear almost as puppets on a mock stage. Despite this rather shallow and simplistic rendering, emptied of any deeper emotional content, Retzsch's compositions achieved great popularity not only in Germany but in France and England as well.[20] Exercising considerable influence on artists, and serving as models for the design of stage productions in Europe, they almost assumed the function of a pattern book which could easily be adapted for a variety of purposes.

Retzsch included in his sequence two scenes which became an integral part of all later illustrations, epitomizing an altogether new concept: *Faust in his Study* (ill. 10) and *Margaret at the Spinning Wheel* (ill. 11). The first became the model for numerous scenes showing Faust as the old scholar brooding over his books in desperate search of the ultimate truth; the second provided an appealing image of Margaret as the virtuous young woman in a typical Northern interior. It was a well-chosen contrast, which betrayed the bourgeois ideals of the century: the speculative-metaphysical realm as an appropriate setting for the man, the safely confined domestic interior as suitable for the vaguely longing young woman. As in all of Retzsch's line drawings, the nature of his compositions provided the molds which could easily be filled by later artists which anecdotal detail, emotional drama, and psychological tension.

As in Cornelius's prints, the setting of Retzsch's compositions is Northern, but the selection of episodes and the emphatic gestures of the protagonists are of a far more theatrical nature than the austerity and psychological tension of the earlier scenes. It might well be for this lack of psychological penetration, of metaphysical allusions, and political con-

notations that Goethe ultimately preferred the more neutral rendering of
Retzsch to the intensity of Cornelius: the artist had not even attempted to
invent images which would evoke, or compete with, the poetic tone of the
text.

While Retzsch's *Umrisse zu Goethe's Faust* had a great impact upon
the rather sentimental depiction, especially of the Gretchen tragedy,
during the years of the Biedermeier, their function remained that of a
pattern book conveniently providing a canon for the standard illustrations of Goethe's text. It was Cornelius's political interpretation and,
foremost, his vision of a strong, dynamic, and almost Olympian Faust
which inspired the image of Faust as a Germanic hero in the second part
of the 19th century. The ideological appropriation of Goethe's *Faust* as a
German drama seems to have been forged simultaneously in the reading
of the text and in the creation of its illustrations. In 1864, Heinrich
Düntzer emphasized this "Germanness" in the introduction to *Gustav
Nehrlich's Zeichnungen nach Goethe's Faust:* "Ein Werk von so wunder-
barer Anziehung, so tiefem Gehalt, wie die reiche Welt des Goetheschen
Faust, worin deutsches Leben, deutsches Sinnen und Fühlen so ergrei-
fend sich spiegeln, mußte vor allem den bildenden Künstler mächtig
anregen. . . ."[21] And indeed, this Germanic reading of the text immediately found its pictorial counterpart. Even though Cornelius's vision
was a powerful inspiration, there should be no confusion between the
patriotic spirit of the anti-Napoleonic movement and the increasingly
nationalistic tone of the second part of the 19th century.

While such outright Germanic readings of Goethe's *Faust* became
consistent only during the 1860s and later, its roots reach as far back as
the *Vormärz.* During the period of the *Vormärz,* the agitated years
leading to the revolution of 1848, Wilhelm von Kaulbach (1805–1874)
was commissioned by Cotta to execute drawings for Goethe's collected
works.[22] As early as 1836, Kaulbach had been asked to execute twelve
drawings for steel engravings to illustrate a "Prachtausgabe," a luxury
edition, of Goethe's works. This project, however, had been abandoned,
and only twenty-five years later, around 1865, the Munich publisher
Bruckmann produced Kaulbach's famous *Goethe-Galerie,* a portfolio of
twenty-one photographic reproductions.[23] This new and most direct
technique of reproduction achieved a clarity and authenticity of the
original drawings which elicited the artist's enthusiastic approval. Kaulbach executed the twenty-one chalk drawings for his *Goethe-Galerie*
during the years from 1857 to 1864, but the concept and many of the
pictorial ideas hark back to his earlier compositions for the steel engravings of the 1840s and to his frescoes for the Munich *Residenz.*[24] During
the second half of the 19th century, Kaulbach's *Goethe-Galerie* became

perhaps the most popular series of *Faust* images in Germany, a "cultural icon" of the educated bourgeoisie.[25] Kaulbach's drawings already display those decisive traits which would determine, in the near future, the new Germanic interpretation of Goethe's *Faust* as a strong-willed man of action with whom the public was able to identify during the crucial years of German unification: the intrepid look and the determined and tense pose of *Faust in his Study* (ill. 12)—with clenched fist—not only contradicts but eradicates the traditional gesture of contemplation with the head resting on one arm. It is no surprise, then, that the relationship between Faust and Mephistopheles casts Faust in the dominant and active role, leaving Mephistopheles with the part of servile seducer.

During the same years, Cotta commissioned Engelbert Seibertz to execute the drawings for the steel engravings of the richly illustrated editions of *Faust I* and *Faust II* which appeared in 1854 and 1858.[26] Whereas Kaulbach still vacillates in his definition of Faust, his pupil Seibertz consciously turned away from the romantic and Biedermeier interpretations, choosing as his main source of inspiration Cornelius and only those aspects of Kaulbach which fit his concept of heroic nationalism. In his study "Goethe's *Faust* in der modernen deutschen Kunst," published in 1900,[27] Alexander Tille recognized in Seibertz's prints the turning point in the history of *Faust* illustrations. Himself in tune with the nationalistic tendencies of the Wilhelminian Empire, the author admired Seibertz's transformation of Faust into the Germanic blond hero, correlating the artist's characterization with the changes in German history. The scene depicting *Faust and Wagner Before the City Gate* overlooking the countryside (ill. 13) sets the tone for the entire sequence of illustrations: Framed by a decorative border, Faust's powerful figure is *the* center of the composition. This is not an elderly scholar philosophizing with his student, but a virile, energetic man whose commanding gesture and determined posture are those of an *imperator* rather than a philosopher. Fitting this interpretation are the two lines of text chosen as a title at the center top of the decorative frame:

> Ja wäre nur ein Zaubermantel mein
> Und trüg er mich in ferne Länder.

Seibertz effectively translates Faust's longing for new experiences and his escape into far and foreign lands from spiritual imagination into the historical and material world. The artist departed radically from the romantic mood of Carl Gustav Carus' painting of the *Osterspaziergang* of 1821 (ill. 14):[28] Faust and Wagner, two small figures seen from the back, are contemplating the view over the town, with its Gothic church towers, embedded in a hazy landscape. The change from Carus' rendering of calm meditation to the atmosphere of explosive action in Seibertz's steel engraving could not demonstrate more pointedly the difference in the interpretation of Goethe's text between the 1820s and the 1850s. This is the crucial transformation in the reading of *Faust* to which Tille referred:

> Aus dem Grübler ist im Laufe eines doppellangen Lebens ein Mann der That geworden, . . . weil das Jahrhundert eben auf dem Wege war, dieselbe Wandlung vom Denken zur That zu erfahren.[29]

Seibertz's conception, as well as his composition of the episode of *The Compact* (ill. 15), are derived from Kaulbach's earlier drawing. It is in this scene that the artist defines the relationship between Faust and Mephistopheles: There is no doubt that Faust will play the role of the resolute hero not only controlling but commanding the action. Conforming to this transformation of Faust, Margaret is no longer the innocent young girl of the earlier illustrations, but becomes the blond Northern woman, more theatrical and sentimental than sincerely emotional. Not surprisingly, *Margaret at the Spinning Wheel* (ill. 16) was one of the most popular scenes from *Faust* in German graphics and paintings of the second part of the century. The emotional content of this scene—love and longing—is cast in the traditional image of domestic activity— spinning—thus providing the perfect female role-model for the time.

Seibertz brought Faust from the spiritual and metaphysical realm into the historical-material world. While Cornelius endowed Faust with great emotional intensity and dynamic energy, alluding stylistically to the manner of Dürer, and thereby invoking the new patriotic spirit, Seibertz's Faust appears as a rather plain Germanic hero in authoritative command of the action, but without any traits of the pensive and brooding scholar. It is this almost aggressive explosion of action in the figure of Faust which Tille admired most: "Erst Seibertz hat den rabenhaarigen Christuskopf des Berliner Faust ins Blonde, Germanische übersetzt, ihn dadurch seiner deutschen Abkunft zurückerobert und ihn wirklich zum geistigen Nationalheros des deutschen Stammes gestempelt."[30] By 1900, Faust had become the hero of "our greatest national drama." Tille's interpretation of these images betrays a close political affinity between two movements of acute nationalistic fervor in German history: the strong patriotic drive for national unification and, half a century later, the will to imperialist expansion.

When Alexander Liezen Mayer, a student of Piloty's, illustrated *Faust I* with fifty compositions for an edition in 1876,[31] he was even more conscious of making concessions to the dominant political trends and the popular taste of the day. In his two scenes depicting Faust and Mephistopheles in the Study (ill. 17), he characterizes Mephistopheles as the agile, servile, and glib agent, giving him the features of a Jesuit. Only a few years earlier, in 1872, Wilhelm Busch had published his picture stories of *Die fromme Helene* and *Pater Filucius* (ill. 18), the latter a vicious caricature of a Jesuit:

> Pater Luzi, finster blickend,
> Heimlich schleichend um das Haus.[32]

There is no doubt that Liezen-Mayer was inspired by Wilhelm Busch when he invented his slinking Mephistopheles. The severe anticlericalism of those years is reflected in the literature and visual arts of the 1870s as well as in the writing of German history. Its most outspoken proponent was perhaps the historian Heinrich von Treitschke, who believed that the victory over France in 1871 was above all a victory for Protestantism. The laws passed in Prussia in May of 1873 were mainly directed against the Society of Jesus and "called for the abolition of all supervision of schools," transferring "all disciplinary authority over the Church to state agencies."[33] The Government's persecution of the Roman Catholic Church, its institutions and dogma was motivated on one level by merely political strategies, but it also expressed on a deeper level the widespread anticlerical, that is, antipapal, feelings in North Germany. It is no mere coincidence or merely artistic "borrowing" when Liezen Mayer's creeping Mephistopheles appears as the caricature of a wicked Jesuit: during the years of the so-called *Maigesetze* and the *Kulturkampf,* the artist revealed a clear partisanship for Bismarck's policies by giving his Mephistopheles the features of Busch's *Pater Filucius.*

If political ideology inspired the image of Liezen Mayer's Mephistopheles in an almost propagandistic manner, the overt erotic undercurrent of Wilhelminian painting, photography, and theater penetrates many of his Faust illustrations. The sweet cuteness and pompous theatricality of the scene of *Faust's Dream* (ill. 19) evoke the fantastic and overtly erotic atmosphere so characteristic of the escapist nature of German academic painting during the *Gründerjahre.* This new erotic tone is not restricted to scenes of the Walpurgis Night and the Helena sequence but also permeates the Gretchen episodes.

Margaret's role and her relationship to Faust had to be made consistent with Faust's conversion to a *Mann der Tat* ("man of action"). Around 1900, Franz Stassen created 163 illustrations for *Faust I* and a sequence of 12 scenes—without text—for *Faust II.*[34] A comparison between Radziwill's illustration of *Margaret's Room* (1835) (ill. 20) and Stassen's drawing of the same scene (ill. 21) reveals the profound change that the interpretation of Margaret's role had undergone during the past decades. Radziwill's carefully detailed and cozy interior provides an appropriate setting for the coy young woman who attentively gazes at the viewer. The figure is placed in the middleground of the composition, completely integrated into this neat Biedermeier environment, and thereby keeping a safe distance from the viewer. The mood is one of cautious expectation. In contrast, Stassen draws an image of directness and determination. Margaret's figure is pushed to the very foreground of the composition, directly confronting the viewer. Characterized as the ideal type of the blond Germanic woman, she exhibits gestures signaling action rather than hesitation.

Franz Stassen did not only propagate the Germanic elements but also a new erotic atmosphere. A comparison of the Garden Arbor (ill. 22) with Seibertz's illustration (ill. 23) demonstrates this shift in focus. Whereas Seibertz carefully integrates the figures of Faust and Gretchen into a typically ornamental Biedermeier composition—almost hiding the scene of the embrace in the decorative frame—Stassen depicts the ideal Nordic pair in a forcefully direct manner: eliminating all associations to the related figures of Mephistopheles and Martha, he focuses all attention on Faust and Margaret and openly alludes to their sexual relationship in the ornamental *Jugendstil* border.

In Stassen's interpretation of Goethe's text, the blond Nordic elements take on an outspoken nationalistic tone which is also expressed in his ambivalent adaptation of the art nouveau style associated with the more progressive and international artistic movement. In his attempt at creating an appropriate German style, he at once assimilated certain more pleasing features and suppressed the daring and abstract elements of *Jugendstil*. Stassen, a member of the *Werdandibund,* an anti-Semitic and nationalistic group of artists, promoted in his *Faust* illustrations, in concept as well as in style, an outspokenly *völkisch* ideology. In their politics, too, the members of the *Werdandibund* followed these principles: they fought against all modernism, including the Berlin Secession, and they were violently opposed to French Impressionism as an import of foreign decadence. Their goal was a Nordic-German art purged of all foreign, especially French, influence.

Both Seibertz and Stassen also illustrated *Faust II,* and it is in some of these images that the Germanic-imperial reading of *Faust* is most obvious. Faust did not only become a symbol of German virtues in the bourgeois sense, he also served as an inspiring model for the enterprising pioneer in the age of industrial expansion which occurred between 1871 and 1914. Thus, the Philemon and Baucis episode almost assumes the role of an allegory for colonial endeavors. In the years of the Second German Empire, the "Faustian ideology" reached the peak of nationalistic meaning. To illustrate the scene in the High Mountains (*Faust II,* act 4), both Seibertz (ill. 24) and Stassen (ill. 25) design powerful and persuasive images of Faust, the Nordic hero, in full command of his worldly mission. Faust's thirst for action, his sense of fulfilling a mission provide the focal point for the national identification with Goethe's tragedy. Redemption for titanic action fulfilled a well-calculated propagandistic purpose at a time when industry and perseverance were proclaimed as the main virtues of the new German Empire.

The portrayal of Goethe himself did not escape these dramatic changes in interpretation. When Cornelius designed the title page for Radziwill's *Faust* publication of 1835 (ill. 26), he depicted the contemplative poet at his desk in a medieval study surrounded by figures from the drama. The scene is framed by a floral decoration in the manner of Dürer's *Prayerbook of Maximilian* that imitates Gothic vaults dividing the composition into three parts very much in the fashion of a triptych. While the poet is prominently placed in the center of the composition, the episodes of *Faust I* revolve clockwise from the left to the right. Whereas Cornelius sees Goethe as the creative artist at work in the seclusion of his study, Stassen pictures him as the Olympian hero of the nation: in his title page for illustrations of *Faust II* (ill. 27), he designed a large medallion with the portrait bust of the poet framed by the smaller figures of Faust and Mephistopheles to the left and right. The boldly drawn features of Goethe's portrait crowned by a laurel wreath create the effect of a marble bust; the heroic mode, the antique garb, all evoke the association with the portrait bust of a Roman *imperator*. Not only Faust, "der Mann der Tat," but the poet himself had by the end of the century become a national symbol for the *Reich*.

Notes

1 The following studies do not represent a complete bibliography but a list of publications which I found helpful and inspiring for my own work. I will refer to them in an abbreviated form in the following notes. To wit: Alexander Tille, "Goethes *Faust* in der modernen deutschen Kunst," *Westermanns Deutsche Monatshefte* 88 (1900): 762–777; *Goethes Faust, erster und zweiter Teil: Mit Bildern nach 7 Handzeichnungen von Goethe und zahlreichen Illustrationen zeitgenössischer deutscher Künstler, hrsg. und eingeleitet von Franz Neubert* (Leipzig, 2d ed., 1923); *Faust von Goethe: Zwei Teile in einem Band,* hrsg. von E. W. Bredt (Munich [1923]) with numerous illustrations; *Goethes Faust mit einer Einleitung von Max von Boehn: "Faust und die Kunst"* (Berlin, 1924); Franz Neubert, *Vom Doctor Faustus zu Goethes Faust* (Leipzig, 1932); Edwin Redslob, *Goethes Faust und die bildende Kunst* (n.p., n.d.); Heinz Kindermann, *Das Goethebild des 20. Jahrhunderts* (Vienna and Stuttgart, 1952); Wolfgang Wegner, *Die Faustdarstellung vom 16. Jahrhundert bis zur Gegenwart* (Amsterdam, 1962), the most comprehensive overview of images illustrating *Faust;* Hans Schwerte, *Faust und das Faustische: Ein Kapitel deutscher Ideologie* (Stuttgart, 1962); *Goethe im 20. Jahrhundert: Spiegelungen und Deutungen,* ed. by Hans Mayer (Hamburg, 1967); Wolfgang Wegner, in *Reallexikon zur deutschen Kunstgeschichte* (Munich, 1981), 7:847–866; Klaus Popitz,

"Goethes Faust," in *Von Odysseus bis Felix Krull: Gestalten der Weltliteratur in der Buchillustration des 19. bis 20. Jahrhunderts* (exhibition catalogue: Berlin, 1983).

2 Cf. my study "Adolph Menzel's Daguerreotypical Image of Frederick the Great—A Liberal-Bourgeois Interpretation of German History," *Art Bulletin* 59, no. 2 (1977): 242–261.

3 Count Radziwill organized the first private stage productions in 1819 and 1820. Cf. Carl Niessen, "Zu den Ausstellungen 'Faust auf der Bühne' und 'Faust in der bildenden Kunst'," in *Das Buch des Goethe-Lessing Jahres 1929* (Braunschweig, 1929); Boehn, 69.

4 Goethe, *Faust, Tragédie, traduite en Français par M. Albert Stapfer. Ornée d'un Portrait d'Auteur et de dix-sept Dessins composés d'après les principales Scénes de l'ouvrage et exécutés sur Pierre par M. Eugène Delacroix* (Paris, 1828).

5 Ibid.

6 Neubert, ill. p. 3, 86. Wegner, 19, 41.

7 Ibid., 239. According to Neubert, Cotta probably added four engravings to a few copies.

8 Ibid., 240.

9 *Bilder zu Goethe's Faust von P. Cornelius. Gestochen von F. Ruscheweyh. Franckfurt am Main bey F. Wenner. 1816.* For a critical assessment of Cornelius's prints, cf. Alfred von Wolzogen, *Peter von Cornelius* (Berlin, 1867); Hermann Riegel, *Peter Cornelius, Festschrift zu des großen Künstlers 100. Geburtstage* (Berlin, 1883); Alfred Kuhn, *Die Faustillustrationen des Peter Cornelius in ihrer Beziehung zur deutschen Nationalbewegung der Romantik* (Berlin, 1916); *Goethes Faust. Der Tragödie erster Teil mit Zeichnungen von Peter Cornelius,* eingeleitet von Alfred Kuhn (Berlin, 1920); Alfred Kuhn, *Peter Cornelius und die geistigen Strömungen seiner Zeit* (Berlin, 1921); Felix Salomon, *Die Faustillustrationen von Cornelius und Delacroix* (Diss. Würzburg, 1930); Maria-Luise von Graberg, *Die Nibelungen-Illustrationen von Johann Heinrich Füssli und Peter Cornelius* (Diss. Berlin, 1970).

10 *Scenen aus Goethe's Faust in acht lithographischen Bildern nach der Angabe des Fürsten Anton Radziwill* (Berlin, 1835). The artists who provided the drawings for these prints were: Biermann, Cornelius, Hensel, Hosemann, Count Radziwill, C. Schulz and Zimmermann.

11 Cf. Günter Busch, *Eugène Delacroix: Der Tod des Valentin* (Frankfurt, 1973).

12 Neubert, 241.

13 See n. 7 above.

14 Ibid.

15 Quoted from Wolzogen, 23. Cornelius was unaware of the change in Goethe's attitude between the time of the *Faust* fragment and the years when he criticized Cornelius's illustrations around 1811 to 1812. Cf. Riegel, 31.

16 Quoted from Graberg, 65.

17 Riegel, 123; cf. n. 7 above.

18 Riegel, 249; Cornelius in a letter to his publisher Wenner of 24 May 1814; Wegner, 1962, 58–60.

19 *Umrisse zu Goethe's Faust. Gezeichnet von Moritz Retzsch* (Stuttgart and Augsburg, 1836 [dated on the title page: 1837]). The first part consists of 29 plates, the second of 11 plates. Cf. Leopold Hirschberg, *Moritz Retzsch: Chronologisches Verzeichnis seiner graphischen Werke* (Berlin, 1925).

20 Cf. Niessen.

21 *Subscriptions-Einladung zu Gustav Nehrlich's Zeichnungen nach Goethe's Faust. Mit erläuternden Worten von Heinrich Düntzer* (Coblenz, n.d. [1864]); no pagination.

22 Neubert, 245; Wegner, 79; Popitz, 170 and 172; Fritz von Ostini, *Wilhelm von Kaulbach* (Bielefeld and Leipzig, 1906); Evelyn Lehmann and Elke Riemer, *Die Kaulbachs: Eine Künstlerfamilie aus Arolsen* (Arolsen, 1978).

23 Cf. Neubert, 169–173 and Popitz, 172, 179.

24 Neubert illustrates some of the frescoes in the Munich Residenz; cf. 171–172.

25 Popitz, 172. His assessment is largely based on Ostini's studies.

26 *Faust: Eine Tragödie von Goethe. Mit Zeichnungen von Engelbert Seibertz. Zwei Teile* (Stuttgart and Tübingen, 1854 and 1858).

27 Tille, 762–777.

28 Essen, Museum Folkwang.

29 Tille, 268.

30 Ibid., 769.

31 Johann Wolfgang von Goethe, *Faust: Eine Tragödie. Erster Theil.* Illustrirt in 50 Compositionen von Alexander Liezen Mayer. Mit Ornamenten von Rudolf Seitz (Munich, 1876); cf. Popitz, 172 and 180.

32 Gordon Craig, *Germany 1866–1945* (New York, 1978), 74.

33 Ibid., 73–74.

34 *Faust: Eine Tragödie von Goethe mit 163 Federzeichnungen von Franz Stassen* (Berlin, n.d.) and *Faust: 12 Zeichnungen zum zweiten Teile von Franz Stassen* (Berlin, n.d.). Published in *Teuerdank: Fahrten und Träume deutscher Maler. 22. Folge.* This is a sequence of prints without text. Cf. Popitz, 172 and 180.

1. Johann Wolfgang von Goethe, *Appearance of the Earth Spirit,* ca. 1810–12, pencil drawing, Weimar, Nationale Forschungs- und Gedenkstätten der klassischen deutschen Literatur.

2. Peter von Cornelius, *Faust Meeting Margaret on Her Way from Church,* engraving by
Ferdinand Ruscheweyh, 1816, Düsseldorf, Goethe-Museum.

3. Peter von Cornelius, *Marthe's Garden,* engraving by Ferdinand Ruscheweyh, 1816, Düsseldorf, Goethe-Museum.

4. Peter von Cornelius, *Margaret in the Dungeon,* engraving by Ferdinand Ruscheweyh, 1816, Düsseldorf, Goethe-Museum.

5. Eugène Delacroix, *Margaret in the Dungeon,* lithograph, 1828, Düsseldorf, Goethe-Museum.

6. Peter von Cornelius, *Faust and Mephistopheles Speeding Onward on Black Horses round the Raven Stone,* engraving by Ferdinand Ruscheweyh, 1816, Düsseldorf, Goethe-Museum.

7. Eugène Delacroix, *Faust and Mephistopheles Speeding Onward on Black Horses round the Raven Stone,* lithograph, 1828, Düsseldorf, Goethe-Museum.

8. Eugène Delacroix, *Mephistopheles,* lithograph, 1828, Düsseldorf, Goethe-Museum.

9. Peter von Cornelius, *Cathedral Scene,* 1811, pencil drawing, Berlin, GDR, Staatliche Museen, Nationalgalerie, Sammlung der Handzeichnungen.

10. Moritz Retzsch, *Faust in His Study,* line engraving, first edition, 1816, Düsseldorf, Goethe-Museum.

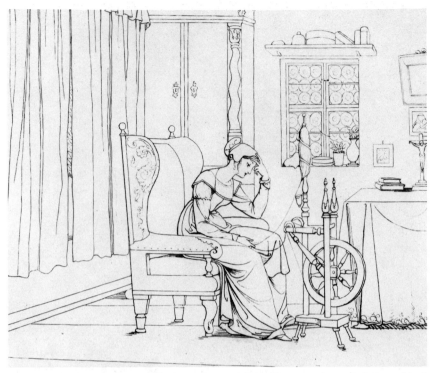

11. Moritz Retzsch, *Margaret at the Spinning Wheel,* line engraving, 1816, Düsseldorf, Goethe-Museum.

12. Wilhelm von Kaulbach, *Faust in His Study,* engraving from: *Goethes poetische und prosaische Werke in zwei Bänden,* Stuttgart/Tübingen, Cotta, 1837.

13. Engelbert Seibertz, *Faust and Wagner before the City Gate,* steel engraving by Adrian Schleich, 1854, Düsseldorf, Goethe-Museum.

14. Gustav Carus, *Osterspaziergang* (Faust and Wagner Before the City Gate), 1821, oil on canvas, Essen, Museum Folkwang.

15. Engelbert Seibertz, *The Compact,* steel engraving by Adrian Schleich, 1854, Düsseldorf, Goethe-Museum.

16. Alexander Liezen Mayer, *Margaret at the Spinning Wheel,* wood engraving, 1876, Düsseldorf, Goethe-Museum.

17. Alexander Liezen Mayer, *Faust and Mephistopheles in the Study,* wood engraving, 1876, Düsseldorf, Goethe-Museum.

Dennoch und trotz alledieſem
Geht die Wirthſchaft doch ſo ſo. —
Aber aber, aber aber

Jetzt kommt der Filuzio.

Nämlich dieſer Jeſuiter
Merkt ſchon längſt mit Geldbegier
Auf den Gottlieb ſein Vermögen,
Denkend: „Ach, wo krieg ich Dir?"

18. Wilhelm Busch, *Pater Filucius,* from: *Pater Filucius: Allegorisches Zeitbild,*
1872, Düsseldorf, Goethe-Museum.

19. Alexander Liezen Mayer, *Faust's Dream,* wood engraving, 1876, Düsseldorf, Goethe-Museum.

20. Anton Radziwill, *Margaret's Room,* lithograph by Eduard Meyerheim, 1835, Düsseldorf, Goethe-Museum.

Abend. Ein kleines reinliches Zimmer.

Margarete, ihre Zöpfe flechtend und aufbindend.

Margarete. Ich gäb' was drum, wenn ich nur wüßt',
wer heut der Herr gewesen ist!
Er sah gewiß recht wacker aus
und ist aus einem edlen Haus;
das konnt' ich ihm an der Stirne lesen —
er wär' auch sonst nicht so keck gewesen. (Ab.)

Mephistopheles. Faust.

Mephistopheles. Herein, ganz leise, nur herein!

Faust (nach einigem Stillschweigen).
Ich bitte dich, laß mich allein!

Mephistopheles (herumspürend).
Nicht jedes Mädchen hält so rein. (Ab.)

21. Franz Stassen, *Margaret's Room,* from: *Faust: Eine Tragödie von Goethe,*
Berlin, ca. 1900, Düsseldorf, Goethe-Museum.

115

22. Franz Stassen, *Garden Arbor,* from: *Faust: Eine Tragödie von Goethe,* Berlin, ca. 1900, Düsseldorf, Goethe-Museum.

23. Engelbert Seibertz, *Garden Arbor,* steel engraving by Adrian Schleich, 1854, Düsseldorf, Goethe-Museum.

24. Engelbert Seibertz, *Philemon and Baucis,* steel engraving by Adrian Schleich, 1858, Düsseldorf, Goethe-Museum.

Bist du Baucis, die geschäftig
halberstorbnen Mund erquickt'?

Der Gatte tritt auf.

Du, Philemon, der so kräftig
meinen Schatz der Flut entrückt'?
Eure Flammen raschen Feuers,

25. Franz Stassen, *Philemon and Baucis,* from: *Faust: Eine Tragödie von Goethe,*
Berlin, ca. 1900, Düsseldorf, Goethe-Museum.

26. Engelbert Seibertz, *In the High Mountains* (*Faust II*), steel engraving by Adrian Schleich, 1858, Düsseldorf, Goethe-Museum.

27. Franz Stassen, *In the High Mountains,* from *Faust: 12 Zeichnungen zum II. Teile von Franz Stassen,* Berlin, n.d.(1902), Düsseldorf, Goethe-Museum.

28. Peter von Cornelius, title page for Anton Radziwill's *Scenen aus Goethe's Faust,* 1835, lithograph by Theodor Hosemann, Düsseldorf, Goethe-Museum.

Feuerdank. Fahrten und Träume deutscher Maler. 22. Folge.

29. Franz Stassen, title page from: *Faust. 12 Zeichnungen zum II. Teile,* Berlin, n.d. (1902), Düsseldorf, Goethe-Museum.

Mallarmé's Faust:
The Politics of Withdrawal

FRANÇOISE MELTZER

In the second half of the previous century, when Mallarmé was writing his difficult texts, the theme of Faust was very "in" in France. Gounod had produced his opera of Faust in 1858; Berlioz his *La Damnation de Faust* in 1846; Delacroix had done a series of seventeen drawings for the new French edition of Goethe's work, which had already been translated and commented upon by Gérard de Nerval and Blaze de Bury, among others, and had been widely read. Mallarmé was most familiar with all of these works, and Faust was by no means a stranger to him.

Yet it is the way in which Mallarmé is drawn to Faust which bears, I think, serious scrutiny. I am not going to try to compare the Mallarmé poems to moments in Goethe's *Faust*—although that could be done, and with relative ease. Rather, I am going to try to show that what Mallarmé likes in Faust, takes from Faust, demonstrates a surprising phenomenon: the ease with which the poet felt capable of turning his back upon the political world surrounding him—indeed, the blithe way in which Mallarmé never even considers the political realm as his. In other words, Mallarmé's Faust is a very specific, limited one: the Faust at the beginning of part 1 of Goethe's work; the Faust who, filled with *ennui,* has had enough of the world, which, since he has read all of its books, seems to have nothing left to offer. While such *ennui* informs in particular the early poetry and correspondence of the French poet, it also motivates his hermetic drama of metaphysical suicide, *Igitur,* and his mature poem, "Victorieusement fui le suicide beau."

Every schoolchild in France, upon reading Mallarmé's early poem "Brise marine" (1865) is told that the first line is "Faustian": "La chair est triste, hélas! et j'ai lu tous les livres." This notion is echoed in Mallarmé's "Crise de vers," in which the poet refers to the modern crisis in verse as belonging to the one "qui semble avoir lu tout." Here is the lassitude of Goethe's Faust at the beginning of part 1: the Faust who laments his knowledge of philosophy, law, medicine, even theology, and adds, "Da steh' ich nun, ich armer Tor,/ Und bin so klug als wie zuvor!"

Mallarmé's "Brise marine" is a desire for flight from things of the world or, as Mallarmé wrote of the poem himself in 1866 to a friend, "that inexplicable desire which occasionally overcomes us to leave those dear to us, to *depart.*"[1] Indeed, the poem's next lines make such a desire explicit: "Fuir! là-bas fuir! Je sens que des oiseaux sont ivres / d'être parmi l'écume inconnue et les cieux" ("To flee! flee over there! I sense that the birds are intoxicated to be in the unknown foam and the heavens"). Nothing will restrain him, says the poet, from his flight, including "the desert clarity of my lamp upon the empty paper which whiteness protects." Even the accoutrements of the scholar, then, even the familiar surroundings of his study, will not prevent his leaving; nor will the young woman breast-feeding her child (biographers are quick to point out that, when this poem was written, Mallarmé's wife had just given birth to their first child). The poet will become a "steamer," lifting anchor for an exotic place far away.

The next stanza of the poem, of course, as always with Mallarmé, destroys such illusions. The steamer can invite storms, lose its mast, be shipwrecked, without ever finding its fertile isles. But the poet's heart still hears the sailors' songs: "Mais, ô mon cœur, entends le chant des matelots!"

No doubt, this poem inspired Rimbaud's famous work, "Le Bateau ivre"; no doubt, "Brise marine" was itself inspired by Baudelaire's obsessive need to escape *(fuir)* or, as Baudelaire puts it—in English—to get "anywhere out of the world."[2] And again no doubt, Baudelaire in turn was inspired by Edgar Allan Poe, whose vision of the world as a claustrophobic kettle with the lid firmly in place—the clouds "hung oppressively low in the heavens," he says in the "Fall of the House of Usher"—will become Baudelaire's "Spleen! quand le ciel est bas et lourd."

But these common literary genealogies point only to similarities, to textually sympathetic souls, as it were. They do not ask a rather simple question: Why is it that for the so-called symbolist poets (particularly Baudelaire and Mallarmé, but also Rimbaud and Verlaine) the notion of the "world" means books and, to some degree, human relations, and that if these are exhausted there is nothing left of the world at all? *Ennui* is ever close, ever "gnawing," as Baudelaire puts it—ready to devour these poets at every turn, in every activity. The world is too much with them— but it is a paltry, flimsy thing, this world, and that makes their imprisonment within it all the more frustrating. Hence, Baudelaire's and Mallarmé's obsession with the idea of *là-bas,* the vague "over there"—a theme which already haunts old Provençal literature (Jaufré Rudel's *de lai*) but which, with these later poets, becomes a concept of such metaphysical urgency that suicide, as in *Faust I,* seems a more felicitous alternative to the grim prison of books and scholarly pursuits that were to have served as a refuge from the commonality of the world.[3]

It is no accident, then, that the theme of Icarus is prevalent in Mallarmé's poetry; nor is it an accident that the Faust Mallarmé understood from Delacroix's drawings and from translated excerpts of Goethe's work became one of the unacknowledged heroes of the protagonists in Mallarmé's *poésie pure*. Hérodias, the sick old man in the poem "Les Fenêtres," and Igitur, the narrator of "Un coup de dés"—all of these have in common a desire to attain supreme knowledge, to recapture a moment and hold on to it, to escape the tawdriness of the world. The myth of Icarus appears in Mallarmé as through the painted glass which Faust says obstructs him from the light of heaven: it is the flight of birds which the poet joins in "Brise marine," the prevalence of airy things in general in Mallarmé's verse—handkerchiefs, sea foam, fog, mists, clouds, embroidery, candles—all of which are dissolved in one way or another by the power of the sun to which they aspired.

The "real" Doktor Faustus of the 16th century is said to have died in a demonstration of flying. This motif—the Icarus motif of the man who wants to fly, to be superman, but whose ambition is foiled by the very presence of the all-powerful sun—appears in *Faust I* as an echo: Faust wants to fly, like the sun: "O daß kein Flügel mich vom Boden hebt / Ihr nach und immer nach zu streben! / Ich säh im ewigen Abendstrahl / Die stille Welt zu meinen Füßen . . ."[4] There is an inner human impulse, Faust tells Wagner, to fly like the birds—even though the prison of the body makes this impossible: "Doch ist es jedem eingeboren, / Daß sein Gefühl hinauf und vorwärts dringt, / Wenn über uns, im blauen Raum verloren, / Ihr schmetternd Lied die Lerche singt. . . ." Of course, Wagner says that *he's* never wanted to fly—books are enough for him. This pedant, for whom books are, precisely, sufficient, is rendered ridiculous by the implied comparison to the obviously (to put it mildly) more intelligent and more complex Faust. Such a contrast creates as well an ironic distance between the reader and the type of posing Wagner exemplifies. But now, as the two are walking outside the city, Faust tells Wagner that he wants to fly off to distant foreign lands. The tenor is exactly what Mallarmé tries to achieve in "Brise marine," with its theme of flight, its *Fuir, fuir là-bas:* "O gibt es Geister in der Luft / . . . führt mich weg, zu neuem, buntem Leben! / Ja, wäre nur ein Zaubermantel mein / Und trüg' er mich in fremde Länder . . ." And this magic coat, of course, is conveniently what Mephistopheles will provide. "Wir breiten nur den Mantel aus," he says to Faust: "Der soll uns durch die Lüfte tragen." And yet, there is a part of Faust which knows, after a brief consideration of suicide, that he has flown too high. This recognition is emphasized, of course, by that which saves him: the choir of angels singing in celebration of Easter. It is Christ who has risen, not Faust.

The Icarus symbol in Goethe's *Faust* is as if split into two parts:

Mephistopheles and Faust himself. In Mallarmé, the satanic instinct to be a superman is at once internalized, insisted upon—and rendered absurd as well as hateful. Like the narrator in Mallarmé's "Le sonneur," the poet pulls in vain at the bell rope to hear the bells, to see the sky. But it is the nonchalant, indifferent child who can hear the bells, and the mindless birds who can pierce the sky. The bell-ringer keeps ringing—in a hopeless, Sisyphean task. But he says: "O Satan, one day when I am tired of having pulled in vain, I will loosen the stone from the rope, and I will hang myself." Or, like the narrator in Mallarmé's "Les Fenêtres," who tells of an old, sick man in a hospital. He is dying and struggles to the window. There, for one brief moment—again, thanks to the brilliance of the sun—he sees himself as he believes himself truly to be: an angel. But the tone quickly shifts, and the narrator cries: "But alas! Here below is master . . ." And he asks, Icarus-like, "Is there a way for me to escape, with my two featherless wings—at the risk of falling throughout eternity?" This final question is a significant one, for it links the classical myth of Icarus—he who would challenge the gods by flying, by attempting to be a superman—to the story of Mephistopheles guilty of the same sin of pride: an angel whose sin led him to fall for all of eternity.

Flight with wings, but also flight as escape, is the major theme which draws Mallarmé to Faust. Rémy de Goncourt noted once that there is in the Louvre an *Andromeda* by Cellini. It shows a terrified woman, her entire pose seemingly crying out, "Whence can I flee?" That, says Goncourt, is the poetry of Mallarmé: *Où fuir?*[5] If Baudelaire is obsessed, as he clearly is, by the notion of sin without redemption, Mallarmé is obsessed with flight to avoid the world. The notion of redemption is not even a possibility for him, and that of sin is an entirely metaphysical, essentially nontheological one. Like Faust, Mallarmé shows a disdain for the rabble, a hatred of all materiality. Even when he begs materiality to offer him the escape of forgetfulness—as in the poem "L'Azur"—failure is the necessary result, and the poet is left with the same loathing of mankind and commonality as he experienced before his plea.[6]

Like Faust, Mallarmé dares to change the word: that is, both the notion of language and the Bible—the Word in its theological sense. "Im Anfang war das Wort," mutters Faust, and he adds: "Ich kann das Wort so hoch unmöglich schätzen, / Ich muß es anders übersetzen." And Mallarmé: "The verse which, by means of several vocables, remakes a word—entire, new, a stranger to the language, almost incantatory—achieves that isolation of speech . . . and causes that surprise of having never heard such an ordinary fragment of elocution, while at the same time the memory of the named object breathes in a new atmosphere."[7]

In Mallarmé, there is great emphasis upon sorcery: words are a book of magic, a *grimoire.* That is, when they are used in their purest sense, they are no longer accessible; they become hermetic symbols, as in a book of magic. If properly deciphered, they may unlock a bit of knowledge for the poet, and afford him a glimpse into the secrets of the mocking azure. The occult intrigues him; Hamlet is one of his heroes; the sinful Hérodias is his symbol of metaphysical sterility and passionate indifference to violence and death. And Igitur, the drama of a suicide—a metaphysical, calm suicide—is Mallarmé's hero surrounded only by books and the phantom voices of his ancestors who whisper to him the lost events of the past and the promises of the hidden future in death.

No wonder, then, that Mallarmé is drawn to this "Urfaust"—this Faust of the *Studierzimmer* who says, "Im Anfang war die Tat," and wants to lose himself in the night. It is Mallarmé, too, who says he wants to "advance as deeply as possible into the absolute of darkness." And the tradition continued: ten years after Mallarmé's death, the poet Valéry, who had sat at the feet of Mallarmé, writes to his wife, "I am creating my Faust in the middle of this desert haunted by words."[8] In Mallarmé, Faust is never named nor acknowledged. But he is everywhere, haunting the poet's texts like one of the spirits which Faust himself both fears and hopes to encounter.[9]

And yet, everything is missing. He is all wrong, this Faust of Mallarmé, this tired scholar who is overwhelmed with the greatness of his task, the complexities of his mind, the sterility of books, the hopelessness of words, the *ennui* which destroys even the possibility of passion and sensuality. It will perhaps have been noticed that throughout my essay, whereas I refer to Goethe *and* to Faust, I have only said "Mallarmé" (or, at most, the narrator of a Mallarmé poem) when referring to the French poet's work. This is not merely a narratological naïveté on my part: there is, very simply, a transparency between Mallarmé and his poetry. Gone are the ironic stance separating Goethe from his Faust and the distance Goethe's irony grants us between the world as Faust sees it and the world as it is—or perhaps, more accurately put, the way Goethe sees it. Gone is the humor which such distance generates; gone, too, the polity, the government and its corruption and inequities. Gone are the Shake-spearean touches of humor: Auerbach's Keller, with its moments of realism ("The Holy Roman Empire," says Brander to Frosch, "isn't your affair"). Finally—although there are many other examples—gone is Goethe's prelude in the theater, with its dialectic between director and poet, sublated by the diplomatic actor.

This is not to say, let me hasten to add, that I am for some peculiar reason trying to make Mallarmé more like Goethe. Rather, I am trying to demonstrate that Mallarmé uses those parts of *Faust* which necessarily attract him, and that such a choice serves as a type of barometer showing what one of the major French poets assumes—indeed, even insists upon—in the ideology of his poetics.

We need but cast a brief glance again at the way in which Valéry sees Goethe, in order to demonstrate that, underlying this French poet's use of the *Faust* texts, there is (to the contrary of Mallarmé) political concern. On 30 April 1932, Valéry gave a "Discours en honneur de Goethe" at the Sorbonne. The occasion was, of course, the centennial of Goethe's death. Valéry begins immediately by talking of the "politics of mind" in his speech. The mind has its own government, bureaucrats, traditions, and notions of power. It is clear from the outset that, for Valéry, Goethe is not only a literary genius, but also a political figure. Valéry emphasizes the political by concentrating upon Goethe's meeting with Napoleon: the two great powers of Europe conversing as equals—for, says Valéry, if one can manipulate the kings of Europe, the other can manipulate Homer, Virgil, Shakespeare at will. For Valéry, Napoleon would make for a good third Faust, and, for that matter, so would Goethe himself. Both men shared, according to Valéry, a professed hatred of ideology: Goethe claimed not to like thinking about thought; Napoleon deplored thought without action. Moreover, Valéry sees *Faust II* (utterly absent from Mallarmé) as a possible prefiguration for the "difficulties" which Europe is already beginning to experience in the early 1930s: "Tu as écrit [he apostrophizes Goethe] dans le second Faust des pages où l'on peut bien trouver quelque préfigure de notre politique égarée, de notre économie bouleversée, de notre état paradémoniaque."[10] What would Goethe think, asks the French poet, of this new, troubled Europe? The implicit question Valéry also asks is whether new tensions between France and Germany will serve to cause Goethe's "real" death—that is, to expunge him from the French canon of great literature for unspoken political reasons: "Même il n'a point manqué à ce jubilé le sentiment de ceux qui trouvent que l'empire de cette gloire est extenué et que cette œuvre, jugée immortelle, ne répond plus aux besoins spirituels du monde terriblement neuf qui se déclare si peniblement en nous et autour de nous . . ." It should be clear from this short summary of Valéry's views on Goethe and his *Faust* that the same text which can be seen as the spiritual ancestor of Mallarmé's poetry of *impuissance* and withdrawal is viewed—by a poet for whom Mallarmé was mentor—as a timeless document of political wisdom and even prophesy. Valéry concludes by suggesting another *Faust III*—now, no longer that of Napoleon, but the very discourse which the ghost of Goethe perhaps is overhearing at the jubilee celebration of his death. This Third Faust will be ours, while we await others—"en attendant les autres Faust, en attendant le Faust que l'on écrira peut-être à la fin des temps, le dernier livre possible!" The last possible *Faust* will be the last

book, because it will augur the end of history. That is how Valéry sees
Goethe's *Faust:* embedded in politics, able even to foreshadow the tensions mounting in the Europe of the early 1930s, inextricable from the
world, and, like its author, utterly devoted to what Valéry calls "exter-
iority."

On the other polar extreme, we have Mallarmé, the poet of utmost
interiority, and for whom thinking about thought is the last and first goal
of the mind when it is capable of action. The ideology of Mallarmé is
entirely a politics of withdrawal: withdrawal from the masses, from
society, from the acceptable poetry of Victor Hugo, from conventional
honor, from what we call today a "job," from anything that smacks of
government or of "the world." Why does Mallarmé's poetry say over and
over again that, once books have been read and a woman loved, there is
nothing left except the lamentation of the loss of *l'Idéal* and of the
potency of poetry? And why do most critics think that such withdrawal is
either fascinating and terrific or something to be assumed without
question?

Once more, Mallarmé is a great poet; of that there can be no doubt.
My questions have not to do with his value or genius as a poet, but rather
with the reasons for which a poet in late 19th-century France would find
commerce with the world and its people heinous at best; and why critics
do not bother to ponder such an attitude. While it may come as no
surprise that most bourgeois critics rush to deny, or refuse to question,
withdrawal, the way in which they and others institutionalize such a
rejection of the world bears serious consideration.

Many critics have noted with a certain flair the hermeticism, both
textual and biographical, that characterizes what is called "symbolist"
verse (I say "what is called" because "symbolism" is a label invented by
critics who feel the need to lump together such disparate poets as the four
French writers I listed previously). Edmund Wilson's *Axel's Castle,* for
example, takes hermeticism as a given in late 19th-century French
poetry. "Let our servants do our living for us," is Axel's cry to his lover,
and is as well Wilson's starting point for the writers in his book—their
common ground. His study traces the various forms of escape which
writers such as Rimbaud, Baudelaire, Villier de l'Isle Adam, Huysmans,
and so on, chose in their flight from the world. The flight itself, however,
is described but barely questioned. So, too, Anna Balakian in her book
The Symbolist Movement is surprised by the escapism into the occult and
into mysticism which, in her eyes, characterizes at once the Romantics
and the later "Symbolists." In discussing the impact of Swedenborg's
doctrines on the Romanticists, Balakian notes: "It is strange that, in the
midst of the Age of Enlightenment, such literal enunciation of immortality should have become a popular philosophy." While this comment

specifically describes the Romantics, such reasoning would remain equally perplexed by the analogous situation of the mysticism of Mallarmé "in the midst" of the age of positivism, as Auguste Lecomte was to dub it. The first *Faustbuch,* let us remember, was published in 1587, at a time of great Renaissance skepticism. It seems worth noting, then, that an epoch of skepticism and rationalism, such as the Renaissance, an epoch of enlightenment, such as the early *Goethezeit,* and an epoch of positivism, such as the time during which Mallarmé was writing—that in all of these epochs insisting upon reason and clarity, there arises a clear nostalgia for the occult. In Goethe, this nostalgia is both ironized and, at times, sympathetically depicted in the figure of Faust; in Mallarmé, this nostalgia for a mystical *au delà des choses* is never seen at a distance, the longing being one and the same in his texts and in his letters. The irony in Mallarmé, when it is there at all, appears mainly on the side of the *au delà:* it is the azure which is contemptuous of man, looking down upon him with what Mallarmé calls "indolent indifference" or, at other times, outright cruelty.

But an atmosphere of scientific positivism, with its concomitant literary naturalism, is insufficient and inadequate to explain why, with Mallarmé, the poet has reached the point of total withdrawal. One might retort, of course, that other poets before Mallarmé also withdrew. What is curious about Mallarmé, however, and what distinguishes him, is that his isolation becomes a cult, becomes glorified, becomes the trademark of his *kind* of poetry. And this is true not only for the elite *cénacle* which surrounded Mallarmé during his famous *soirées*—it is, more significantly, true as well of the reams of critical texts written about the French poet. They simply do not put his isolation into question, do not problematize it nor the glorification it engenders. It is all very odd. A cursory run through some of the major critical approaches to Mallarmé will, I think, demonstrate what I mean.

Few authors have generated as many texts from critics as has Mallarmé, and this is especially true of late, when symbolism studies in general and Mallarmé studies in particular abound. I have broken these critical approaches down into seven groups—not because the categories comprise in any sense a real structure. They are provisionally hypostatized by me solely for the sake of expediency, and should in no way be construed as an effort on my part to quantify or programmatize literary criticism. Any of these categories can be deconstructed—and probably should be. But many of the labels I am imposing are used by the critics themselves; it is in this sense that they "situate" themselves, and it is in that spirit that I somewhat reluctantly employ such labeling.

The first of these critical camps, then, is the "traditional" approach to Mallarmé—represented by such varied (in all senses) figures as

Edmund Wilson, Thibaudet, Valéry, Hugo Friedrich, Guy Michaud, A. G. Lehman, Wallace Fowlie, and even Robert Greer Cohn. These critics, useful though many of their insights may be, content themselves with a descriptive, programmatic approach to the poet. It is, if you will, an *explication de texte* combined with a general framework of French literary history—a framework which is either provided, as in Valéry's brilliant if subjective essays on Mallarmé's symbolism, or assumed, as in Thibaudet's somewhat obsequious prose.

The second group I shall call the "linguists." Concerned with language and rhetoric, these include, among others, Jean-Pierre Richard, and even Julia Kristeva. They all try to make sense of, to systematize, the maddening syntax and vocabulary of Mallarmé. This most useful approach unravels some of the syntactical webs which Mallarmé delights in spinning. But it never really questions or considers the poet's relation to the world.

The third group of critics of French symbolism are the Marxists. Among these number Lucien Goldmann, Frederic Jameson, Richard Terdiman. But again, these critics describe the conditions for 19th-century literature in France overall. Moreover, their interest is generally focused on the novel. It is almost as if poetry by definition were not considered sufficiently realistic or historical to act as a valid gauge of social climates. Hence, by this prejudice alone, Marxist critics of French literature have further hermeticized the poetry of symbolism, which had already begun by proclaiming itself as being apart. A *Catch 22,* in other words.[11]

The fourth type of critical perspective might be labeled "sociological." Some of the critics from the previous category also fall into this group (like Goldmann, for example). Here, we find such writers as Walter Benjamin and Lionel Trilling. Benjamin's essays on Baudelaire are, in fact, unsurpassed in their brilliant move between Baudelaire's poems and life of the *flâneur* in Paris, which so greatly informs the rhythm and social texture of Baudelaire's poetry. Mallarmé, unfortunately, is largely missing from Benjamin—as he often is from sociological approaches. Is it perhaps that to be an antisocial (indeed, antipolitical) poet constitutes a nonsociological phenomenon? That would seem at best, I should think, to be tautological.

Fifthly, there is the Geneva School of criticism, with Georges Poulet as its leader, and including such other critical giants as Marcel Raymond, Jean Rousset, Jean Starobinski. Their approach, there can be no doubt, has produced invaluable studies of symbolism—beginning with Georges Poulet's *Études sur le temps humain.* This criticism of consciousness compellingly strains to place the critic into the mind of the poet so as to reenact for the reader the poet's deepest mental movements, which will in turn produce the geometry of his poetry. Sensitive though this criticism is—and I believe that it has given us some of the finest criticism since the 19th century—it is far too close to the poet himself to even attempt an understanding of his position in the political world. And yet, it is a Poulet who would best ferret out the unacknowledged presence of a Faust in Mallarmé.

So, too, of our sixth category: the psychoanalytic approach. Charles Mauron's exhaustive study of Mallarmé retraces the obsessive myths of Mallarmé's psyche in order to uncover them once again in the configurations of the Mallarmean text. Mallarmé's fatigue with the world is explained convincingly—but as a phenomenon of his personal psychology. In other words, the isolation becomes (as with much pre-Lacanian psychoanalytic criticism, I would argue) an ineluctable, foreseeable necessity stemming from certain childhood dramas, the structure of which continues to unfold itself into the adult texts. The outside world as a notion is then by definition an extension of Mallarmé's psychic lens—it is a narcissistic lens which can grant the world neither autonomy nor objectivity. Nothing can finally be held accountable.

Philosophical approaches, comprising the seventh (arbitrary) group, frequently look to the texts of Mallarmé. Maurice Blanchot's criticism is perhaps the first best example. His brilliant works subtly, and somewhat impressionistically, retrace the philosophical implications of Mallarmé's project. More recently, the *Nouvelle critique,* which comes out of philosophy, has devoted a surprisingly enormous amount of time and effort to an understanding of Mallarmé's texts. Jacques Derrida, of course, at the forefront; but also the late Paul de Man and Barbara Johnson. Derrida concentrates on showing how Mallarmé fits into the "machine" of Western metaphysics.[12] While this reading of Derrida's is both elegant and singularly useful to our understanding of Mallarmé, it once again does not take the polity—what I am calling the "world"—into account.

Well, perhaps there *is* no world. Yet people have spoken of Goethe's *Faust* as an answer to political changes in Germany; of Helena as Goethe's poetic expression of history; of Faust as a protest against the German misery of the times (we think here of Gretchen and the jewels she longs for but does not dare keep). These things have to do with, or are referential to, what we call the "world" around us—the political and economic realm, the external environment of social structures in which we live. Why is all of this missing from Mallarmé, and why does no critic probe this lack? Why is Mallarmé's apolitical, reclusive stance simply taken for granted?

What kind of Faust is this whom French teachers of literature see in Mallarmé's verse? *Faust I,* for example, is rich with the world: the director at the beginning who wants the play to *sell;* the citizens outside the city gates, who complain about the mayor; the "News of Turkey"; the freshman worried about courses and Mephistopheles' brilliant satire on the scholar; the bawdy discussions in Auerbach's cellar ("thank God I'm not the Kaiser," and so on); allusions to the plight of the poor. Where in Mallarmé is Faust's risk to *encounter* the world? For that is Faust's gamble: to *return* to the world with the Devil in search of a moment that lives—that lifts off the veil of *ennui* which initially pervades Faust as surely as it does Mallarmé. In other words, Faust is at the point of "Brise marine" *until* his pact with the Devil—a pact which agrees to a lengthy exploration of *ici-bas* in search of the famous moment.

But Mallarmé does not ever risk encountering the world. His letters are filled with his hatred for his job (teaching English in *lycées* in the provinces). Summer for him is a mercy, a release from quotidian existence. Autumn is for him the death knell—the return to the dreaded classes of unruly and uncooperative students (who make great fun of his poetry). Far from Paris, where there are those few who understand him, and whom he wants to have understand him, the poet feels so cut off that he suffers a nervous breakdown (in 1866). When he returns to Paris at last, in 1871, it is to lead a contented life of utter seclusion from everything except his group of followers. "Beim Propheten" by Thomas Mann could be as well about Mallarmé as about Ludwig Derleth.[13]

The political world in Mallarmé does not exist except as a constant threat to the poet's retreat. Now, Huysmans's *A Rebours* tells a story of such extreme seclusion. But I wish to stress that it is the story of an aesthete, Des Esseintes, for whom *life* is an art form—and who (like Heinrich von Ofterdingen, although one still has hope for him) does not produce a line of verse. There is some of Des Esseintes in Mallarmé—but that is by no means all there is. Mallarmé is first and foremost a poet, a poet for whom the act of writing poetry means isolation. That is *his* striving, his *Streben:* an Icarus-like aspiration, but one which the poet already knows is doomed to failure. Each poem brings him too close to the sun, destroys him. Of his poem "L'Azur," Mallarmé writes to his friend Cazalis in 1864, "I was barely able to overcome my sterility to write this work." And to Eugene Lefébure, in 1867, Mallarmé writes, "I have created my work only by elimination . . . and each writing advances me further into darkness. Destruction has been my Beatrice."[14] Writing poetry consumes the poet—as does music the composer in the Berglinger episode of that ill-named little volume, *Herzensergießungen eines kunstliebenden Klosterbruders,* an episode which helped, as much as *Faust,* to inspire Thomas Mann's *Doktor Faustus.*

For Mallarmé, poetry is the absolute: the myth toward which the poet must always strive. If Faust could not be condemned in an Age of Enlightenment for seeking absolute knowledge, Mallarmé believes himself to be condemned by his human condition alone *a priori*. Salvation does not exist; there is no promised land; the azure will never be attained; thought will never be expressed accurately—and, especially, not by crass language. The world is the first empty shell to be discarded in the search for understanding while we strain for an absolute we cannot attain. If Goethe's utopia has been called capitalistic by critics (and mercantile by Novalis), Mallarmé's utopia participates in no such materiality: for him, utopia is the poem never written, the one endlessly destroyed by the words the poet writes with his black ink on the pure page. If Mallarmé has a passion, it is not one for supreme knowledge; it is rather the passion to strain away from the rabble toward an understanding and a refinement of man's mental and metaphysical *impuissance* in the face of the serene, porcelain sky—that wall between man and the *au delà*. It is thought thinking itself—that which Goethe rejected, and which Valéry person-ifies in the sterile and suicidal intensity of his *Monsieur Teste*.

How do we know that Mallarmé was attracted to Faust? I have said that he never mentions Goethe's *Faust* directly in any of his works, essays, or letters. And yet, everywhere in his early poetry—until his return to Paris—are instances of what many critics of French literature couch in terms of what we might call the Faust motif in Mallarmé's work. French critics (by which I mean here Mondor, Thibaudet, Blanchot, Richard, Mauron, and many others) imagine the Faust motif to mean the turning away from the world, the politics of withdrawal in favor of a search for pure beauty. This is what Faust has come to "mean" in one area of French letters—more than the pact with the Devil; more than the great love with Gretchen. It is Faust—the myth of Faust—which runs like a current of nostalgia in French literary criticism, and is used as an explanation for the reclusiveness of Mallarmé and his *poésie pure*.[15] But, of course, this may have nothing to do with Mallarmé at all. In his essay on the origins of mythology (an essay which is partially a translation of the work of the Englishman Cox, partly the product of Mallarmé), the French poet notes that myths are singular in that they reappear in different countries as a form of obsessive repetition. Their traits, indeed their sources, are the same, though their names may change.[16] The insistence on the part of French critics—even French schoolteachers—to suggest a subtext of Faust in Mallarmé's early poetry demonstrates, therefore, not only what Faust means in France, but also the nostalgia and sentimentality which criticism itself unconsciously clings to in the form of a displacement upon, in this case, Mallarmé. If Mallarmé can be shown to be "Faustian"—in the sense that I have explained it—then there is no need, criticism would seem to be saying, to go further with Mallarmé's rejection of the world in his poetry; no need to probe more deeply into the politics of Mallarmé's withdrawal. If we may say that in

Mallarmé the mythical transfiguration is that of poetry into an unattainable absolute, then I believe we must also acknowledge that criticism's willed blindness to Mallarmé's hermeticism is criticism's own myth of literature: that which must, at times, be left its secrets, must not be entirely unveiled lest the myth be revealed to be what a myth always is, what Mallarmé himself says a myth is—a consensus among the people to explain away that which frightens them, that which they cannot explain. If this consensus be uncovered, the nudity of what remains puts meaning far more into question than the despairing poetry of Mallarmé itself. Moreover, the privileged notion of individuality, which criticism must to a large degree maintain, is then put at risk.[17] It is for this reason, I would argue, that literary criticism in France insists upon retaining, even if implicitly, a "Faust motif" in Mallarmé. As with all myths, such an insistence is a consensus designed to veil that which is neither understood nor finally acceptable. The motif of Faust may well be an undercurrent in Mallarmé—I believe that it is—but it is also an undercurrent of the myth of criticism itself, designed to maintain the partial mystique of literature. Once that mystique is established as ineluctable, forever sealed from the mind's eye, criticism can comfortably go about its business of professing to unveil the very core of things which it has carefully masked. "La chair est triste, hélas, et j'ai lu tous les livres," may be a Faustian cry. But it is also the cry of a criticism which seeks to maintain the meaning it has decided upon for the texts which it has exhausted, and from which it is, at times, exhausted as well. In conclusion, I would say that Mallarmé's politics of withdrawal from the world *and* from literature is doubled by criticism, is too close to criticism for comfort. It is for that reason that such a withdrawal must remain unacknowledged or, at best, mystified— lest criticism see itself in what it prefers to call, without acknowledging it, Mallarmé's Faustian crisis.

Notes

1 8 February 1866 to Madame Le Josne, cousin of Mallarmé's closest friend, Henri Cazalis (Jean Lahor); cf. *Corréspondance 1862–1871,* ed. by I. H. Mondor and J. P. Richard (Paris, 1959). All translations are mine.

2 "Brise marine" may also be read as a response to Baudelaire's "Parfum éxotique," which describes the sailors' songs mixing with the odor of tamarinds in the poet's soul.

3 The transformation of such a tendency into a cult of withdrawal is perhaps best exemplified by the hermetic figure of Des Esseintes in *A rebours,* the celebrated novel by Huysmans. Withdrawal in itself becomes gradually confused, in criticism, with symbol-

ism and "decadence," as evidenced for example in *Axel's Castle* by Edmund Wilson. In that study, Wilson essentially uses the two terms interchangeably.

4 The present essay limits itself for the most part to *Faust I,* although Mallarmé was equally familiar with *Faust II.* Both parts of Goethe's work were translated quite early (1828 and 1840) by Gérard de Nerval. *Faust II* was not translated again until 1947, well after Mallarmé's death, by Alexandre Arnoux. Mallarmé did not read German, and thus had to rely upon translations. His Faust is Nerval's.

5 Cited by Mondor in his edition of the *Œuvres complètes* of Mallarmé (Paris, 1945), 1433: "Il y a au Louvre, a écrit Rémy de Goncourt, dans une collection ridicule, par hasard une merveille, une Andromède, ivoire de Cellini. C'est une femme éffarée, toute sa chair troublée par l'effroi d'être liée; *où fuir!* et c'est la poésie de Stéphane Mallarmé."

6 From the poem "L'Azur":

> —Vers toi, j'accours! donne, ô matière,
> L'oubli de l'Idéal cruel et du Péché
> A ce martyr qui vient partager la litière
> Où le bétail heureux des hommes est couché . . .
> En vain! l'Azur triomphe . . .

7 Mallarmé, *Œuvres complètes,* 368.

8 In fact, Valéry did write his Faust. *Mon Faust* was published in 1940.

9 The word *Faust* is used exactly three times by Mallarmé in his writings, and each time in connection with opera. See "La dernière mode," in his *Œuvres complètes,* 772, 785, and 841. Goethe is mentioned once by Mallarmé, in a letter which refers to Villiers de l'Isle Adam's prose drama *Elèn.* But Mallarmé's use of "Goethe" refers indirectly to Faust in precisely the terms indicated in the present essay. Mallarmé writes: "Je vous envoie un drame en prose pour lequel le théâtre serait trop banal, mais qui vous apparaîtra dans toute sa divine beauté, si vous le lisez, *sous la clarté solitaire de votre lampe: Elèn,* par mon ami Villiers de l'Isle Adam. *La conception est aussi grandiose que l'eut rêvée Goethe,* c'est l'histoire éternelle de l'homme et de la femme. Les personnages y sont incomparables, depuis Samuel Wissler, ce grand philosophe qui se donne la peine d'avoir du génie quand il parle, et n'est pas le grand homme de parade qu'on a inventé pour ces drames, jusqu'à cette fatale Elèn; et Tanuccio, perfide comme la lune italienne." *Corréspondance,* 153 (my emphases). It should be clear from this passage that Mallarmé is tracing in Villiers de l'Isle Adam, insisting upon seeing, the same structure as in *Faust:* the philosopher, his beloved Helen, and the devilish third figure. And even the admonishment to the recipient of Mallarmé's letter—the beauty of the drama *Elèn* will appear "if you read it in the solitary clarity of your lamp," the poet writes—evokes the very atmosphere of the opening of *Faust I* (I am grateful to the database program ARTFL at the University of Chicago for scanning all of Mallarmé's work for any mention of Faust).

10 "Goethe," in *Vues* (Paris, 1948), 156; for the following quote, see p. 142. The speech in honor of Goethe originally appeared in *Variété IV.* The text I am using contains additions and revisions.

11 The Marxist prejudice against poetry has also been remarked upon recently by Andrew Parker, who is working more from the point of view of Marx himself on poetry. Parker's lecture was given at the 1985 MLA Convention in Chicago, and is entitled, "Why Western Marxists Don't Like Poetry."

12 I am, because of the constraints of this essay, being reductive about what is a brilliantly compelling and enormously innovative reading of Mallarmé. See Jacques Derrida's "The Double Session," in his *Dissemination,* transl. by Barbara Johnson (Chicago, 1981).

13 I am grateful to Reinhold Grimm, who pointed out to me that "Beim Propheten" is in fact a satire upon Derleth. I had originally been taught that it was upon Stefan George, and had never probed the matter further.

14 *Corréspondance 1.*

15 I wish to make clear here, lest my argument be misunderstood, that the critics I cite do

not speak directly to a Faust theme in Mallarmé. But the genealogy is so obvious that the evocation of the "Faustian theme" needs no explicit mention. Gérard de Nerval's translation of Goethe's great work was accompanied by an introduction in which Nerval "interpreted" *Faust.* Thus French poets became acquainted with Nerval's *Faust,* especially his *Faust II.* Moreover, Nerval's *Imagier de Harlem* is an overt imitation of *Faust II.* Gautier was tremendously influenced by this French rendition of the German figure. He, of course, was to inspire Baudelaire, who in turn was one of Mallarmé's first spiritual teachers. As Georges Poulet puts it: "Ainsi ce que Goethe lui avait donné, ce que Nerval lui avait transmis, Gautier le transmettait transfiguré aux symbolistes. Déjà en 1859, Baudelaire reconnaissait qu'il avait appris, grâce à Gautier, l'existence de cette 'sorcellerie évocatoire' dont, si l'on se reporte au texte de *Fusées,* la langue et l'écriture devaient constituer les opérations magiques—opérations par lesquelles, après Baudelaire, Mallarmé devait un jour arriver 'au ciel antérieur où fleurit la Beauté." Cf. his *Études sur le temps humain,* vol. 1 (Paris, 1949), 304. The idea of the search for pure beauty becomes associated in French letters with the theme of Faust, and so it is by no accident that Mallarmé mentions "divine Beauty" in his letter on Villiers de l'Isle Adam cited previously. It should be understood, then, that when contemporary French critics speak of the notion of beauty in Mallarmé, and of his idea of language as a book of sorcery *(grimoire),* they are assuming a tradition which begins with Nerval's translations and readings of Goethe's *Faust;* a tradition which was to create the *topoi* and metaphors for a good deal of the metaphysical "crisis" forming the basis of Mallarmé's verse and, in turn, Mallarmean criticism.

16 Mallarmé, *Œuvres complètes,* 1164ff.

17 Marxist criticism does not uphold the bourgeois notion of individuality (one which the "romantic" movement cultivates), nor that of reified traditionalism—quite to the contrary, obviously. But in avoiding the politics of poetry, or the lack thereof (a politics in itself, as Sartre reminds us), Marxist criticism lends added weight to the "mainstream" critical voices which would see poetry in a 19th-century light: that is, as a type of transcendence of the individual; as a process which necessarily entails a retreat from the world. Benjamin on the mechanistic age clearly sketches out the problematic interplay between individuation and the ambivalence of aesthetic modernism. And although Hannah Arendt's preface to the English edition tells us that Benjamin "understood language as an essentially poetic phenomenon," and although Benjamin opens his wonderful essay "The Task of the Translator" with a quotation from the French poet, the citation is from Mallarmé's *prose* ("Crise de vers," in *Variations sur un sujet).* Moreover, Benjamin remains descriptive rather than analytic about Mallarmé's withdrawal: in his essay on the mechanistic age, mentioned above, he talks about the idea of "pure" art, "which not only denied any social function of art but also any categorizing by subject matter" (in poetry, Mallarmé was the first to take this position). Cf. "The Work of Art in the Age of Mechanical Reproduction," in his *Illuminations* (New York, 1969), 224. In his brilliant essay on Baudelaire, Benjamin cites poetry quite frequently. But Baudelaire turns out to be the author of "the last lyric work that had a European repercussion; no later work penetrated beyond a more or less limited linguistic area" (192). And Baudelaire already believes that the poet has lost his halo. Benjamin, meanwhile, believes that the modern age which reproduces beauty marks the "decline of the aura." Thus we might say that a criticism such as that of Benjamin, which sees the poet (with Baudelaire) as having lost his halo, and the age as having lost its aura, inadvertently returns the halo and aura to both by steering mostly clear of subsequent poets, such as Mallarmé, and thus permitting bourgeois criticism to mystify the poet and to refuse, concomitantly, to probe the possible reasons for denial of the world and withdrawal on the poet's part. It is rather in the interest of bourgeois criticism to encourage such a precisely *uncritical* stance so that the aura can be maintained, and criticism continued.

The Masses and Margarita:
Faust at the Movies

RUSSELL A. BERMAN

A recent study of Faust films includes more than forty entries, and even this surprisingly long list is incomplete. The most obvious examples are literary films, cinematic adaptations of canonic plays and novels: *Faust,* directed by Peter Gorski and Gustaf Gründgens, based on Goethe's play (1950); *Doctor Faustus,* directed by Nevill Coghill and Richard Burton, who stars with Elizabeth Taylor in a version of Marlowe's drama (1967); and Aleksander Petrovic's treatment of Bulgakov's novel, *The Master and Margarita* (1973). Others retell the Faust story in contemporary settings: *L'homme qui vendit son âme* by Jean-Paul Paulin (1943) and John Farrow's *Alias Nick Beal* with Ray Milland as the Devil (1949). Still others focus on the central female figure, like Claude Autant-Lara's *Marguerite de la nuit* (1955), or they transform Faust into a woman: *Faustina* by José Luis Saenz de Heredia (1958); *Faustina* by Luigi Magni (1968); and *Faustine et le bel été* by Nina Companeez (1975).[1]

Interestingly, nearly half of the recorded Faust films were produced before the First World War, during the earliest period of cinematic history. The Lumière catalogue of 1897 lists a *Faust* by Georges Hatot, which lasted little more than a minute, and included two shots: the appearance of Mephistopheles and the transformation of Faust with the image of Gretchen. The first Méliès version, *Le cabinet de Méphistopheles,* was made in the same year; three more followed by 1904. Clearly, the Faust material fascinated the first generation of filmmakers and has continued to attract the attention of directors ever since.

In "The Work of Art in the Age of Mechanical Reproduction," Walter Benjamin remarks on how Faust films necessarily surrender the literary-historical specificity that adheres even to the worst performances on stage.[2] This loss of aura, however, sheds light on the character of the cinematic process as well as on the ramifications of the Faust theme. Three issues are especially crucial: mass culture and the masses, whose role Benjamin underscores in his seminal essay; the role of Margarita, or the representation of women in narrative cinema; and the aesthetic specificity of the movies—the wish-filled illusions—that is set in relation to the diabolical power to produce images. I want to discuss these issues in five Faust films, each of which transforms the material both in terms of its own historical context and within the institutionalization of commercial mass culture.

After his successes with *Nosferatu* in 1922 and *Der letzte Mann (The Last Laugh)* in 1924, Friedrich Murnau had considerably less luck with *Faust: eine deutsche Volkssage* in 1926. On the eve of his move to Hollywood, the project, which, as the subtitle indicates, was understood as a cinematic rendering of the German national epic, turned into a financial flop, grossing only half of its production costs of two million marks. Conservative critics, who measured the film against its literary models, resented the eclectic mixture of elements from the 16th-century chapbook and Goethe's drama. Others, like Herbert Jhering, pointed to the insipid performance of Gösta Ekman in the title role, upstaged by Emil Jannings as Mephisto and Camilla Horn as Gretchen (a role initially planned for Lillian Gish). In this atmosphere of critical hostility, the Prussian Interior Ministry was able to declare the film unfit for minors in 1927, a strange echo of an earlier conservative antipathy to Goethe's alleged immorality.[3]

Murnau's *Faust* found a somewhat warmer reception abroad; but there, too, a negative tone prevailed. A critic for the *National Board of Review Magazine* bemoaned that "we find ourselves descending from the masculine version of Marlowe and the philosophical concept of Goethe to the level of the libretto which inspired Gounod to write his opera." Siegfried Kracauer, who cites this remark in *From Caligari to Hitler,* concurs and continues: "*Faust* was not so much a cultural monument as a monumental display of artifices capitalizing on the prestige of national culture. The obsolete theatrical poses to which the actors resorted betrayed the falsity of the whole. . . . The Germans of the time did not take to Faustian problems and, moreover, resented any interference with their traditional notions of the classics."[4]

Without adopting these critical judgments, one can recognize them as evidence of the early reception history in which two allegations predominate: a feminization of the Faust material and the triviality of cinematic renditions, contrasted with traditional high culture. These claims are based on broad sexual, political, and cultural conservative assumptions, which could serve as evidence for a general cultural history of the period. However, they also indicate features of the cinematic culture industry during the 1920s, and of Murnau's film in particular.

The accusation of a feminized Faust is not adequately explained by pointing to the unequal performances of Ekman and Horn. Consider instead the structure of the narrative: the initial prologue, in which the battle between good and evil is announced; the medieval city, beset by Mephisto's plague that forces Faust to sign the fateful pact; the brief erotic episode with the Duchess of Parma; and, finally, the lengthy vicissitudes of love played out between Faust and Gretchen. After the first three sections, which amount to fragmentary vignettes, albeit richly detailed, it is through the Gretchen material that the film develops suspense and cohesion, and the victimized female lover is indisputably the center of attention. In this sense, Murnau's *Faust* is no exception: commercial narrative cinema generally involves a love story which, as feminist critics like Laura Mulvey and Teresa de Lauretis argue, demands the sacrifice of the woman.[5] When Faust goes to the movies, Gretchen comes to the fore, if only to go up in flames.

This shift in the sexual economy of the narrative, resulting in the relative dwindling of the Faust figure, is compounded by an additional factor. Three years after the era of astronomical inflation and the profound political crises that nearly toppled the Weimar Republic, the first German democracy had achieved a relative stability. Murnau presents his *Faust* as a German *Volkssage,* a legend of the people; and while it is hardly a democratic *Faust* it is definitely a *Faust* of the *demos.* Excluding for a moment the dialogue between Satan and the heavenly forces at the beginning and end of the film, one notes that the popular masses frame the film and define the action: the crowds at the fair; the victims of the plague; the throngs at the Easter mass; and the irate populace, outraged by Gretchen's crimes, swarming forward to watch her burn at the stake. The culture industry mobilizes the masses in representation, in order to march them in reality past the ticket counter. Poor Faust, the individual, is nearly forgotten. Instead of his singular crisis of faith or knowledge, to which earlier accounts attribute his willingness to enter the diabolic pact, Murnau's version ascribes priority to the needs of the people suffering from the scourge of the plague, while Faust's decision assumes a secondary, derivative status. It is almost as if sovereignty derived from the people; but the democratization of the culture industry remains inauthentic insofar as ultimate authority is located in the metaphysical debate and celestial power, Murnau's popular counterpart to the fundamental ontology of his philosophical contemporaries.

The ideological context of the Weimar Republic explains why Murnau could try to sell his film by foregrounding the masses, in turn eroding the centrality of the Faust figure, which is one of his critics' major complaints. Their other complaint, the negligible quality of the cinema when compared with the Goethean legacy, also strikes right to the heart of the legitimation problem of the film industry. Murnau's film itself incorporates the tension between a high culture of verbal literacy and a popular culture of visual imagery. The simple masses at the fair are entertained by acrobats and a shadow theater, while the isolated scholar Faust, looking like an Old Testament patriarch, is surrounded by books and words. When he is overcome by despair, he casts his books into the fire, forsaking the word of God. Mephisto, characteristically, approves of this transition when he later asserts that Faust's earlier life had only been "Bücherstaub und Moder," the dust of books and mold. Instead of verbality, Mephisto offers illusions, the deceptive imagery of youth, wealth, and eros; and he can generate these images thanks to his control over fire, the power of light, the same force that produced the initial shadow theater.

Faust succumbs to Mephisto because he rejects books, and he is saved at the end by love, designated as "the one word," an obvious reference to Luther's "ein Wörtlein." Mephisto can enact compelling visual images, but they are always deceptive. This line of argument suggests that the message has to do with the victory of the divine word over the sensuous illusions of diabolical pleasure, a plausible if unoriginal homily. Yet that is indeed a strange message for a film, and especially a silent film that depends so centrally on the montage of images. But perhaps it had strategic value: when conservative critics attacked the film by referring to traditional high culture, they were already caught in the logic of the film, which denounced images in the name of books. Mephisto, as the master of illusions, is Murnau's cinematic principle— which, however, always subverts itself since Murnau, as director, never questions the priority of the word. The culture industry attempts to legitimate itself by pledging allegiance to the same high culture it opposes: clearly, a case of Mephistopholean legerdemain.

This self-critique of the film medium is thematized in the double courtship between Faust and Gretchen and between Mephisto and Marthe. The affairs are initiated in similar manners. Mephisto hides a box in Gretchen's dresser, and he carries another one with him to Marthe. Each metaphoric *camera obscura* contains a chain on which the illusions of love are spun, a constellation of images repeated in the chains of children and the chains of flowers. When Gretchen counts petals to determine Faust's love, Mephisto acts out a parodic inversion, plucking at a sunflower, in order to play with Marthe's fantasies and, implicitly, to reveal the hopelessness of Gretchen's dreams. Yet his own machinations sparked those dreams; it is his mise-en-scène that stages the delusions. In Murnau's cinematic Faust, Mephisto's prestidigitation becomes a self-critique of the magic of the silver screen.

After his cinematic death in the role of Valentin in Murnau's film, Wilhelm Dieterle turns up in Hollywood in 1941 as the director of *All That Money Can Buy,* also known as *Here is a Man* and, more generally, as *Daniel and the Devil,* based on Stephen Vincent Benét's story *The Devil and Daniel Webster* published in 1937. The history of American Faust films begins with Edison's *Faust and Marguerite* of 1900 and includes at least one *Faust* in 1909, a film of Gounod's opera in 1910, a parody of Gounod, entitled *Bill Bumper's Bargain,* in 1911, and *Faust and the Lily* in 1913. Charles Hackett's 1929 *Faust* drew on Gounod's music and treated the hero as a businessman, and for the Goethe centennial in 1932 Howard Higgins presented a twenty-minute-long education film, *Walpurgis Night.*[6] Interestingly, this tradition is much older and more varied than the German lineage, which does not begin until 1926 with Murnau, unless one counts the integration of certain Faustian elements in *Der Student von Prag* of 1913, remade in 1926 and 1935.

Dieterle's film borrows from the American tradition by maintaining a humorous tone and, in the wake of Higgins, by using the Faust material to examine the business ethics of capitalism. On both these points, he follows his literary model closely; in fact, Benét, who had already transformed his story into a play, collaborated on the script. In the original version, Jabez Stone, a poor New Hampshire farmer, is constantly beset by bad luck. When he cries out that enough is enough, and offers to sell his soul to the Devil, a stranger shows up and a contract is signed, replete with the obligatory spot of blood and the seven-year term. Jabez prospers of course; but as the due date of the mortgage draws near, he begins to worry and appeals to the popular hero Daniel Webster, who, as an accomplished rhetorician and skilled lawyer, agrees to represent the worried farmer.

But the Devil, Mr. Scratch, has an ironclad contract, and Webster is forced to leave civil law and torts behind and invoke constitutional grounds: "Mr. Stone is an American citizen, and no American citizen may be forced into the service of a foreign prince. We fought England for that in '12 and we'll fight all hell for it again." Scratch can counter, however, that no one has a better right to American citizenship than he himself: "When the first wrong was done to the first Indian, I was there. When the first slaver put out for the Congo, I stood on her deck." Faced with this state of affairs, Webster calls for a trial by jury. Scratch quickly complies and conjures up quite a hellish crew: ". . . there was Walter Butler, the loyalist, who spread fire and horror through the Mohawk Valley in the times of the Revolution; and there was Simon Girty, the renegade, who saw white men burned at the stake and whooped with the Indians to see them burn. . . . There was Teach, the bloody pirate, with his black beard curling on his breast." And so on—the judge, Justice Hathorne, presided at the Salem witch trials.[7]

Things look bad for Daniel and worse for Jabez Stone, but Webster's words work wonders. Beginning with descriptions of simple human experiences, he goes on to talk of American history and its promise, then of Stone as an example of a man who had had bad luck and made a wrong choice, but now wanted to change. He convinces the jury, that acquits Stone, and Webster can banish Scratch.

Although Dieterle's version follows this plot line closely, different sorts of changes are evident. Some have to do with the specificity of the film medium. For example, the populist language of the story disappears—there is no voice-over narration—but a similar effect is achieved through a plethora of shots displaying the details of rural life: farm animals, wagon wheels, a barn dance, and the like. This cinematic realism is compounded by an expressionist use of lighting, evidence of Dieterle's training with Murnau. In the opening shot, Webster sits at his desk while behind him, a giant shadow, the Devil, looms ominously, whispering: "Don't write that speech." In addition, the visual potential of the film allows for the direct representation of supernatural phenomena generally omitted in the story: Scratch can suddenly appear out of nothing; bags of gold coins can pop out of the ground, and ghostlike visitors besiege Jabez.

A more significant change involves the age of the farmer: in the story, he is an older man while the film presents him in his mid-twenties. This transformation may seem curious because it prevents the Devil from granting his victim youth, the cinematic representation of which had worked so well for Murnau. However, given the character of the culture industry, the change from Benét's senior citizen to Dieterle's young man is crucial since it makes room for three female roles grouped around Jabez: his mother, played by Jane Darwell, remembered for her remarkable performance as the matriarch in *Grapes of Wrath;* his wife Mary; and the maid Belle, a demonic temptress who provides Jabez with Faustian pleasure while introducing discord into the Stone household. Only the wife is mentioned in the story (and she remains nameless there): the other two women are cinematic innovations. As with Murnau's *Faust,* it appears that the cinematic appropriation of the narrative leads to a feminization of the material.

More generally, Dieterle transforms Benét's terse legend through the addition of background details, minor figures, and subplots. The initial story simply recounted the origins of the pact, Stone's despair, and Webster's plea to the jury. The film traces the character of Stone's affluence: his sudden wealth, his success at farming, his growing importance in the village, and his increasingly luxurious life-style. This expansion was undoubtedly necessary to magnify the short story into a feature-length film. It also conforms to an additional imperative of the commercial cinema: the possibility of audience identification. Benét's story of an exemplary case employed distanciation with a didactic intent, reminiscent of Benjamin's comments on epic narration. The film invites an empathetic reception from its first title: "This is a story they tell in New Hampshire, but it could happen anywhere. Yes, it could even happen to you."

Yet the major consequence of the integration of the new material involves the political substance of the film. Benét's story vaguely invokes a progressive American tradition. It designates the treatment of Indians and the slave trade as evil while invoking as a normative ideal the inalienable right to the pursuit of happiness, the grounds on which Stone is acquitted. References to Webster's political horizon—his antagonist John C. Calhoun, the Missouri Compromise, and the impending threat of the Civil War—are never fleshed out and, ultimately, only provide local color. Dieterle maintains the historical setting, even dating it specifically as the period 1840–1847; but his treatment of the Faust material clearly displays the tensions in progressive American politics on the eve of the Second World War.

While Jabez Stone is as unlucky in the film as he was in the story, Dieterle transforms his financial crisis into a typical case of rural life during the depression. All the farmers are impoverished; all suffer from loan sharks and the banks. Mary and Jabez's neighbors repeatedly implore him to join the grange; but, after concluding his deal with Scratch, he insists that he will "take care of himself," and separates himself from community solidarity. As he grows increasingly wealthy, the other farmers become his debtors and, later, his wage laborers. When Mary begs Webster for help, she describes how her husband turns the poor away from their door despite his own past. As Jabez pursues an upward social mobility, he loses all his initial rural social virtues.

In Benét's story, Webster's politics, in spite of loose references to antebellum debates, remain unclear. In contrast, Dieterle makes him an explicit opponent of the banks and an advocate of the debtor farmers. This characterization of Webster as a New Deal reformer runs throughout the film and culminates in the speech to the jury. Because its members were greedy, Webster asserts, they believed in Scratch and lost their freedom. Jabez did so, too; but he has recognized his error. Every man has a right to rebel against his fate, and Stone therefore deserves another chance. Webster concludes with a ringing exhortation: "You can't be on his [i.e., Scratch's] side, the side of the oppressor. Don't let this country go to the Devil. Free Jabez Stone." Dieterle turns the struggle for Faust's soul into a political trial with social implications. For the Devil represents the principle of unfettered capitalist accumulation, the law of contracts which the liberal Webster wants to modify, if not abolish. The line from the story regarding Stone's American citizenship is expanded in the film to include Webster's apodictic assertion: "A man is not a piece of property." The rhetoric of the politician articulates the objective goals of the populist grange, which Jabez joins at the conclusion of the film.

Dieterle's Webster may be a Roosevelt reformist, but the historical problem of American populism is its proximity to nativism. The film treads a thin line here. The coins which Scratch kicks up out of the ground are described as "Hessian gold," lost by an ambushed convoy on its way to Saratoga during the Revolutionary War. Is lucre thereby associated with counterrevolutionary forces, the mercenary soldiers whose origin is described parenthetically in Schiller's *Intrigue and Love*? Or is the designation of wealth as "Hessian" an attempt to mobilize anti-German sentiment in 1941? A similar semiotic ambivalence recurs in the case of the devilish lady Belle, who speaks with a French accent but who describes her home simply as "over the mountain," and later herself, as "I am not anything."

Both story and film are thick with Americana, and the émigré director has included signs of foreignness that may be negatively charged. Recall, by the way, how Murnau treated his *Faust* as a specifically German legend and how his hero, after the erotic vacation in Parma, yearns to return to his *Heimat*. The question of national identity is inherent in the Faust material while presenting a specific problem for progressive politics, especially at the historical juncture where the New Deal is about to become the war effort. Dieterle may not have an answer, but he at least poses the question in a clever way. Benét's story ends with Scratch's exile. The film ends with Scratch sitting on a fence, pondering where next to ensnare a gullible soul. He looks to the left and to the right and then straight forward. As the camera zooms in for a closeup shot, he points his finger at the viewer and grins. He is of course the ever-present Devil, waiting for the spectator, as indicated at the outset of the film. Yet with his hat, scruffy beard, bushy eyebrows, and the pointed finger, the resemblance to the Uncle Sam of recruitment and war-bonds posters is unmistakable. Or is the military Uncle Sam the mechanism with which the Devil will put an end to Webster's reformism? For Dieterle, cinematic representation simultaneously critiques and reproduces a vernacular American iconography. The ambiguous meaning is indicative of the political paradoxes of 1941.

Both *Faust: eine deutsche Volkssage* and *Daniel and the Devil* locate the Faustian hero within a social collective. After the experiences of the Second World War, this characteristically modernist faith in community loses its credibility, and cinematic renditions of Faust turn to explorations of individual autonomy. This transition reflects the privatization of public culture in the consumer society of advanced capitalism, as well as the growing intellectualization of the cinema due, in part, to the competition with the new mass medium, television. An early example of this neoindividualist Faust is provided by René Clair's *La Beauté du diable* of 1949, where the masses appear only briefly as a threat, and the heroic scientist insists on severing his ties to the state. Against the background of contemporary existentialism, Clair uses the Faust material to demonstrate an irreducible human freedom and the priority of immediate experience over conceptual knowledge.

Attempting to emancipate the narrative from religion and metaphysics, Clair shifts attention away from the consequences of the pact and toward the initial duel between a rationalist Faust and Mephisto. The Gretchen material consequently loses importance and becomes little more than a plotty embellishment. An aging professor in a small Italian principality in the 17th century, Henri Faust is besieged by the "second-class demon," who cannot convince him to relinquish his soul. In order to accelerate the negotiations, Mephisto rejuvenates Faust while himself taking on Faust's old body. Henri learns about the long-forsaken pleasures of life and continues to resist Mephisto's entreaties. Inspired by his master Lucifer, Mephisto sets out on a new course: he grants Henri fame and success, attributing to him the alchemistic discovery of a method to transform sand into gold. The court adores him, the princess loves him, and Henri exclaims: "I'm the happiest man in the world."[8] At this point, Mephisto whisks him away; believing all his happiness was an illusion, Henri signs the pact on the understanding that he would regain what was lost. But it was never lost; Mephisto has succeeded on the basis of a ruse.

Although all of his wishes are granted, Henri grows melancholy and insists that Mephisto show him the future. In images conjured up in a mirror, he sees his undying love for the princess rapidly giving way to other amorous affairs; his political leadership leads to war; and the scientific progress in which he places so much faith ends in mass destruction. He commands Mephisto to undo all he has done; in the ensuing crisis, the latter tries to ensnare Marguerite, the innocent Gypsy girl who loves Henri, by showing her the pact with Faust's signature. She grabs it and throws it to the angry mob, which responds by chasing Mephisto— remember, he has exchanged bodies with Faust—who must jump to his death from a window, a victim of mistaken identity. As the film ends, a Gypsy caravan moves off through an idyllic countryside, and one can only assume that Henri and Marguerite will live happily ever after.

In an afterword to the screenplay, Clair explains that Henri's exclamation, "It's never too late," sums up the message of the play: an emphatically human "refusal to accept the yoke of destiny."[9] Although the scientist has spent decades in ascetic self-denial, the rejuvenation permits him to rediscover the joys of physical existence. Unlike Murnau's Parma episode or Dieterle's temptress Belle, which both present sensuality negatively as diabolical pleasure, Clair treats the physical experience of sense-certainty as an authentic reality superior to all abstract claims. Because the world is perpetually open and indeterminate, no material necessity compels Faust to enter the pact. On the contrary, Mephisto must deceive him, at the turning point in the plot, with the assertion that the world is a place of suffering and joy is only imaginary; and precisely that claim turns out to be mendacious. For Clair, existence precedes essence, and no necessity binds human creativity. Accidentality is therefore an ever-present grace, and the illogical defeat of Mephisto and salvation of Faust make sense precisely as nonsense.

The Heisenbergian critique of determinacy is articulated specifically by the rejuvenated Faust as a denunciation of institutionalized science: "Plato used to close men inside a cavern in order to explain to them the secrets of the earth. . . . Later . . . the astronomer Newton flew off among the stars to explain to men the secrets of the sky. Well, the philosopher and the astronomer were wrong. It's a third sage who is telling you. I, Henri! Because there is only one secret to know. It's the secret of youth! It's the secret of happiness. It's the secret of joy. It will be revealed to you inside. Come in, ladies and gentlemen!"[10] Attacking science and idealist philosophy in the name of experiential immediacy, Henri stands in front of the Gypsies' circus tent, suggesting that aesthetic representation, too, provides an alternative to deterministic knowledge and the authoritarian state. That aesthetic dimension certainly includes the cinema as well, the medium which Clair employs in order to elaborate his critique of a system of domination based on an alliance between government and the universities. In a film made four years after the attacks on Hiroshima and Nagasaki, the most vivid accounts of the destructive potential in scientific progress are consequently found in the cinematic images provided by Mephisto when Faust inquires into the future. Like Murnau, Clair uses the diabolical production of illusions as a metaphor for his own medium of representation.

Multifold contradictions beset Clair's œuvre. The director insists on the rationality of an irreligious Faust but denigrates philosophical reason. He scorns the Gretchen material but preserves Marguerite for the conclusion. He attacks Newtonian mechanics from the advanced standpoint of indeterminacy but constructs a plot organized in terms of the conservation of matter: for Faust to grow young, Mephisto must become old; sand turned into gold must return to its original state; everything must be paid for; and all supernatural elements in the tradition are reduced to a clumsy realism. A mythic eternal return of the same coexists with a faith in freedom raised to the level of dogma. The political passions of the previous decades have receded and the privatized consumer retreats into the creativity of a world of do-it-yourself accumulation. The postwar Faust renounces the Faustian projects of universal emancipation, but his postmodern quietism cannot disempower a hellish objectivity simply by denying it.

Clair's secularization of the Faust story continues in Louis Pauwels's *Président Faust* of 1974. Because of the hero's atheism, the Devil, whose classical proposal makes no sense, complains: "Now it's up to me to convince men that they have a soul before I can seize it. You just have to do everything yourself. God has abandoned me." A ruthless industrialist, President Henry Faust is locked in combat with Boucard, a left-wing leader. Marguerite and Valentin are Boucard's children. Faust advocates unlimited technological modernization, while Boucard insists on social welfare and organizes strikes. A scientific invention promises a utopian reduction of oil dependency. Although Faust initially opposes utilization of the discovery, he falls in love with Marguerite, who tempers his avarice and teaches him humanity. He breaks up his monopoly and concludes by telling the disappointed Devil that he has no desire but to become "un homme parmi les hommes," as he disappears into the crowd.[11]

Against the background of the energy crisis, the spread of environmentalism, and an increasing hostility toward traditional models of economic growth, Pauwels emphasizes the problematic character of Faustian progress. In contrast to Clair's private escapism, however, his rendition at least touches on some possible political and economic reforms. The theological component has all but disappeared, and Marguerite, the traditional vehicle of grace, operates as a metaphor for human love rather than as a catalyst for divine intervention. Freedom depends on a dismantling of hypertrophic political, economic, and scientific structures. Moreover, Pauwels thematizes the debilitating effects of the culture industry: the Devil's dwelling is full of television sets. The mass media thoroughly control the conditioned reflexes of the manipulated viewer. With its episodic structure, *Président Faust* attempts to counteract this reception process by underscoring the necessity of choice and creativity.[12]

The examination of the culture industry and aesthetic representation in Faustian terms, evident in the works of Murnau, Dieterle, Clair, and Pauwels, occupies the thematic center of István Szabo's film *Mephisto* (1981), based on Klaus Mann's 1936 novel of the same name. As in the case of *Daniel and the Devil,* the film follows its literary referent closely, yet also makes extensive changes. It is always crucial to examine such changes, but not in order to determine whether a film accurately adapts the prior text; the notion of accuracy is here untenable methodologically. The terms of the transformation can, however, tell us something about the alternative media and the differing concepts of author and director.

The novel begins in 1936 with a festive celebration of the Nazi elite, in which the actor Hendrik Höfgen plays a central role. The subsequent narrative begins by returning to the early years of the Weimar Republic and proceeds to trace the rise of Höfgen's career: i.e., his personal history constitutes the main concern of the novel, a roman à clef in which Mann attacks his former colleague Gustaf Gründgens for collaborating in the Third Reich. While Szabo cannot omit the Gründgens material, his film redirects attention to another issue. The party, with which the novel commences, is transported to its appropriate chronological place near the end of the cinematic narrative; the film opens with an aesthetic spectacle, an operatic performance in the Hamburg Arts Theater during the 1920s. The film cuts to a dressing room where Höfgen is crying. In the novel, the corollary performance is described as a "successful middlebrow drama," and the actor's tears are shed because of unrequited love.[13] By reorganizing this material, Szabo foregrounds the triviality of the traditional theater and suggests that Höfgen's despair refers to the low quality of the stage. In place of Mann's opportunist careerist, Szabo presents the actor as an aesthetic innovator anxious to modernize the theater, no matter what the cost. This Faustian pursuit of progress leads him to his success as Mephisto and his alliance with the diabolical powers of the state.

The differing perspectives of novel and film become particularly evident in the alternative treatments of Höfgen's aesthetic leftism during the Weimar Republic. In the novel, he promises to join a revolutionary theater project, but constantly postpones actual participation. When he finally does appear on stage, he merely utters a *pro forma* declaration of solidarity. The narrator quickly points out the perfunctory character of this engagement: "The day is approaching. That blazing conviction drives [the fascist and communist activists] Hans Miklas and Otto Ulrichs forward, consuming them and millions of other young people. But for what day is Hendrik Höfgen waiting? He never waits for anything but a new part."[14] In contrast, the film shows Höfgen as actor and director attempting to institute a new aesthetic practice grounded in left-wing thought; in a passionate speech, he calls for a "total theater" for the working class, described in terms reminiscent of Brecht.

Disappointed by Gründgens's collaboration, Mann presents a vacillating Höfgen ready to sacrifice all political integrity. In 1936, the author wishes the actor had been as much of a leftist as he had once promised. In 1981, Szabo has a very different position intimately tied to the postwar Eastern European experience. He not only distrusts any politicization of art, that apparently always threatens to lead to totalitarian results. He also scrutinizes the manner in which the aesthetic avant-garde easily mobilized revolutionary political ideologies in order to demolish traditional modes of aesthetic representation—the operatic performance at the opening of the film, which the avant-gardist Gründgens so detests. Therefore, Szabo himself presents a traditional narrative film, a standard period piece concerned with the dangers of aesthetic modernism.

Consider also the two conclusions. Mann confronts Höfgen with a mysterious revolutionary emissary, the harbinger of a better day. Needless to say, that figure is absent in the film. More importantly, the two versions culminate in radically divergent treatments of *Hamlet*. In Mann's account, fascist aesthetics push Höfgen to Shakespeare as a purportedly Aryan genius, and the Danish prince represents Nordic profundity and the exigency of action. At the close of the film, the Göring figure drags the actor in the middle of the night to the Olympic stadium and, blinding him with spotlights, calls out his name again and again. Höfgen is the Hamlet who has no identity and can no longer act because, in the course of aesthetic modernization, he has destroyed all substantive values and traditional legitimacy. He is Faust, Mephisto, and Philemon and Baucis all at once.

The hostility to the aesthetic avant-garde ends up close to a neoconservative nostalgia for traditional art and bourgeois individualism. Yet Szabo fails to comprehend how individualism initially emerges as a protest against a reified traditionalism, Höfgen's Faustian despair, even if the erosion of that tradition also undermines the possibility of subjectivity. This dialectic of individuation runs like a red thread through all Faust films, cinematic narratives of the autonomous subject in the age of a culture industry that produces the collective mass of consumer recipients. "The work of art in the age of mechanical reproduction" (Benjamin's optimistic circumlocution for the capitalist modernization of culture) promises stories of individuals—Faust is a case in point—only to negate them. It is almost as if the notion of Faust films were always a contradiction in terms. But the immanently contradictory character of aesthetic representation is the esoteric trace of contradictions present in society: "Am farbigen Abglanz haben wir das Leben."

Notes

1 Ernest Prodolliet, *Faust im Kino: Die Geschichte des Faustfilms von den Anfängen bis zur Gegenwart* (Fribourg, 1978), 83–91.
2 Walter Benjamin, *Das Kunstwerk im Zeitalter seiner technischen Reproduzierbarkeit* (Frankfurt, 1969), 52.
3 Prodolliet, *Faust im Kino,* 59–52; Ludwig Greve et al., *Hätte ich das Kino! Die Schriftsteller und der Stummfilm,* catalogue of the Deutsches Literaturarchiv (Stuttgart, 1976), 260–261.

4 Siegfried Kracauer, *From Caligari to Hitler: A Psychological History of the German Film* (Princeton, 1971), 148–149.

5 Teresa de Lauretis, *Alice Doesn't: Feminism, Semiotics, Cinema* (Bloomington, 1984).

6 Prodolliet, 53–54.

7 Stephen Vincent Benét, "The Devil and Daniel Webster," in his *Thirteen O'Clock: Stories of Several Worlds* (New York and Toronto, 1932), 172–174.

8 René Clair, *Four Screenplays,* transl. by Piergiuseppe Bozzetti (New York, 1970), 174.

9 Ibid., 213.

10 Ibid., 145.

11 Louis Pauwels, *Président Faust* (Paris, 1974), 46, 168.

12 Jean Kerchbron, "La réalisation militante," in Pauwels, 15–17.

13 Klaus Mann, *Mephisto,* transl. by Robin Smyth (New York, 1983), 22.

14 Ibid., 151.

"Faust im Braunhemd":
Germanistik and Fascism

Kirsten Belgum,
Karoline Kirst-Gundersen,
and Paul Levesque

Of the works devoted to the history of Goethe reception in the 19th and 20th centuries which have appeared since 1945, Hans Schwerte's book *Faust und das Faustische* of 1962 covers the *Faust* reception in particular during these centuries.[1] Yet, as detailed as Schwerte is in his presentation of the ideological uses made of the Faust figure over the years, he has little to say concerning *Faust* reception under National Socialism (NS). It was during the period of the Fascist dictatorship, however, that the interpretative manipulation of literary texts such as *Faust* became openly political and ideological. Not only did some German scholars in the Third Reich perceive of themselves as spokespersons of German identity, but historically, too, they must be considered representative of, and instrumental for, national socialist ideology.

Our original interest in pursuing the topic of *Faust,* the drama and the man, as they appeared under national socialist guise, was encouraged by the fact that where we expected to find ideological uniformity, or agreement, among scholars in Germany of the 1930s, we did not. We discovered that the figure of Faust and his reputation (i.e., the "Faustian") were contested in the 1930s—and even, to some extent, by various committed Nazis. We also realized that *Faust* interpretations under the NS regime did not take place in a historical vacuum, and that our discussion would have to retrace the legacy of Faust leading up to this period. In view of these considerations, we shall begin with references to *Faust* in the 1910s and 1920s by the cultural critics Houston Stewart Chamberlain, Moeller van den Bruck, and Oswald Spengler. A second section of our study will discuss the central importance of those works for a later Fascist reading of Goethe's *Faust.* Finally, we shall turn to interpretations from the 1930s and 1940s that diverge from such Fascist models in varying degrees. In looking at the reception of *Faust* during the Third Reich and the period preceding it, we have not come to a conclusive definition of what a Fascist interpretation is—i.e., of the exact boundaries of a Fascist interpretation of *Faust*—but we have identified some qualities, or emphases, which appear necessary for a Fascist *use* of the Faustian. In particular, we want to demonstrate that the terms used to describe Faust in the Third Reich, such as his essential Germanness, his "grand personality" *(große Persönlichkeit),* and his dedication to the "community" *(Gemeinschaft)* experienced a development of their own which paralleled the rise of a chauvinistic nationalism and *völkisch* anti-Semitism in Germany.

In reaction to the overwhelmingly positivist, empirical investigations of Goethe published in the late 19th century, several monographs appeared in the early part of the 20th century which offered a more personal, subjective reading of Goethe's life. Moeller van den Bruck in 1907 and H. S. Chamberlain in 1912 specifically state their purpose as one of educating the public about Goethe, the German man, by offering their own "experience" of the poet. The works of Moeller (an art historian) and Chamberlain (a cultural critic) defend a conservative German cultural heritage which functioned as an ideological legitimization of the Wilhelminian Empire. Although neither author was a literary scholar, they were important for later Germanists in popularizing this conservative, nationalist approach to German culture. Both authors utilize their positive interpretation of Goethe's *Faust* as a cry for German nationalism. Their works, both published before the First World War, are full of the idealism and nationalistic righteousness which sent so many German men enthusiastically to the battlegrounds. They instilled and legitimized a sense of duty for the German people—the will to realize a global plan—-and the feeling of Germanic cultural, even racial, superiority. In other words, they laid the groundwork for later Goethe studies which stressed these nationalistic ideals even more.

Moeller van den Bruck published the sixth and final volume of his series, *The Germans: Our History of Humanity,* under the title *Goethe.*[2] In this book, Moeller presents his view of Goethe as the first man knowingly to portray the vision of a "leading" Germany, an accomplishment which made Goethe the ultimate German. Moeller defines as particularly German Goethe's and Faust's passion to work, and their feelings of social responsibility. The poet is set up as prophet of the German people. Moeller subordinates humanist ethics to a radical nationalism by elevating the figure of Faust to a state beyond good and evil. He makes mention of only one tragic aspect in *Faust,* the Gretchen tragedy of the part 1, and even here Faust transcends the guilt of seducing Gretchen by aspiring beyond the personal realm:

> No human who has truly accepted the feeling that it is his duty to lead an active life can be harmed by the guilt which he perhaps burdened himself with in his youth.[3]

Faust is able to rid himself of his moral guilt through his dedication to the communal good; or, to put it another way, no price is too high to pay for the benefit of the masses. The Faustian vision, "to stand on a free ground with a free people" *(auf freiem Grund mit freiem Volke steh'n),* and Faust's radical method of self-realization are symbolic of the Germanic mission. Moeller argues that Goethe has prophetically unveiled the German future in his tragedy *Faust.* Faust, the model man, the magus, is beyond morality by virtue of his communal efforts. All Germans should aspire to the Faustian idealism in order to become as a whole the leading nation they are meant to be.

Chamberlain's depiction of Goethe is every bit as programmatic as is Moeller's. Yet he carefully points out that he is less concerned with the poet's literary accomplishments than with the man himself. "The most important part of Goethe's poetry," he writes, "is undoubtedly his own life."[4] In a manner characteristic of the conservative cultural elite of Wilhelminian Germany, Chamberlain seeks to rescue the classical tradition in the face of the threatening, chaotic phenomenon of modernism. Pessimistically, he defines his time as one of spiritual and cultural decay. Modern science and the Jews, he argues categorically, are responsible for the growing political unrest among the lower classes, the decline of religiosity, and the lack of spiritual unity in the German nation.[5] The only possible defense against this cultural decay lies in a proper understanding and internalization of Goethe's philosophy of life.[6] To be instrumental in protecting Germany against the Jewish danger, he argues, one must pursue the Goethean spirit, the spirit of Germanness. The anti-Semite Chamberlain draws on the reader's veneration for Goethe and Goethe's work in his argument for the superiority of the Germanic people and his call for nationalist action.

Faust is endowed with a truly German spirit. The old Faust, as the old Goethe, gains wisdom through a continuous internal battle between rationality and sensuality. This discord, or inner struggle, between the will of the individual and the pressure of the community, between the idea and the concrete is characteristic of both Goethe and Faust.[7] It is a struggle for the realization of an ideal within its practical limits. Faust's duty was to attempt the fulfillment of his dream, even at the expense of others. Draining the swamps is an act of utmost communal importance: creating *Lebensraum* for the "free people." "Every individual man must be ready to make any sacrifice . . . out of duty."[8] The real driving force behind this duty can be read in Faust's words, "In the beginning was the deed." Chamberlain leads the reader through an examination of the Faustian personality and an exoneration of the Faustian enterprise. He argues in favor of the Faustian as the grand German plan for social, *völkisch,* and nationalist action.

While these two authors try to identify the German quality in Faust, Oswald Spengler's *The Decline of the West*[9] is dedicated to defining the Faustian in the German character. His book is an exposition of the way in which Faustian man can and will shape his own fate. Spengler divides mankind into three categories, each representative of a time in history and a geographical position: the Apollonian, the Magical, and the Faustian. The Faustian age is the history of Western man from the 13th century to the present. At the center of the Faustian personality and the Spenglerian thought, there lies what Nietzsche called "the will to power": an unquenchable thirst for power, even for total control, that fuels a belief in the absolute necessity of human action. Faustian man is propelled by the presumptuous mission to submit all others to his own will and truth:

> Will to power even in ethics, the passionate striving to set up a proper morale as a universal truth, and to enforce it upon humanity, to reinterpret or overcome or destroy all who are otherwise constituted—nothing is more characteristically our own than this.[10]

Spengler follows the social-Darwinist argument that throughout history the strong peoples have overtaken the weaker ones. In addition, the peoples dedicated to action have always overcome those dedicated to justice or morality.[11] In his introduction, Spengler outlines the most direct route to domination of history. However, not just any people, or *Volk,* is capable of this. Spengler's work is meant to lend credence to the notion of Nordic racial and moral dominance. According to his model, the Faustian man is the savior of the Western world. Upon realizing that the West is in a crisis, the Germanic people must assume its inherent Faustian calling and set out to shape a new world. Spengler traces the Faustian mission through the history of Western Europe to prove the legitimacy of the Germanic claim to world rule. He calls this rule, which is achieved by overcoming all obstacles, even at the expense of others, "socialism." It is the inevitable fate of the German people. Clearly, this brand of socialism differs fundamentally from the classical notion of socialism. It is a program of systematic elimination of those opposed to Germanic dominance, which stems from an intolerance toward all non-Western, all non-Faustian peoples, ethics, and moral or political structures. The goal of history as the absolute rule of the Faustian, or German, allows Spengler a total disregard for all who stand in the way of Western man.

So far, we have seen three exemplary efforts by representatives of German conservatism to utilize the classical heritage of Goethe's *Faust* in their design of a German nationalism. Goethe—and, more specifically, Faust—have been idealized as examples for a political policy of tremendous national and racial chauvinism. The Fascist works of the 1930s and 1940s were deeply indebted to the likes of Moeller van den Bruck, Chamberlain, and Spengler in their characterization of Faust as the Fascist prototype, Faust the brownshirt.

Before moving on to a treatment of *Faust* reception during the 1930s, it is important to stress the fact that Goethe's privileged place in the literary canon was not as secure during this period as the representative use of Goethe and, especially, his *Faust* in the 1910s and 1920s would have us believe. From the period around 1900 onward, and in the wake of the First World War in particular, figures from the Storm and Stress and Romantic periods such as Herder, Hölderlin, and Heinrich von Kleist were increasingly being presented as members of a new canon which would break the dominance of the old Weimar Classicism under the aegis of Schiller and Goethe. This new, more "romantic," canon with its mythic, nationalistic, and irrational tendencies seemed more representative of the German character to some of the fervently nationalistic and increasingly *völkisch* literary critics of the 1920s than did the works of the Olympian Goethe. One such critic, Joseph Nadler, argued his case against Goethe in his essay "Goethe oder Herder."[12] For Nadler as well as for other extreme nationalists, it was inconceivable that Goethe, the "good European," was being presented as the one truly great and representative German. His status as the great individual smacked of bourgeois liberalism and seemed, according to Nadler, irreconcilable with any true identification with the German *Volk* as a whole. Finally, in light of Goethe's "unpatriotic" stance during the Wars of Liberation and his acknowledged admiration for Napoleon, one can see that Goethe presented some problems for literary critics belonging to the extreme Right.

Nadler's charges were not the only ones leveled against Goethe. One of the most contested issues during the 1920s and 1930s, which even inspired a *Faust* interpretation of its own, was Goethe's known membership in a Freemason Lodge in Weimar. In 1931, the Ludendorff publishing house—a violently anti-Semitic concern run by the ex-First World War general Erich Ludendorff, and devoted to unmasking the "crimes" of Freemasonry—brought out Else Rost's *Goethe's Faust: Eine Freimaurertragödie.*[13] This pamphlet, following the line set forth in other books published by Ludendorff, put forward the hypothesis that Goethe, as a Freemason, must either have participated in, or have had knowledge of, the Freemasons' "secret murder" of Friedrich Schiller. Rost's innovation lies in her claim that Goethe's *Faust,* supposedly Germany's greatest dramatic work, was in fact a barely disguised hymn to the Freemasons' ongoing project of delivering the world over to Jewish control. In her interpretation, Mephisto emerges as an established Brother of the Lodge who leads Faust through the necessary initiation rites in order to prepare him for full membership. One of these rites involves seducing Gretchen, who is recognized as a symbol of the once hardy German people rendered weak and pliable by the centuries of debilitating Christianity. Faust's "salvation" at the end of the drama is merely a representation of his acceptance into a decidedly Masonic heaven.

Even in the face of such criticism, however, Goethe retained his privileged place in the German cultural heritage claimed by the Nazis. One need only scan the numerous publications of minor party functionaries and Nazi sympathizers within the discipline of *Germanistik* to find a coherent picture of Goethe's usefulness for the NS regime. Titles such as *Goethes Sendung im Dritten Reich* ("Goethe's Mission in the Third Reich") by August Raabe; *Goethe im Lichte des neuen Werdens* ("Goethe in Light of the New Becoming") by Wilhelm Frehse; and *Faust im Braunhemd* ("Faust the Brownshirt") by Kurt Engelbrecht reveal the same veneration of Goethe familiar to the 1910s and 1920s.[14]

A leading example of this is the 1937 speech, "Goethe in unserer Zeit," delivered by Reichsjugendführer Baldur von Schirach on the occasion of the Weimar festival of the German youth.[15] Schirach, one of the few high-level Nazi functionaries to devote a public speech to Goethe, begins with the obligatory defense of Goethe which culminates in the rousing cry: "German, name the unmistakably German book, it is *Faust.* Name the unmistakably German poet, it is Goethe."[16] Quoting from Goethe, and taking liberties with his original words, Schirach represents him as an admirer of the Hitler Youth (before the fact) and as sympathetic to the policies of the National Socialists. While Baldur von Schirach provides a paradigmatic example of the Fascist appropriation of Goethe the man, Georg Schott, in his 1941 study *Goethes Faust in heutiger Schau* ("Goethe's *Faust* in Today's Perspective"), performs the same service for Goethe's most famous drama.[17] For Schott, the Faust figure represents all the virtues and vices of the Nordic or, more specifically, the German man.

He is the "genial man," dissatisfied with mere material possessions, and constantly striving after higher goals. Faust is ruthless when it comes to achieving his desired objectives and joins up with the Devil himself if necessary to reach them. Possessing a deep understanding of nature, he relies more on feeling than on intellect in his dealings with the world. This intuitive understanding of the world brings him into conflict with the conventional moral order, however—a situation Schott designates as "tragic." Faustian man's constant striving must necessarily disrupt the closed, ordered world of bourgeois sensibilities, as Faust's dealings with Gretchen can attest. It would be wrong, though, to judge Faustian man by using conventional moral standards, for, in a sense, he is beyond morality. The true sign of Faustian man is the fact that he strives not for himself, but rather for his people, the *Volk,* and any crime committed on this path of striving must be seen in such a perspective. Faust reveals his true genius when, in the last act of *Faust II,* he recognizes his responsibility to the people and undertakes his massive land reclamation project, creating a safe haven for what Schott refers to as his "Volk ohne Raum," his people without land. "Auf freiem Grund mit freiem Volke steh'n," perhaps the most quoted *Faust* line of Fascist *Germanistik,* serves as Faust's glowing epitaph and final justification for his, at times, less than exemplary life.

Ruthless, striving, beyond good and evil, dedicated to the *Volk:* these are the qualities Schott admires in Faust. They are also the qualities he admires in the Faustian men of the 1930s. And yet, Faust is not the only character of the drama Schott brings up to date. Mephisto is revealed as the quintessential Jewish intellectual, a master of "Talmudic" logic who ridicules Faustian man's higher strivings. Faust's colleague Wagner represents the German philistine, a pedantic scholar who lacks Faust's ties to the people and, consequently, would not have appreciated Faust's later vision of a free and happy *Volksgemeinschaft.* Gretchen, while definitely a part of the conventional moral order, is nevertheless heralded as a model German woman, dedicated to home and hearth and blessed with an intuitive understanding of the differences between the Faustian and the Mephistophelean, i.e. Jewish, man. Philemon and Baucis, the victims of Faust's grand vision, represent a social class unwilling or unable to adapt themselves to the changes any kind of struggle must bring with it. Schott's general intent is clear: Goethe's *Faust* must be represented as a profoundly German work which prophetically addresses the issues and concerns of the National Socialist state.

Schott's reliance on simplistic analogies and his pointed references to the relevance of Goethe's *Faust* for his contemporaries strike today's reader as rather obvious propaganda ploys. But his rhetoric and argumentation do capture the essence of a certain strand within *Germanistik* of the 1930s. With him, a not unimportant group of second-rate talents showed their willingness to propagate the most orthodox National Socialist line on Goethe in countless essays, speeches, and pamphlets. The mediocrity of their output is readily apparent nowadays; their names have been relegated to the dustbin of history; yet, in sheer numbers, they far outweighed that group of Germanists from the 1930s whose names are still remembered.

Nevertheless, any survey of *Faust* reception in *Germanistik* of the period must make it clear that the paradigmatic Fascist interpretation found in Schott was not followed blindly by all members of the discipline. There were divergences from this model, divergences which were equally sympathetic to Fascist ideals but couched in a more sophisticated language. An exemplary case in point is Heinz Kindermann. His 1941 collection of essays, *Kampf um die deutsche Lebensform* ("A Battle for the German Form of Life") is the most programmatic work of a writer given to programmatic statements.[18] Kindermann felt that he had a mission, that he, as a Germanist, should work to illustrate the ways in which German literature had fostered the cultural, spiritual, and political growth of the German nation.

Kindermann's *Faust* interpretation is contained in the essay "Persönlichkeit und Gemeinschaft in Goethes dichterischem Werk" ("Personality and Community in Goethe's Poetic Work"), an essay which attempts to portray Goethe's own particular contribution to the growth of the German nation. He begins by stressing Goethe's roots in the Storm and Stress movement, seeing in his early writings an explicit critique of the dominant Enlightenment mentality of the late 18th century. Kindermann goes on to argue, however, that Goethe's *Faust,* the poet's crowning achievement, ventures beyond the earlier Storm and Stress critique of the German Enlightenment. The earlier works had successfully shown that the "omnipotence of feeling," not the omnipotence of reason, rules men's lives, but they had also concentrated on the Promethean, titanic figures who seemed isolated from the community at large. Kindermann also views Faust as a Titan linked to Goethe's earlier creations; however, Faust does not suffer the fate of isolation common to Goethe's earlier titantic figures. At the end of the drama, Faust realizes that his individual striving must ultimately serve the good of the community as a whole. This idealistic, communal activity is symbolized by his colonization project. Once again, the line from *Faust,* "Auf freiem Grund mit freiem Volke steh'n," is used to characterize the drama as a whole. It is reduced to a representation of the need of the individual, the "personality," to channel his energies and make sacrifices for the good of the community, the *Gemeinschaft.* A platitude, perhaps, but in the context of National Socialist ideology, a rather ominous one. Although Kindermann does not rely on Schott's forced analogies in order to come up with this rather banal interpretation of *Faust,* the final conclusion is as implicitly Fascistic as are Schott's explicit ones. The individual must be sacrificed for the good of the National Socialist state.

Up to this point, we have outlined the roots of a Fascist interpretation of Goethe's *Faust* and traced their development into the 1930s. Parallel to this development, there also appeared studies of *Faust* which, standing in the tradition of *Geistesgeschichte,* are more difficult to characterize. As texts, they often evade any clear historical categorization, which is mostly due to an appeal in them to supposedly timeless, eternal, universal qualities they claim to find in *Faust* in particular and in the German *Volk* in general. In an essay of 1980, Beate Pinkerneil makes a strong case for the continuity in the scholarly work of many of the major Germanists between the Weimar Republic and the Third Reich.[19] This methodology, she claims, presented little threat to the Fascist framework of the 1930s. On the contrary, due to its dedication to the so-called eternal laws of genre, and its rejection of historical, political, or social considerations, this methodology lent itself well to a mystification of the cultural heritage and the construction of an irrational *völkisch* myth. Pinkerneil is not alone in her judgment. The thesis has been formulated by others that these literary scholars even supplied the Nazis with useful tools in the development and expansion of their ideology.[20]

While the latter may be debatable, we do consider it central to a study of *Faust* reception under Fascism to present some evidence of this "continuity" as it existed with respect to *Faust* interpretations in the 1930s. A useful example is H. A. Korff, who wrote on *Faust* both before and during the NS period. Along the same lines, however, we shall also discuss the nonaffirmative continuity which existed within the ranks of *Geistesgeschichte* as evinced by the writings of Ernst Beutler, Wilhelm Böhm, and the Catholics Karl Kindt and Reinhold Schneider.

Korff's landmark work from the late 1920s was entitled *Geist der Goethezeit.*[21] In his chapter on Goethe's *Faust,* he makes the general assertion that life is not to be understood or questioned, but is rather a paradox which is inaccessible to reason; its mystery can only be broken by the strength of the individual's *Lebenswille.* The ability of Faust to do exactly this in Goethe's drama makes him an admirable, great personality. His will to life constitutes the strength of his personality; it excuses all the less than admirable deeds he commits. Korff describes Faust as a criminal at one point, but greater than that is the *trotzalledem,* the "nevertheless," written over his entire existence, justifying everything: "Life, we could say, needs the mistake for its completion."[22] This excuse applies *a priori* to all great personalities. Their greatness provides them with a completely different ethical system in which power is an absolute good. "Faust takes the risk to do evil because he feels the power to turn evil into good. In that case, then, evil endures for right."[23] That is to say, actions do not need justification through reasons; they are justified by their "grandness." It is just a small step to Fascist acceptability when Korff, in his 1932 essay "Goethes deutsche Sendung," adds the component of chauvinistic nationalism to his *Faust* interpretation.[24] As the title implies, Korff's purpose is to demonstrate Goethe's truly German nature. The German and the Faustian essences become synonymous. The explanation of Faust's behavior and the justification for his evil are now applied to the German people, the *deutsches Volk.*

In a work of 1938, *Faustischer Glaube,* Korff uses the Faustian motif to outline a "way of life" for contemporary Germans.[25] Under the chapter heading "The New Life," the pieces of his *Faust* interpretation coalesce. We might call this the striving-man ideology, according to which ruthlessness and egotism are couched in philosophical, supposedly neutral, terms, and where the side effects of the striving man's actions are insignificant compared to the ultimate "good" of his will to power. Clearly in the tradition of a Nietzschean "Übermensch," and echoing what we found in Spengler, Korff describes Faust as a Titan whose natural constitution makes all others bow to his predominance: "Great personalities devour the smaller ones, that is the law of nature."[26] What many have called the tragic ruination of Gretchen and Philemon and Baucis at Faust's hands is here an act of nature. The "genius" of Goethe's poem consists in inspiring a "horrified amazement" in its audience of the Faustian personality and the Faustian project; it "annuls our ethical misgivings against our will."[27]

These emphatic quotes from Korff are similar to statements made by Schott and Kindermann with respect to Faust's role as a leader and as the ultimate German. What is missing from Korff's interpretation, however, is the community. In overtly Fascist interpretations, Faust's "greatness" resides in the ultimate good he does for the *Volk,* the *Gemeinschaft.* This is too plebeian an interpretation for Korff, whose praise of Faustian titanism and egoism is too individualistic for a *völkisch* appeal. Therefore, we cannot easily place him into the ranks of an outspoken Fascist *Germanistik* as represented by Schott and Kindermann. Korff does not work with simplistic characterizations of Mephistopheles as the evil Jew and Faust as the political leader *(Führer)* of the German people. And yet, we do find elements in his writings on *Faust* which move beyond a glorification of the heroic individual, and which, in the context of National Socialism in Germany, cannot be read other than as a sympathetic recognition of the ideology of Fascism. For Korff, the struggle in Faust's soul corresponds to the struggle in the German nation, the history and future of which must be accepted as fate even if it involves the use of terrorism by the strong against the weak. While lacking an expressly anti-Semitic or racist moment beyond the glorification of the "German" or of "Germanness," Korff does extol a project of rampant expansionism for the German, i.e., Faustian, being.

This was, however, not the only direction taken by *Geistesgeschichte* in *Faust* interpretations during the Third Reich. In his 1941 essay "Goethes *Faust:* ein deutsches Gedicht," Ernst Beutler's tone is decidedly nationalistic, but some of the ideas he presents take issue with the standard Fascist interpretation of *Faust.*[28] Before examining Beutler's essay in any detail, however, it might prove instructive to place him and his reading of *Faust* in context. Beutler, a longtime director of the Goethe Museum in Frankfurt, was one of the most prominent Goethe specialists of the 1930s and 1940s. He also represented a certain strand within *Germanistik* whose members, while not sympathetic to Fascist ideology, nevertheless decided to remain in Germany during the Third Reich and continue in their profession. Like other members of the so-called inner emigration, he tried to continue his work as if the National Socialists had never come to power.

Such a position was difficult to maintain. Beutler and other like-minded scholars pointedly avoided controversy by concentrating on collecting biographical information, turning to a positivist approach to Goethe reminiscent of the late 19th century. Such apolitical tendencies, however, were controversial in their own right. Bernhard Kummer, in his 1935 pamphlet "Germanenkunde im Kulturkampf," rails against those scholars who place objectivity before commitment to National Socialist ideals, accusing them of protectively flying the symbol of the "international quest for truth over the racial stain of Jewish-blooded Germanists," and lambasting "objectivity" as a "shield against a lack of sense of the fatherland."[29] Kummer's rhetoric is menacing and gives a good idea of the pressures exerted on Beutler and others. However, it was not until the outbreak of the Second World War that the option of producing apolitical, positivistic studies of Goethe seemed no longer available. *Germanistik* was called upon to participate in the war effort, which meant in effect that prominent scholars were compelled to write explicitly nationalistic studies for government-sponsored anthologies. One such anthology was *Von deutscher Art in Sprache und Dichtung,* a five-volume work compiled in 1941 by the editorial team of Gerhard Fricke, Franz Koch, and Clemens Lugowski.[30] Beutler's essay first appeared in this work. At the end of this essay, when he discusses Faust's colonization project beloved by so much of Fascist *Germanistik,* his own view of the drama's essential Germanness becomes clear: "The *Faust* drama would never have been a German poem if the final conclusion of wisdom had been that one can create new land with devilish powers."[31] When compared with other interpretations, the uniqueness of Beutler's becomes apparent. Philemon and Baucis are rarely even discussed in most interpretations, much less represented in stirring terms as victims of Faust's grandiose schemes. The uniquely German aspect of *Faust* for Beutler is the play's implicit condemnation of Faust's colonization project, because of its reliance on "devilish powers." Faust is presented as a failure, a *Scheiternder,* a genuinely tragic figure. We have heard Schott describe Faust as a tragic figure, but his definition of a tragic situation—one in which the innocent must necessarily suffer due to the strivings of a noble hero—lacks the moral force of Beutler's usage. Whether or not Beutler was in his own way drawing a comparison between Faust's pact with Mephisto and the "devilish powers" of National Socialism—it is clear that his interpretation questioned the distorted Fascist appropriation of Goethe's *Faust*.

A related, but earlier, critique of the Fascist emulation of Faust appeared in a work entitled *Faust der Nichtfaustische* (1932/33) by Wilhelm Böhm, the renowned Hölderlin scholar.[32] In this book, Böhm discusses the discrepancy between Goethe's dramatic character Faust and the long tradition of misinterpretations of that figure which had led to a false use of the term *Faustian*. His project consists in defending Goethe's *Faust* as a literary work against the misconstruing readings of critics, beginning with Goethe's contemporaries, and continuing up to the present. He especially attacks the "cultural missionaries" of the 1920s, as he calls them.

In contrast to Korff, Böhm argues that Goethe made Faust a "big-time criminal," an "incorrigible Titan," whose method of operation is making mistakes rather than striving. Böhm offers a pointedly negative picture of Faust which emphasizes his tragic flaws, without the admiration for his excesses displayed by Korff. This characterization of Faust as *Unmensch* is part of Goethe's attempt to paint an "apocalyptic picture of the hellish forces of exploitation."[33] *Faust,* as a dramatic poem, should shock and upset us; we should be "tragically shaken by the way this man without measure cloaks his entrepreneurial lusts with stoical humanistic ideals."[34] The emulation and glorification of the deed *(die Tat ist alles)* is mere seduction, according to Böhm. He ridicules the notion that Faust's scheme to win back land from the sea in act 5 of part 2 is a grand *Vollendungsplan*. It was, he argues, only a banal principle of water management which was generations old, and certainly not an act of genius.

Böhm's phrase, "the apocalyptic picture of the hellish forces of exploitation," is decidedly anti-Faustian in the sense of Faust as a mighty, heroic, genial, even godly personality. Faust the character is an example of what should be avoided, *Faust* the play, a moral lesson in the dangers of that personality and mentality. In 1932, this is as close as Böhm comes to saying what he does formulate more explicitly in 1949: *Faust* is Goethe's warning to modernity and modern man. "History has taught us the bitter lesson of what dangers the Faustian . . . holds. In *Faust,* Goethe gives us the antidote."[35] Böhm implicitly links the Faustian to Fascism. More simply put: Fascism is the Faustian gone wild. It is important to note that Böhm did not write on *Faust* during the Third Reich itself. We found a harsh condemnation of the Faustian, as the Fascists had praised it during the 1930s, only in a critique by authors of what we might call a Catholic "inner emigration."

Karl Kindt, in his 1938 book entitled *Geisteskampf um Christus,* devotes a chapter to Faust, or, in particular, to the Philemon and Baucis scene in the last act of Goethe's *Faust*.[36] Instead of commending Faust for his destruction of the backward Philemon and Baucis, along with their little chapel, during his land reclamation project in the name of progress for the *Volk* and the *Gemeinschaft,* the Catholic interpretation offers a challenge to this Fascist praise of progress. For Kindt, the old couple's chapel represents the Christian idyll, the world of tranquility. Goethe, he argues, set up this scene "in order to achieve the full *Fallhöhe* of the tragical,"[37] i.e., the more idyllic their situation, the more demonic is Faust's use of Mephisto in their destruction, the more tragic Faust's project. The "chapel on the dune" need not resist in order to disturb the Faustian project; its mere existence presents a challenge to the "drawing-board order" of modern society. In contrast to this peaceful enclave, Faust, the man of activity, appears as a ridiculously overwrought figure: "He remains only a bundle of nerves of organizational energies of the highest tension, which wear themselves out in self-consuming dynamics."[38]

Reinhold Schneider, in his 1944 essay "Fausts Rettung" (published in 1946), also places a "good, true relationship to the creation" as the Christian ideal in Goethe's work.[39] As with Kindt and Böhm, the emphasis here is on Goethe's critique of the Faustian, of Faust's striving aided by Mephistopheles. And yet, Schneider laments, recent decades have instead chosen to idolize, or deify, Faust. Schneider poses the rhetorical question: "Didn't *Faust* make history in the last one hundred years, and perhaps call up just those terrors that have been making us tremble?" The reason for this lies in the interpretations of *Faust,* not in the work itself. It was precisely against these terrors that Goethe's *Faust* was warning with "portentous wisdom."[40] Writing in 1944, in the crisis of the world war, Schneider repeatedly draws parallels between Faust and the present horror in Germany. In accordance with his Catholic confession, the solution for both Goethe's and Germany's tragedy is to be found in an act of grace: "The heavenly Mother will deliver Faust; she will heal the world, which suffered because of Faust."[41] The only escape from rampant Faustianism is salvation through the intercession of the heavenly powers; the only alternative to the Faustian is unlimited, religiously conservative respect for God's creation. In other words, their critique of Fascism is a conservativism with an anti-industrial, antitechnological bent. It is a private, personal resistance to a political phenomenon.

We have come to see that during the 1910s and 1920s there was a trend to make Goethe the prophet of German nationalism. A variety of conservative authors stressed the factor of nationalist, social struggle in Goethe's *Faust.* This school of German cultural interpretation rapidly developed into a more pronounced, even chauvinistic, nationalism. That a later group of *Faust* critics could incorporate this nationalism into their own work which became ideologically important for Fascism has been shown in the examples of Georg Schott, Heinz Kindermann, and, to a certain extent, H. A. Korff. In 1933, numerous respected Germanists pledged their cooperation with the cultural goals of the National Socialists. Korff expresses this sense of duty in an essay entitled "The Demands of the Day":

> Es genügt nicht, theoretische 'Kunde' zu haben von deutschem Wesen. . . . Diese Kunde muß durchblutet sein von einem leidenschaftlichen Gefühl— und darum leidenschaftliches Gefühl erregen. . . . nicht wertfreie Wissenschaft, sondern Wissenschaft, die all ihr *objektives Wissen* in den Dienst einer *subjektiven Wertung* stellt, aber einer Wertung, deren Wertmaßstäbe aus dem völkisch-organisierten Leben stammen, weil sie eben im Dienst des Lebens stehen.[42]

This quote seems to support the thesis put forward by some critics on the Left at the outset of the Third Reich, in particular during the Goethe celebrations of 1932: namely, that the Fascistization of Goethe was a project in which bourgeois Germanists, or "liberal theoreticians" as Georg Lukács called them, were active. From our historical vantage point, however, we have been able to show that Goethe and Faust remained contested figures in Germany throughout the 1930s and 1940s. We have seen that some critics were intent on rejecting this ready appropriation of Faust for Fascist ideology. Their alternative interpretation— the one of Beutler, Böhm, Kindt, and Schneider—resisted, or even critiqued, the positive reception of the Faustian figure by emphasizing Faust's tragic character and Goethe's own distance to him. This focus, however, ultimately limited them to a position of resignation in the face of German Fascism.

Notes

1 Hans Schwerte, *Faust und das Faustische: Ein Kapitel deutscher Ideologie* (Stuttgart, 1962).
2 Arthur Moeller van den Bruck, *Goethe* (Minden, 1907).
3 Ibid., 194.
4 Houston Stewart Chamberlain, *Goethe* (Munich, 1912), 106.
5 Ibid., 286, 678.
6 Ibid., 710.
7 Ibid., 718.
8 Ibid., 728.
9 Oswald Spengler, *The Decline of the West* (New York, 1926). We have changed the translation where we saw fit.
10 Ibid., 344.

11 Ibid., 507.
12 Josef Nadler, "Goethe oder Herder," *Hochland* 22 (1919): 1–15.
13 Else Rost, *Goethes "Faust," eine Freimaurertragödie,* 2d ed. (Munich, 1936).
14 August Raabe, *Goethes deutsche Sendung im Dritten Reich* (Bonn, 1934); Wilhelm Frehse, *Goethe im Lichte des neuen Werdens* (Braunschweig, 1935); Kurt Engelbrecht, *Faust im Braunhemd* (Leipzig, 1933).
15 Baldur von Schirach, *Goethe an uns: Einige Gedanken des großen Deutschen* (Munich/ Berlin, 1938).
16 Ibid., 7.
17 Georg Schott, *Goethes Faust in heutiger Schau* (Stuttgart, 1940).
18 Heinz Kindermann, *Kampf um die deutsche Lebensform* (Vienna, 1941).
19 Beate Pinkerneil, "Trennung von Geist und Politik: Literaturwissenschaft im Bann der Geistesgeschichte," in *Am Beispiel Wilhelm Meister: Einführung in die Wissenschafts- geschichte der Germanistik.* Band 1: Darstellung, ed. by Klaus L. Berghahn and Beate Pinkerneil (Königstein, 1980), 54–74.
20 Cf. Eberhard Lämmert, Walther Killy, Karl Otto Conrady, Peter von Polenz, *Germanistik—eine deutsche Wissenschaft,* 3d ed. (Frankfurt, 1968); Hildegard Brenner, *Die Kunstpolitik des Nationalsozialismus* (Reinbek, 1963).
21 H. A. Korff, *Geist der Goethezeit,* vol. 2 (Leipzig, 1930).
22 Ibid., 416.
23 Ibid., 418.
24 H. A. Korff, *Goethes deutsche Sendung* (Leipzig, 1932).
25 H. A. Korff, *Faustischer Glaube: Versuch über das Problem humaner Lebenshaltung* (Leipzig, 1938).
26 Ibid., 163.
27 Ibid.
28 Ernst Beutler, "Goethes Faust, ein deutsches Gedicht," in *Von deutscher Art in Sprache und Dichtung,* ed. by Gerhard Fricke, Franz Koch, and Clemens Lugowski (Stuttgart, 1941), vol. 4.
29 Bernhard Kummer, *Germanenkunde im Kulturkampf* (Leipzig, 1935).
30 See n. 28 above.
31 Beutler, "Goethes Faust," 279.
32 Wilhelm Böhm, *Faust, der Unfaustische* (Halle, 1933).
33 Ibid., 64.
34 Ibid., 60.
35 Wilhelm Böhm, *Goethes Faust in neuer Deutung* (Cologne, 1949), 347.
36 Karl Kindt, *Geisteskampf um Christus* (Berlin, 1938), 90–121.
37 Ibid., 101.
38 Ibid., 102.
39 Reinhold Schneider, *Fausts Rettung* (Berlin, 1946).
40 Ibid., 4f.
41 Ibid., 31.
42 H. A. Korff, "Die Forderung des Tages," *Zeitschrift für Deutschkunde* 47 (1933): 344.

Amazing Grace:
Thomas Mann, Adorno, and the Faust Myth

HANS RUDOLF VAGET

"... wie sollte ich kein Gläubiger
der Gnade sein, da sie mir im Alter
gewährte, dies Buch zu schreiben?"
Letter to Agnes E. Meyer,
March 17, 1948.

Unequivocal Negation?

Shortly after completing chapter 46 of *Doctor Faustus,* the penultimate, Thomas Mann read it to Theodor Wiesengrund Adorno. He had been in the habit of trying out each new chapter before a small, sympathetic audience ever since he began writing this most German of his novels in Pacific Palisades on 23 May 1943. On this occasion, however, 12 January 1947—very late in the game—there was no longer any question of simply testing the effectiveness of the writing. This reading was a truly crucial event in the genesis of the novel; this, after all, was the culminating and decisive chapter. By reading it to Adorno, Mann submitted his work once again, and for the last time, to the judgment of the man whom he had accepted as the supreme authority on all matters concerning modern music.

Adorno—Mann's junior by almost thirty years—had become his collaborator beginning with chapter 7 of *Faustus.* "This was my man," he realized at once after reading the manuscript, as yet unpublished, of Adorno's *Philosophie der neuen Musik,* which the author, eager to be of assistance, had given to Mann on 23 July 1943.[1] Though insignificant as a composer himself, Adorno was regarded, even then, as a formidable theoretician, and was soon to be considered, by some at least, as "undisputably the most important and most competent philosopher of music since the Pythagoreans."[2] Adorno—and this represents perhaps his most controversial position—practically identified modern music with the so-called Second Viennese School of Arnold Schönberg and his followers, particularly Adorno's own teacher, Alban Berg. Mann, whose understanding of modern music did not extend beyond the level of an "ini-

tiated ignorance," came to rely almost completely on his "privy coun-
cillor," as he would call him.[3] Adrian Leverkühn's astonishing fictitious
compositions are simply unthinkable without the ideas and suggestions
of the Frankfurt philosopher. His role in the genesis of *Doctor Faustus*
exceeds considerably the rather limited extent that Mann acknowledged
in the published version of his *The Story of a Novel.*

On occasion, Adorno could be somewhat intimidating. He did not
like what Mann read to him. He objected, even "rebelled,"[4] and insisted
on drastic changes. Understandably, Mann's initial irritation was great.
"Strained nerves," his diary entry from that time reports.[5] He had been
led to believe that he was in tune with Adorno's thoughts on Leverkühn.
A year earlier, he had shown Adorno the entire manuscript, which by
then had reached chapter 33, and had received his complete approval
and encouragement. Subsequently, Adorno was granted an increasingly
stronger voice in Leverkühn's development. He "collaborated" on Leverkühn's Violin Concerto and the Oratorio *Apocalypsis cum Figuris.* More
importantly, he persuaded Mann to drop the idea of giving Leverkühn's
last composition, *The Lamentation of Doctor Faustus,* a fragmentary
form.[6] For philosophical reasons, this work, the culmination of Leverkühn's œuvre and of the whole novel, had to be a complete, full-scale
composition. Adorno prevailed. He also suggested, brilliantly, that the
work's basic row, its "Grundreihe," should represent the old Doctor
Faustus's final statement—which happens to be dodecasyllabic: "For I
die as a good and as a bad Christian."[7] Mann had gratefully accepted this
and other suggestions. All the more troublesome, then, was Adorno's last-
minute objection to *The Lamentation.* Clearly, this was a point of the
utmost delicacy and importance. A fault here would suggest a crucial flaw
in the whole design of the novel. And that would affect the far-reaching
historical implications inscribed in Mann's revision of the Faust myth.
Mann and Adorno eventually "harmonized" their conceptions of Leverkühn's last composition, but the mere fact of their clash must be regarded
as indicative of important and substantive differences between their
positions—differences that merit our closest attention.[8]

Remarkably, Adorno's objections did not concern the musical par-
ticulars of *The Lamentation* but rather its philosophical purport. In
retrospect, Adorno wrote that he found the weighty pages evoking Leverkühn's last composition simply "too positive, too unabashedly theological. They seemed to lack what was demanded in that crucial passage: the
impact of unequivocal negation as the only permissible cipher of the
Other."[9] Mann, for his part, remembered Adorno crying: "No, no—no
such reconciliation. You must not degrade despair; it must not sound as
though the archsinner had grace and forgiveness already in his pocket."[10]
In the published version of *The Story of a Novel,* Mann toned down this

little scene in his study considerably. The passages concerning grace and hope, he writes, had simply "gone wrong. I had been too optimistic, too kindly, too pat, had kindled too much light, had been too lavish with the consolation. I had to grant that Adorno's criticisms were justified."[11]

One is reminded here of Nietzsche's comically sarcastic description of the dilemma Wagner found himself in upon his discovery of Schopenhauer, and of Wagner's attempt at harmonizing the originally optimistic conception of *The Ring of the Nibelung* with the pessimism of Schopenhauer's world view that he now found much more plausible. "What happened?" Nietzsche asks. "A misfortune. The ship struck a reef; Wagner was stuck. The reef was Schopenhauer's philosophy; Wagner was stranded on a contrary world view. What had he transposed into music? Optimism. Wagner was ashamed."[12] It does not appear that Mann actually felt ashamed of the secretly "positive" thrust of his Faust novel, but he did seize the opportunity to satisfy Adorno and, at the same time, to bring *The Lamentation* more in line with the novel's basic pattern of equivocation and paradox. It should be noted, however, that Mann admitted only to an excess of hopefulness, whereas Adorno had demanded a complete absence of consolation. Here is the final version of the passage in question:

> No, this dark tone-poem permits up to the very end no consolation, appeasement, transfiguration. But take our artist paradox: grant that expressiveness—expression as lament—is the issue of the whole construction: then may we not parallel with it another, a religious one, and say too (though only in the lowest whisper) that out of the sheerly irremediable hope might germinate? It would be but a hope beyond hopelessness, the transcendence of despair—not betrayal to her, but the miracle that passes belief. For listen to the end, listen with me: one group of instruments after another retires, and what remains, as the work fades on the air, is the high G of a cello, the last word, the last fainting sound, slowly dying in a pianissimo fermata. Then nothing more: silence, and night. But that tone which vibrates in the silence, which is no longer there, to which only the spirit hearkens, and which was the voice of mourning, is so no more. It changes its meaning; it abides as a light in the night.[13]

It is evident that Mann followed Adorno in stating explicitly that Leverkühn's final musical utterance allows for no consolation. At the same time, however, he invokes the "religious paradox" of "hope beyond hopelessness" and has *The Lamentation* end on a high G—an all too transparent cipher of grace. Still, when Mann read this new version of chapter 46 to Adorno and his wife, the effect was tremendous. "We could not conceal our emotion," Adorno remembered, "and I think it made him happy."[14] He seems, finally, to have approved of Leverkühn's last composition. He must have felt that *The Lamentation*—despite that concluding high G—now ended indeed on the very note of "unequivocal negation" that he had demanded.

Adorno's prime concern was with the fictitious music of the novel—music that was to serve as the paradigm for the desperate situation of modern art and for the course of modern history.[15] He was, naturally, less concerned with the other fundamental dimension of the novel, its embeddedness in the history of the Faust myth. There can be no doubt, however, that he viewed Mann's novel as a radical revision of the optimistic Goethean version of the myth—its revocation, so to speak—and as a return to the original 16th-century version of the Faust myth. Goethe's sophisticated scheme for Faust's redemption—itself a radical transformation of all previous Faust literature—was to be "taken back." To Adorno, the Goethean (and also Wagnerian) formula had lost its credibility and artistic validity. Leverkühn, like his 16th-century model, had again to be forbidden to love. "Thou shalt love no human being" (249) becomes again part of the pact; it is the unalterable prerequisite for Leverkühn's extraordinary creativity. Whereas Goethe discarded the theological framework of the Faust myth almost completely, Mann and Adorno, in the light of recent history, saw fit to revalidate the original, strongly hortatory, version in which a pact with demonic powers is tantamount to eternal damnation. Goethe rejected the seven deadly sins that still appear in Marlowe's tragedy, and to great effect. The only "sin" in the Goethean universe appears to be sloth, the refusal to participate in the eternal activity and motion of creation. Mann, on the other hand, by identifying *superbia* as the sin of sins, returns to the original position of the myth. It is Leverkühn himself who admits to an abysmal *superbia*. In his moving final address to his friends, he confesses that "arrogance" (499) motivated his turn from theology to music, and that even the original choice of theology was an act of arrogance. Given these and many other overt signals of a reactivation of the original "negative" vision of the Faust myth, it seemed inevitable—at least to Adorno—that Leverkühn's last composition, which reveals his identification with the *damned* Faustus, had to end in despair and negation.

In Defense of Germany

The critical reception of *Doctor Faustus* has, on the whole, tended toward Adorno's "negative" view of Leverkühn. Conservative and Marxist critics alike have read this novel as an indictment of Germany. Consequently, Mann was attacked for his allegedly lock, stock, and barrel condemnation of German culture. In Marxist readings, from Ernst Fischer to Gert Sautermeister, Mann is charged with mystification of

German history. He failed, so the argument goes, to account for the economic basis of Kaisersaschern, and to give Germany credit, as it were, for three attempted revolutions.[16] Presumably, for these critics, references to the Peasants' War and to the aborted revolutions of 1848 and 1918 would have rendered Mann's notion of the course of German history more plausible than does the hackneyed device of the pact with the Devil—which in historical reality, according to Fischer, was a pact between the German bourgeoisie and the Junkers.[17] In essence, these critics affirm the existence of another, completely undemonic, Germany that did not embrace the forces of evil and did not deserve the wholesale condemnation which Mann's novel appears to imply.

One-sidedness was also the charge leveled against *Doctor Faustus* by the conservative critic Hans Egon Holthusen. What Holthusen missed, however, was not the representation of the emancipatory, progressive elements in German history but some depiction of the supposedly healthy, blessed Germany of Goethe and Mozart. But his most urgent concern was with the lack of "true religiosity." In Mann's work, he claimed, in contrast to Dostoevsky's, there was not even the slightest perception of the ontological-metaphysical locus at which the idea of God could be imagined.[18] This is a truly baffling assertion in view of the substantive theological discussions in *Doctor Faustus,* and there are good reasons to suspect that Holthusen's overtly religious argumentation was, at bottom, politically motivated. He protested, above all, against the notion of a whole people being fetched by the Devil. To him, this made no theological sense; he therefore branded the book as anti-German "propaganda."[19]

Holthusen now insists that he is a dyed-in-the-wool admirer of Mann, and he considers *Doctor Faustus* one of the most important examples in German literature of a critical discussion of National Socialism.[20] Ernst Fischer, the distinguished Austrian critic, was a much more emphatic admirer of Mann and his work than was Holthusen. In order to understand their rejection, we have to recall the politically charged atmosphere of 1947 when *Doctor Faustus* burst upon the scene. Though arguing from opposite ends of the ideological spectrum, both Fischer and Holthusen attacked the book with the painful passion that has been characteristic of all debates about the "German catastrophe," from 1945 down to the Reagan-Bitburg episode of 1985. In a sense, Fischer and Holthusen reacted to the same irritation. Both rejected what they saw as a condemnation of Germany as a whole—the notorious thesis of Germany's collective guilt. They shared Adorno's negative perception of Mann's new Faust figure, but they denied its representativeness, protested its historical implications, and spoke in defense of their respective ideas of the "other Germany."[21]

Together, Fischer and Holthusen may be seen as paradigmatic of the predominantly negative German reception of Mann's novel. Their critical reactions throw into relief, and underline, the problem that had emerged during the genesis of the novel, in the clash between the author and his collaborator. Indirectly, they help us see more clearly what kind of a book *Doctor Faustus* is and is not.

Montage and Intertextuality

Banal though it may sound, we must remind ourselves again and again that *Doctor Faustus* is a novel and not a dissertation about the origins of German Fascism. Mann's concern was not to set forth a rational discourse on the economic and political causes of the German catastrophe. Nor could he have contemplated developing a complete etiology of that historical catastrophe. Clearly, this is not a historical allegory offering an account of Germany's road to Fascism.

What stands in the way of our inclination to read *Doctor Faustus* as a historical allegory is its specific textuality, which is impervious to direct mimetic representation of verifiable historical events and processes. The rich archival evidence we have of the novel's composition points in a different direction. It tells us that the basic elements of the *text,* of the novel as opposed to its ideological purport, were distilled neither from historical reality nor from the author's own imagination, but rather from other texts. This procedure accords completely with Mann's "growing inclination to look upon all life as a cultural product taking the form of mythical clichés, and to prefer quotation to independent invention."[22] By far the most important "mythical cliché" on which Mann drew is the old *Faustbuch* of 1587.

In recent years, the validity of the Faustian frame of reference has been repeatedly called into question.[23] But such arguments are not altogether convincing. *Doctor Faustus* was conceived—first in 1904, and when Mann returned to the subject in 1943—as a *Faust* work in the full sense of the term. The *Faustbuch* was, however, not the only source to furnish a pre-text for *Doctor Faustus.* Dante, Shakespeare, and Dostoevsky provide further significant intertextual references, and so do many other written sources pertaining to musical and theological matters from Luther to Nietzsche.[24] In *Doctor Faustus,* the technique of intertextual montage, which can be traced to the beginnings of Mann's literary career, reaches its most advanced stage of development; the reader is confronted with intertextual configurations of uncommon complexity. All the decisive elements of the novel are, in a sense, overdetermined. Leverkühn and Kaisersaschern provide particularly telling examples. Kaisers-

aschern is the result of a skillfully calculated montage of various themati-
cally relevant locations.[25] And Leverkühn owes his literary identity not
only to the old Faust figure but also to the biographies of Nietzsche,
Robert Schumann, Hugo Wolf, and, of course, Mann himself. Such a
text, constituted as it is through montage and intertextuality, tends to
sabotage all attempts at locating any palpable historical reference in the
biography of this German "Tonsetzer"—Zeitblom's regular comments
on the events of the Second World War notwithstanding.

   Mann was constantly plagued by doubts about the appropriateness
and feasibility of his method, though in *The Story of a Novel* he hardly
expresses any of them. His diaries, however, contain a complete record of
those nagging self-doubts. They chiefly concern the problem of integrating the disparate intellectual fields surveyed in this novel, especially
the task of inventing credible musical compositions to serve as vehicles
for a maximum of symbolic references. Here Adorno's encouragement,
after he had read the manuscript through chapter 33, played a decisive
role. Still, Mann was well aware that this kind of writing resembled "a
tense, sustained, neck-breaking game played by art at the edge of impossibility" (218). I cite one of Zeitblom's observations regarding Leverkühn's
music, but it can also be understood as a comment on the textuality of
Doctor Faustus itself. Such observations are part of the pervasive self-
consciousness of this novel which pretends to furnish its own poetics and
even its own critique.

   The complete self-consciousness of *Doctor Faustus* has led to the
assumption—widespread in the critical literature—that Mann strove for
a congruence of literary and musical poetics, for an approximation, that
is, of the novel's narrative method to the compositional method of the
music it describes.[26] But this hypothesis is difficult to substantiate for the
simple reason that Leverkühn's music encompasses several different
musical styles. The model of twelve-tone music, which Mann developed
from Adorno's *Philosophie der neuen Musik,* forms the basis for only one,
though the most important and final, stage in Leverkühn's development.
He refers to it as the idea of the "strenger Satz," the "strict style" (191),
which allows for no note that "does not fulfill its thematic function in the
whole structure"; in short, a completely nonornamental style in which
"there was no longer any free note" (486). But such a strict congruence
and mutual reflection of musical and literary structures has not been
achieved here and could not have been seriously envisaged by Mann.

   Nonetheless, the narrative of *Doctor Faustus* does follow certain
musical techniques. They are derived, not from serial music but, as Carl
Dahlhaus has reminded us, from the familiar model of the Wagnerian
web of motifs.[27] In *Doctor Faustus,* Mann continued his lifelong practice
of emulating the Wagnerian technique of the leitmotif. To be sure, this

technique had been considerably refined since "Tonio Kröger," but its characteristic strategies and gestures remain clearly recognizable in *Doctor Faustus:* to wit, a set of motifs of different types relating to physical and psychological attributes (Leverkühn's eyes, his coldness); gestures (laughter) and ideas (the breakthrough); the development of these motifs on the various thematic levels of the narrative; the repetition, as in Wagner's *Ring* and *Tristan,* of whole blocks of the narration (Buchel—Pfeiffering); and the climactic clustering of the principal motifs in certain privileged passages of the text (as in the portrayal of Kaisersaschern, the conversation with the Devil, and *The Lamentation of Doctor Faustus*). There are other unmistakably Wagnerian hallmarks of *Doctor Faustus*—for example, the paraphrase of the prelude to act 3 of *Die Meistersinger* in chapter 15 and the comparison of the role of music in Leverkühn's life with Kundry's role in *Parsifal* (61). These elements illustrate and confirm Mann's frank admission that, at heart, he did not love the music championed by Adorno, and that the diatonic cosmos of Wagner's *Ring* remained his true musical homeland.[28]

We have to conclude, then, that two conflicting aesthetic orientations govern the narrative of *Doctor Faustus:* a modernist, constructivist model based on Adorno and Schönberg, and reflected in some of Leverkühn's compositions; and, to a much greater measure, an essentially conservative, organic model derived from the Wagnerian technique of musical narration, and recognizable in Mann's œuvre from the beginning.[29] A similar aesthetic as well as ideological conflict is apparent in Mann's treatment of the specifically Faustian material. The attempt at making two conflicting aesthetic models cohabit in the same narrative may be seen as an indication of the risks the late Mann was willing to take in this book. I would submit that the stature of *Doctor Faustus* as Mann's most daring and "wildest" book rests primarily on the existence of these inner tensions that tear at its very fabric and at the same time impart to it its characteristic vibrancy.

Mann vs. Adorno: Wagner and Kierkegaard

In light of the conflicting aesthetic orientations of *Doctor Faustus,* we can now pursue Mann's clash with Adorno over Leverkühn's last composition. There are good reasons to suspect that Mann harmonized his position with Adorno's only superficially, and that, in fact, he merely disguised their aesthetic and ideological differences.

Mann never really thought of himself as a spokesman for Adorno's view on music and music history, no matter how eagerly and gratefully he sought the younger man's guidance and advice. His own musical culture was sufficient to maintain his independence even vis-à-vis the formidable Adorno. Thus Mann would turn to Schönberg personally, to sound him out, rather than rely completely on the master's prophet. As a result, some of the positions taken by Leverkühn are—as again Dahlhaus has shown[30]—closer to Schönberg than to Adorno, whose *Philosophie der neuen Musik* Schönberg refused to endorse.[31] Nor was Schönberg happy with the dubious uses—as he saw it—to which "his" new twelve-tone music was put by Mann. (This, as is well known, led to the embarrassing and notorious charges of plagiarism.) In addition to Schönberg, Mann also sought advice from other composers and musicians he knew in Los Angeles, such as Ernst Krenek, Hanns Eisler, Ernst Toch, Otto Klemperer, and, surprisingly, Igor Stravinsky, Adorno's *bête noire,* whom Mann found delightful, and to whom he paid homage by modeling one of Leverkühn's early works on *L'Histoire du soldat.* Mann did indeed follow the principle of "Je prends mon bien où je le trouve"—as he wrote to Adorno, not without guile.[32]

It is the work of Wagner, of course, that marks the point of their most sensitive disagreement. Mann read Adorno's brilliant and incisive critique of Wagner while he was working on *Doctor Faustus.* His first impression was: "extraordinarily intelligent and insightful."[33] He noted with interest a certain kinship with his own essay on Wagner of 1933: "the same critical reservations and rebelliousness without ever turning completely negative."[34] Privately, however, he expressed misgivings about Adorno's analysis of Wagner's music and sneered at Adorno's own efforts as a composer—though not so overtly as did Schönberg. Even in one of the covert portraits of Adorno in *Doctor Faustus* itself, Mann did not refrain from alluding to his lack of creativity. When the Devil takes on the appearance of Adorno, he is introduced as follows: "a theoretician and critic, who himself composes, so far as thinking allows him" (238). One very specific and important difference existed between their interpretations of Wagner's *Ring.* To Adorno, the message of redemption sounded at the end of *Götterdämmerung* was merely the "ultimate phantasmagoria"—an insincere gesture to disguise an underlying sense of utter nothingness.[35] Mann, on the other hand, linked the Wagnerian idea of "redemption through love" to Goethe's *Faust* and maintained that "the final words of *Faust* and what the violins sing at the close of *Götterdämmerung* are one and the same, and what they sing is the truth: 'Das Ewig-Weibliche zieht uns hinan'."[36]

Adorno's "demand" that Leverkühn's music end on a note of hopelessness was bound to provoke in Mann the same deep-seated disagreement he had over Wagner's *Ring.* And it could only be widened by Adorno's "Habilitationsschrift," *Kierkegaard: Konstruktion des Ästhetischen* (1933). Mann began to read this densely written, provocative study when he was working on chapter 20. He learned more about Kierkegaard by reading Georg Brandes. Soon thereafter, he began to read *Either—Or.* He was immediately fascinated by Kierkegaard's definition of music as "sensuous genius" ("sinnlich erotische Genialität") and as the "realm of the demonic."[37] To his surprise, he also discovered a remarkable "congruence" between Kierkegaard's philosophy and his own novel.[38] It is not difficult to see where this "Christian enamoured of esthetics" (242) left his imprint on the novel—namely, at the beginning of chapter 25 where it is suggested that Leverkühn's reading of Kierkegaard's thoughts on "The Musical-Erotic" directly triggered his conversation with the Devil. The congruence of the novel as a whole with Kierkegaard's philosophy is a more subtle and covert matter. As such it has some bearing on the decisive question of grace.

Adorno's study of Kierkegaard contains what is perhaps his most scathing critique of the Christian idea of redemption as a self-deception characteristic of the bourgeois age. In his analysis, Adorno reconstructs the paradoxical "image of hope" as it appears "in all its strength" in Kierkegaard's writings[39]—only to denounce it as false. Kierkegaard evokes the "night of hopelessness before death" and describes how, through the mediation of the Spirit, a new hope, directed at eternity, can be gained. To him, this is hope in the truest sense of the Christian faith— hope beyond hopelessness;[40] it is grace itself. Adorno rejects this kind of thinking, contemptuously labeling it "that sublime banality of redemption." In a somewhat surprising turn of thought, he likens Kierkegaard to Wagner, asserting: "The twilight of the Kierkegaaardian idea of hope is the pale light of *Götterdämmerung;* what it announces is the futile end of an old age and the aimless beginning of a new one—but not redemption."[41]

Mann, as I have said, had his own thoughts about the ending of *The Ring.* They can only have reinforced his resistance to Adorno's critique of Kierkegaard and to his whole philosophy of negativity. Mann therefore maintained his position even as he appeared to accede to Adorno's demand. He merely toned down his original conception, according to which Leverkühn's creative life was to end on a note of hope, and retained in the final text of *The Lamentation* the paradoxical Kierkegaardian formulation of "hope beyond hopelessness, the transcendence of despair" (491)—the very ideas that Adorno had attempted to discredit. Rather than "proving" Mann's compliance with Adorno, *The Lamentation* actually accentuates the philosophical distance between them. It is, therefore, highly misleading to suggest that Adorno literally dictated all the essential points about *The Lamentation* to Mann, and that the author was simply unaware of precisely what Adorno had told him to write.[42]

The Theological Impasse

What this analysis suggests, then, is a revision of the still prevalent reading of *Doctor Faustus* as an unequivocal indictment of Leverkühn and, by extension, a condemnation of Germany. To be sure, the subject of *The Lamentation* is the damned, not the redeemed, Faustus; but this does not necessarily imply that the judgment of its creator must be the same. Unlike the orthodox Lutheran author responsible for the original damnation of Faustus, Mann could never really bring himself to condemn Leverkühn. This same hesitation and revisionary impulse has also to be postulated for the author/composer of *The Lamentation.* The resulting suspension of judgment—of the protagonist of *Doctor Faustus* and of *The Lamentation*—can in no way be attributed to confusion or indecisiveness on Mann's part. On the contrary, it reflects a historical consciousness that discards popular clear-cut solutions and challenges the reader/auditor to confront the theological and historical paradox of *Faustus,* and to recognize it as his own.

When the subject of sin and grace is brought up for the first time, in Leverkühn's conversation with the Devil, Mann refers to chapter 12 of the *Faustbuch,* the "Disputation von der Hell und ihrer Spelunck." From this point on, the discourse on grace proceeds within a tight framework of intertextuality, in which shift of accent and semantic nuance assume far-reaching meaning. Leverkühn, following the footsteps of his mythical model, inquires about the objective conditions of life in hell. The Devil, now in the guise of Schleppfuß, the unsavory professor of theology at Halle, proves to be just as sophisticated a reader of the old text as his host. He immediately smells treachery when he senses that Leverkühn's interest in hell might imply a somewhat different, almost Kierkegaardian reading. He suspects that Leverkühn is attempting "to summon up the *attritio cordis,* the heartfelt anguish and dread of what is to come, of which you may well have heard, that by it man can arrive at the so-called blessedness" (246). There follows a delightful and brilliant exchange, in which the ex-theologian Leverkühn and the self-proclaimed last true theologian, the Devil, attempt to discredit each other's positions on grace as shallow and outdated. The Devil points out that Leverkühn, because of his pride and his love of the extravagance of the creative life, is quite incapable of achieving *contritio,* "the real and true protestant remorse for sin," the complete "religious conversion." Leverkühn, on the other hand, insists on the possibility of a "prideful *contritio,*" contrition without hope, which he claims to be the "true theological way to salvation." With the characteristically Faustian readiness to gamble away his salvation, Leverkühn speculates that "Everlasting Goodness" will find cases such as his the most irresistible of all. This the Devil will not, and cannot, accept.

Such sly and "conscious speculation on the charm which great guilt exercises on Goodness," the Devil assures his host, renders salvation utterly impossible; it is "precisely heads of your sort" that "comprise the population of hell" (247). The argument arrives inconclusively at a theological impasse. What emerges, however, is a clear realization of the deeply paradoxical nature of the whole question of grace and guilt.

In *The Lamentation of Doctor Faustus,* this theological paradox is reaffirmed and maintained—against the grain, as it were, of the cantata's literary sources. In his last composition, Leverkühn's daring speculation on the irresistibility of his sinfulness in the eyes of God is translated into a musical statement of the paradoxical idea of "hope beyond hopelessness" (491). It manifests itself in the miraculous turn of a completely constructivist music to a new expressivity, in the transformation of utter darkness to abiding light. As noted earlier, Mann's use of the concept of "hope beyond hopelessness" must be understood as an endorsement of Kierkegaard and thus as a distancing from, if not a rejection of, Adorno's demand for unequivocal negativity. Such insistence on Leverkühn's theological paradox also throws into relief the contradictory relationship of the *Lamentation* to the *Faustbuch.* Apparently a reaffirmation of the old text, Leverkühn's reappropriation of it, on a deeper level, actually questions and undermines its theological certainties. Whereas the old *Faustbuch* simply pronounces the damnation of Faustus with self-righteous rigor, Leverkühn's *Faust* cantata and Mann's *Faust* novel propose to suspend the earlier verdict.

Duping the Devil

The *Faust* cantata is by no means Leverkühn's only work to state and develop the theological dilemma of the modern Faust, although, in a sense, all of his work can be subsumed under this formula. But there are two earlier compositions which address the question of grace with special urgency. The setting of Klopstock's ode "Die Frühlingsfeyer," though not one of Leverkühn's major works, is remarkable for having "contributed very much to the fact that at the latest in the twenties an aura of fame began to unfold about the name" (265) of its composer. It also merits attention for its strong religious sentiments. This composition, the first to be completed after his conversation with the Devil, marks "an outburst of religious feeling" in an artist whose previous work was preoccupied with the fateful role in his life of the erotic. Undoubtedly, Leverkühn chose this text precisely for its religious enthusiasm. It seems that he begins to address his own situation in the same spirit. His situation is, of course, a desperate one; he is, after all, in league with the Devil—as he was reminded in no uncertain terms by his uncanny guest in that stone-floored room in Palestrina. Ever since then, it seems, he is seeking redemption in and through his work. The Klopstock setting is characterized as seeking "grace in praise" (265). It is praise inspired by fear, but praise nonetheless of the Lord's "majesty and mildness" as manifested in the glorious appearance of the rainbow after a mighty and terrifying thunderstorm. Clearly, the formal characteristics of this work are to be taken as a first indication of the artistic excellence and modernity that were promised him. Scored for baritone, organ, and strings, the composition displays a very modern "restraint and absence of cheap effects," notably a complete disdain for the "hackneyed tone-painting" (265) of a Richard Strauss. The sparseness of the musical idiom reflects the "purer and more pious" attitude with which Leverkühn now pleads for reconciliation with God—offering his work as a token of his *attritio cordis.*

The simultaneous development of musical style and religious sentiment is carried decisively forward in Leverkühn's puppet opera on the birth and life of Saint Gregory, the "holy sinner." The choice of subject itself reveals Leverkühn's innermost concerns. He turns to a tale of multiple incest that is both "extraordinarily sinful" (319) and an extraordinary manifestation of God's amazing grace, by which Gregory, the fruit of his parents' knowing incest and himself the unknowing perpetrator of incest with his mother, is chosen to become the Holy Pope. Obviously, Leverkühn is drawn to such extreme and hair-raising sinfulness because it asserts the possibility of grace at the edge of impossibility. Like *Die Frühlingsfeyer,* Leverkühn's puppet opera may be viewed, at bottom, as a plea for grace. It is again the style of Leverkühn's music that testifies to the sincerity and authenticity of his musical plea. Even more pointedly than in the Klopstock setting, Leverkühn turns against the dominant late Romantic paradigm. Although his opera maintains a certain teasing and ironic contact with Wagner (the medieval source, the motif of incest) it displays in all other respects an openly "destructive" (319) relationship to the Wagnerian model: puppets, not Gods and heroes, are the protagonists; the "farcically erotic" replaces quasi-religious pontification; and, instead of a powerful Wagnerian orchestra, the score calls for only a band of eight players who are given a music of sophisticated simplicity, a "sort of musical children's trumpet style," in which irony and mockery have taken the place of romantic emotionalism. In terms of music history, Leverkühn's *Gregory* has traveled the distance from Wagner to Stravinsky—the Stravinsky of *L'Histoire du soldat,* to which Mann here pays homage. Once more, this score manifests a kind of artistic asceticism; it rejects the stale idiom of post-Wagnerian Romanticism and seeks a new, authentic musical language in the union of the musically advanced with the genuinely popular. Leverkühn's music apparently achieves this union, and with it a much desired and desperately needed breakthrough from the "solemn isolation" of art in Wagnerianism to the "touch-and-go world of new feeling" (321) in which art can again speak to the common man. Zeitblom, it is true, casts doubt on the sincerity of Leverkühn's denial of his innately aristocratic intellectualism, his typically Faustian spiritual arrogance, but it is obvious nonetheless that this work marks a decisive step toward the ultimate breakthrough of modern art from constructivism to expressiveness.

Surveying Leverkühn's work from *Die Frühlingsfeyer* to *The Lamentation,* one is struck by the consistency of its aesthetic and spiritual concerns. Paramount among them is the question of grace. Even the *Apocalypsis cum Figuris,* a terrifying evocation of apocalyptic despair, testifies to the primacy of that concern. This oratorio, Leverkühn's penultimate work and one of his two towering achievements, breaks through the chill of musical constructivism and achieves a deeply affecting expressivity which, as Zeitblom assures us, "could bring tears to the eyes of a man more callous than I am" (377). Its secret object is to be accepted as a "prayer for a soul": that is, it, too, is meant as a plea for grace.

What are we to make of this insistent concern with grace in Leverkühn's work? Is he merely fantasizing about grace as a man dying of thirst would about water? Or is he speculating that, the Devil's sinister assurances notwithstanding, he might obtain grace, after all, in and through his work—an œuvre in which he has taken "the guilt of the time upon his own shoulders" (499)? Zeitblom suggests the latter, thus providing another important indication of the position of this novel in the history of the Faust myth. In the *Faustbuch* and in Marlowe's tragedy, the Devil reacts quickly and decisively as soon as he suspects that Faustus might be double-crossing him. When the pious old neighbor reminds Faustus that through contrition he could yet be saved, Mephistophilis steps in, forces Faustus to renew his bond, and sends him a *succuba* in the shape of Helen of Troy who will seal the fate of the "fond worldling." Nothing of this sort happens in Mann's work. The hellish authorities seem to be so sure of Leverkühn that they appear unaware of the shift in his strategy. Leverkühn has transferred the central issue of the Christian faith—how to obtain grace—to the aesthetic realm: how to achieve a breakthrough. He has opted for an indirect route to salvation; like Wagner's Kundry, he has chosen the "heilloser Weg zum Heil" (330) which, as Mann's entire œuvre suggests, is the artist's only way to salvation. In contrast to the older versions of the myth, no one interferes, no one stops Leverkühn on his "unholy way to salvation" (246). On the contrary, an invisible but powerful figure in the background, to whom we shall have to return, actively assures the "success" of Leverkühn's radical new music among the few cognoscenti who matter.

All of this, it seems to me, places Mann's novel in closer proximity to Goethe than one has been willing to admit. In Goethe's version of the myth, sexual love, the very power intended to be Faust's undoing, is eventually revealed to be the source of his saving grace. A comparable dialectic prevails in *Doctor Faustus*. Leverkühn uses his creativity, the diabolic gift intended to seal his damnation, to strive for the break-through to a new musical idiom, and thereby to arrive at a position of "hope beyond hopelessness."

Can one escape the conclusion that Mann has, at least to some extent, reactivated the ancient, pre-Renaissance topos of the "duped devil"? This stock motif of the medieval mystery plays proved so appro-priate to Goethe's redemption scheme that he made of it a whole farcical scene ("Internment") and placed it, for comic relief, between the tower-ing sequence of Faust's death and the mysterious epilogue of the work. In Mann's version of the myth, there is no place for farce and comedy because there can no longer be any certainty of Faust's salvation. Still, there is the strong suggestion that the Devil here, too, against all odds, may have been defeated with his own weapons. And to the extent that Leverkühn dupes his Devil, so, too, may it be said that Mann deceived his exacting collaborator on *Doctor Faustus*. It is hardly an accident that one of the masks of the Devil in chapter 25 is that of the well-known "theoretician and critic" with the familiar "horn-rimmed spectacles" (238).

The Piano in the Brothel

The potentiality of salvation which this text maintains so insistently is considerably strengthened by one of the most memorable episodes in Leverkühn's biography—his visit to the brothel in Leipzig. Aside from his conversation with the Devil and part of a letter to Kretzschmar, this is the only other section of the text which is presented in Leverkühn's own words. His reaction to his first contact with the fatal power that will forever mark his life and work is peculiar and highly revealing. Realizing that the "inn" to which he has been taken by his sinister guide is actually a brothel, seeing himself welcomed there as though he had long been expected, and feeling suddenly the eyes of "six or seven" girls fixed on him, Leverkühn has great difficulty concealing his shock and gaining control of himself. He notices an open piano, his only "friend" in the place, and rushes over to it. Still standing, he strikes two or three chords while one of the girls, who followed him, gently strokes his cheek with her bare arm. He did not then realize what he was playing, he claims in his epistolary report of this adventure to Zeitblom. It was simply something that happened to be on his mind—a particular harmonic effect that interested him. But later, writing about it to his friend, he remembers exactly what it was: the famous half-step progression from B Major to C Major in the finale of *Der Freischütz*.

Clearly, we are invited to probe behind Leverkühn's report in which he downplays the importance of the whole incident. Zeitblom diagnoses this experience as *the* trauma of Leverkühn's life—the trauma suffered by a man of boundless intellectual pride in his first and fateful encounter with sex (148). All the more reason to wonder why at this of all moments Leverkühn reaches out to that particular music. As is so often the case, the analysis of Mann's intertextual montage yields the key. Leverkühn's visit to the brothel is very closely modeled on Paul Deussen's report of a similar episode in the life of the young Nietzsche. There, too, the piano appears as the only refuge from "the half-dozen creatures in tulle and gauze looking at me expectantly."[43] We are not told what Nietzsche played at the keyboard. But Mann supplies the missing piece of information—implanting thereby into the text of the novel a crucial signal that further clarifies the position of *Doctor Faustus* both in the history of the myth and with respect to the central question of grace. The context of the opera from which Leverkühn "quotes," as well as Mann's musico-logical source, allow us to decode the secret meaning of Leverkühn's reaction. For what he recalls is precisely the symbol in Weber's score for the granting of grace to a man in league with the Devil. That "brightening semitone step" to a "glowing C Major," which like "a mighty light floods the darkened stage,"[44] occurs to the words:

> Doch jetzt erhebt noch eure Blicke
> Zu dem, der Schutz der Unschuld war.
>
> (But now lift up your eyes to Him
> who has protected innocence.)[45]

From here on, the opera rushes to a joyful, buoyant ending in which "all" are encouraged to trust in the mercy of the Almighty Father. Max is forgiven for his invocation of the Devil; his transgression is blamed on his adherence to an outdated custom and, implicitly, on a backward-oriented society.

Once again, we are confronted with a paradox—perhaps the most illuminating of all in *Doctor Faustus*. When Leverkühn is touched by Esmeralda, something deep inside him invokes the prospect, if not the promise, of forgiveness. In other words, the invocation of grace coincides with the invasion of the demonic. Well-prepared as that invasion may be, it is significant that Mann's text, through its central musical code, signals grace at the very moment of the first contact with the demonic. An essentially mystical theory is suggested here—the idea that sin does not come without grace; that sin provokes and creates grace; that sin might in fact be identical with grace.

It has been noted before that Leverkühn's spontaneous quotation from Weber's popular opera in the Leipzig brothel "foreshadows the transformation from darkness to light at the end of *The Lamentation*."[46] This is indeed the case. The invocation of the *Freischütz* finale is also linked to Leverkühn's bold speculation about grace during his encounter with the Devil, and to the narrator's prayer for grace—for his friend as well as his fatherland—at the end of the novel. The cumulative effect of this subtext on grace—and here Leverkühn's compositions must be included—is to strengthen the case of "hope beyond hopelessness" and thus to maintain that paradoxical equilibrium between damnation and salvation that is the hallmark not only of the novel's microstructure but also of its historical role as the most significant 20th-century transformation of the Faust myth.

Das Ewig-Weibliche in Twofold Guise

The identity of sin and grace implied in the brothel scene can also be discerned in Mann's general treatment of the theme of love. Here, too, he follows the *Faustbuch* faithfully, even to the letter—at least on the surface. "Thou shalt love no human being" (249): such is the identical stipulation in both pacts. It is the dearest price Leverkühn must pay for his creativity. Not only does his personal life become "cold," as predicted, but all his attempts at countering the diabolic command—by loving a man, Rudi Schwerdtfeger, and a child, his nephew Nepomuk—are cruelly frustrated. Schwerdtfeger and little Nepomuk must die, and Leverkühn is not entirely wrong in accusing himself of having killed both with his love. Nor is marriage an option.

In the *Faustbuch,* marriage, as a holy sacrament, is of course forbidden. That injunction applies likewise to Leverkühn. When he seriously contemplates marriage, disaster inexorably follows suit, and Marie Godeau, his intended wife and companion, is removed from reach. It appears, then, that Mann returned to the uncompromising position of the original myth, and embraced it completely.

But as with all the central motifs of the book, the role of love turns out to be a paradoxical one. Beneath its overt adherence to the *Faustbuch,* Mann's novel—in a strikingly secretive manner—develops a most curious love story which in effect undermines the basic stipulation of Leverkühn's pact. This brings us back to the aforementioned mysterious figure. She is Frau von Tolna. In a letter to Agnes Meyer, written relatively early in the genesis of *Doctor Faustus,* Mann remarked that "a woman" was waiting in the background who could become Leverkühn's redeemer were it not for the Devil.[47] The figure of that woman was thus part of the grand design for *Doctor Faustus* from the beginning. Moreover, she was clearly intended as a redeemer figure, an apparent analogue to *das Ewig-Weibliche* in Goethe's work.[48]

In the text of the novel, the redeemer function of Frau von Tolna is perceptible only in barest outline. There does exist, however, a surprisingly intimate relationship between her and Leverkühn. Fabulously rich, she places her wealth at his disposal. Since he has no use for the money, she uses it for the propagation of his music. She sees to it that Leverkühn's works get reviewed in the right journal—the radical progressive music journal, *Der Anbruch,* the chief publication of the Schönberg school and, incidentally, one of Adorno's earliest outlets. She pays for publication of the music and she arranges performances which she attends in person, though without revealing her identity. How else is one to describe such activities but as acts of love—as manifestations of unconditional devotion? We are also compelled to infer an exceptional spiritual intimacy, as between lovers, when we learn of a voluminous correspondence "in which [as Zeitblom assures us, though on scanty evidence] she showed herself the shrewdest and most initiate connoisseur of his work, the most devoted friend, confidante, and counselor, unconditionally and unfailingly at his service; while on his side he went to the furthest limits of communicativeness and confidingness" (391). Finally, there is the precious ring, a present from Frau von Tolna, which Leverkühn wears faithfully when he composes. That ring holds the secret of Frau von Tolna's true identity. It is made of a pale green emerald—an unmistakable etymological reference to Esmeralda; and its emblematic vignette showing a dragon with an arrow-shaped tongue recalls the image of the arrow in which Zeitblom, referring to Leverkühn's infection by Esmeralda, saw the symbol of the mythical identity of love and poison (154, 393). The story of how the prostitute Esmeralda became the widow of a Hungarian nobleman is never fully told. But the details of that story do not matter. What matters alone is the secret identity of the two figures—that of the aristocratic benefactress and that of the prostitute.

It is part of Mann's narrative strategy to leave his narrator in the dark about the identity of Esmeralda and Frau von Tolna who, as Victor Oswald was quick to recognize, turns out to be, "in a very real sense, one of the key figures of the book."[49] Zeitblom understands, indeed wants to understand, only half of the issue. How could his Adrian love a whore? Yet he admits, though reluctantly and with a trembling hand, that it was love, after all, that drove Leverkühn back to the woman who had touched him in the Leipzig brothel. The crucial point here is the element of choice. One year after their first encounter, Leverkühn seeks out Esmeralda in Preßburg and insists that he receive the "gift" of infection from her, and from no one else. Zeitblom even senses an element of love in her response as she, before embracing Leverkühn, warns him of her infected body. What Zeitblom refuses to realize, however, is the fact that Leverkühn's love for Esmeralda is requited in a truly generous and mutually consoling manner. It is requited by Frau von Tolna by her devotion to his work—a work that bears her imprint in more than one sense. To be sure, this love is denied its fulfillment in ordinary human terms. There can be no physical intimacy, no bodily warmth, between the two. In this respect, the contractual stipulation, "love is forbidden you, in so far as it warms" (249), fully applies. But love it is nonetheless. Most importantly, it is requited love—a response to the love implicit in Leverkühn's return visit to Esmeralda. Leverkühn—and that is the crucial point to be made here—is already in this life the recipient of love. As such, he circumvents, at least in some measure, the strictures of his pact. The importance of reciprocal love in Leverkühn's life can hardly be overemphasized. If human love is indeed but a reflection of grace (452), as Zeitblom comes to believe, then the whole Tolna matter is of central importance for the theological discourse of the book. It foreshadows the grace of which Mann's Faust, not unlike Goethe's, is, after all, deemed worthy.

Of the Contradictoriness of the German Spirit

What seems to be at work in *Doctor Faustus*—at the nerve center of its narrative strategy—is a twofold and potent intertextual orientation: overtly, to the *Faustbuch* and the original, uncompromising Lutheran version of the myth; covertly, to Goethe and his radical transformation of the myth embracing the conciliatory spirit of the Enlightenment. On the face of it, such a procedure appears contradictory. It results in that pervasive system of equivocation, inversion, and paradox that permeates the very fabric of this text. I have considered here only a few of many such oppositions: constructivism vs. expressiveness in musical terms; hope vs. hopelessness, philosophically speaking; grace vs. sin in theological terms; and redemption vs. damnation in terms of the Faust myth. At bottom, Mann's transformation of the Faust myth amounts to a paradoxical statement: openly, it suggests the damnation of this Faust while secretly affirming, and with considerable insistence, the potentiality of grace. It seems as though Mann had set out to affirm both versions of the myth by conceiving a Janus-faced Faust figure in whom the preconditions for damnation and grace coexist and whose work embraces both. Mann's *Doctor Faustus* may thus be described as a diachronic summation—an attempt, that is, at locating, through the prism of the national myth of the Germans, the seeds from which have grown, and will continue to grow, salvation and damnation, sin and grace.

One is reminded here of Mann's plea, in a slightly different context, for a conciliatory recognition of the contradictions of the German spirit—"die kontradiktorischen Ausformungen des vielumfassenden Deutschtums."[50] In the spirit of that appeal, made in 1933, *Doctor Faustus* may be said to embody such a conciliatory vision: "We are both of these Fausts, the damned and the redeemed, for both together are Germany. They seem to be pulling away from each other, and yet we must learn again and again to see in the contradictoriness of their natures an eternally fruitful fount of life and spiritual richness."[51]

Notes

1 See Thomas Mann's recently published *Tagebücher 1940–1943,* hrsg. von Peter de Mendelssohn (Frankfurt, 1982), 603. Cf. also his *The Story of a Novel: The Genesis of "Doctor Faustus,"* transl. by Richard and Clara Winston (New York, 1961), 42f.

2 Günter Anders, as quoted on the cover of vol. 19 of Theodor W. Adorno's *Gesammelte Schriften,* ed. by Rolf Tiedemann and Klaus Schultz (Frankfurt, 1984): "In der Tat ist Adorno in meinen Augen der seit den pythagoreischen Metaphysikern wie Archytas unbestreitbar bedeutendste und kompetenteste Musikphilosoph gewesen."

3 Cf. Mann, *The Story of a Novel,* 222.

4 See Theodor W. Adorno, "Zu einem Porträt Thomas Manns," *Neue Rundschau* 73 (1962): 320–327; here 325.

5 *Tagebücher 1944–1947,* 12 January 1947; quoted by P. de Mendelssohn in his "Nachbemerkungen des Herausgebers," in *Doktor Faustus* (Frankfurt, 1980), 738.

6 "Zu einem Porträt Thomas Manns," 325.

7 Cf. *Das Volksbuch vom Doktor Faust,* 2d ed., ed. by Robert Petsch (Halle, 1911), 119.

8 Adorno's role in the composition of *Doctor Faustus* has been studied before, notably by Gunilla Bergsten, *Thomas Mann's "Doctor Faustus": The Sources and the Structure of the Novel,* transl. by Krishna Winston (Chicago, 1969) [first German edition, 1963]; Bodo Heimann, "Thomas Manns 'Doctor Faustus' und die Musikphilosophie Adornos," *DVjs* 38 (1964): 248–266; Hansjörg Dörr, "Thomas Mann und Adorno: Ein Beitrag zur Entstehung des 'Doktor Faustus'," *Literaturwissenschaftliches Jahrbuch,* NF 11 (1970): 285–322; Hanspeter Bode, "Musik und Zeitgeschichte im Roman: Thomas Manns 'Doktor Faustus'," *JDSG* 17 (1973): 455–472; Jürgen Mainka, "Thomas Mann und die Musikphilosophie des 20. Jahrhunderts," in *Gedenkschrift für Thomas Mann,* ed. by Rolf Wiecker (Kopenhagen, 1975), 197–214; Jan Maegaard, "Zu Th. W. Adornos Rolle im Mann/Schönberg-Streit," ibid., 215–222; Wolf-Dietrich Förster, "Leverkühn, Schönberg und Thomas Mann: Musikalische Strukturen und Kunstreflexion im 'Doktor Faustus'," *DVjs* 49 (1975): 694–720; Karol Sauerland, "'Er wußte noch mehr . . .' Zum Konzeptionsbruch in Thomas Manns 'Doktor Faustus' unter dem Einfluß Adornos," *Orbis Litterarum* 34 (1979): 130–145; Carl Dahlhaus, "Fiktive Zwölftonmusik: Thomas Mann und Theodor W. Adorno," *Jahrbuch 1982: Deutsche Akademie*

188   *Vaget*

für Sprache und Dichtung (Heidelberg, 1982), 33–49. All of these studies are mostly concerned with Adorno's views concerning the Faust myth and the question of grace.

9 Adorno, "Zu einem Porträt Thomas Manns," 325.

10 Quoted by de Mendelssohn in his "Nachbemerkungen," 739 (my translation).

11 Mann, *The Story of a Novel,* 222f.

12 Friedrich Nietzsche, *The Birth of Tragedy. The Case of Wagner,* transl. with commentary by Walter Kaufmann (New York, 1967), 163.

13 Thomas Mann, *Doctor Faustus,* transl. by Helen T. Lowe-Porter (New York, 1971), 491. All page references in my text are to this edition.

14 Adorno, "Zu einem Porträt Thomas Manns," 326.

15 Cf. Sauerland, "'Er wußte noch mehr....'"

16 Gert Sautermeister, "Zwischen Aufklärung und Mystifizierung: Der unbewältigte Widerspruch von Thomas Manns 'Doktor Faustus'," in *Antifaschistische Literatur,* hrsg. von Lutz Winckler (Königstein, 1979), 77–125; here 81.

17 Ernst Fischer, "'Doktor Faustus' und die deutsche Katastrophe: Eine Auseinandersetzung mit Thomas Mann," in his *Kunst und Menschheit: Essays* (Wien, 1949), 37–97.

18 Hans Egon Holthusen, "Die Welt ohne Transzendenz: Eine Studie zu Thomas Manns 'Doktor Faustus' und seinen Nebenschriften," *Merkur* 3 (1949): 38–58; here 49.

19 Ibid., 178.

20 Hans Egon Holthusen, *Opus 19: Reden und Widerreden aus 25 Jahren* (Munich/Zurich, 1983), 68–93; Holthusen, "Das Wiesengrund-Thema," *Ensemble 6: Internationales Jahrbuch für Literatur* (1975): 89–97.

21 The concept of the other, i.e. "good," Germany played a central role in the debates among exiled writers about the origins of German Fascism. See, for instance, Klaus Mann and Erika Mann, *The Other Germany* (New York, 1940); cf. Herbert Lehnert, "Bert Brecht und Thomas Mann im Streit über Deutschland," in *Deutsche Exilliteratur seit 1933: Kalifornien,* ed. by John M. Spalek and Joseph P. Strelka (Bern/Munich, 1976), 1:62–88.

22 Mann, *The Story of a Novel,* 155.

23 For instance, by Käte Hamburger, "Anachronistische Symbolik: Fragen an Thomas Manns Faustus-Roman," in *Gestaltungsgeschichte und Gesellschaftsgeschichte,* in Zusammenarbeit mit K. Hamburger hrsg. von Helmut Kreuzer (Stuttgart, 1969), 529–553; T. J. Reed, *Thomas Mann: The Uses of Tradition* (Oxford, 1974), 395ff.

24 See Bergsten's pioneering study *Thomas Mann's "Dr. Faustus,"* as well as Lieselotte Voss, *Die Entstehung von Thomas Manns Roman "Doktor Faustus"* (Tübingen, 1975).

25 See my earlier essay "Kaisersaschern als geistige Lebensform: Zur Konzeption der deutschen Geschichte in Thomas Manns 'Doktor Faustus'," in *Der deutsche Roman und seine historischen und politischen Bedingungen,* ed. by Wolfgang Paulsen (Bern/Munich, 1977), 200–235.

26 See especially the study by Förster, "Leverkühn, Schönberg und Mann," as well as Henry Hatfield, *From "The Magic Mountain": Mann's Later Masterpieces* (Ithaca/London, 1979), 108–134.

27 See Dahlhaus, "Fiktive Zwölftonmusik," 34f.; cf. especially George W. Reinhardt, "Thomas Mann's 'Doctor Faustus': A Wagnerian Novel," *Mosaic* 18, no. 4 (1985): 109–123.

28 Mann, *The Story of a Novel,* 95.

29 Dahlhaus, "Fiktive Zwölftonmusik," 41f.

30 Ibid., 44f.

31 See especially Maegaard, "Zu Th. W. Adornos Rolle."

32 Letter to Th. W. Adorno, 30 December 1945; *Letters of Thomas Mann 1889–1955,* selected and transl. by Richard and Clara Winston (New York, 1975), 361.

33 *Tagebücher 1944–1947,* 30 September 1944.

34 Mann, *The Story of a Novel,* 94f.

35 Th. W. Adorno, *In Search of Wagner,* transl. by Rodney Livingston (New York, 1981), 149.

36 Thomas Mann, "Das Ewig-Weibliche," in his *Gesammelte Werke* (Frankfurt, 1974), 13:388.

37 Sören Kierkegaard, *Entweder-Oder: Ein Lebensfragment,* transl. by O. Gleiß. 5th ed. (Dresden, 1909), 69f., 99. Thomas Mann read Kierkegaard in this translation; his personal copy of *Entweder-Oder,* which shows numerous revealing markings, is preserved in the Thomas Mann Archive in Zurich.

38 Mann, *The Story of a Novel,* 104.

39 Th. W. Adorno, *Kierkegaard: Konstruktion des Ästhetischen* (Tübingen, 1933), 123.

40 Kierkegaard, *Entweder-Oder,* 60.

41 Cf. Adorno, *Kierkegaard,* 123: "Das Zwielicht der Kierkegaardschen Hoffnung jedoch ist das fahle der Götterdämmerung, die das nichtige Ende eines alten oder den ziellosen Beginn eines neuen Äons, nicht aber Erlösung verkündet" (my translation).

42 See Sauerland, 144.

43 Cf. Paul Deussen, *Erinnerungen an Friedrich Nietzsche* (Leipzig, 1901), 24.

44 See Hermann W. von Waltershausen, *Der Freischütz: Ein Versuch über die musikalische Romantik* (Munich, 1920), 113. This essay served Mann as source for his use of *Der Freischütz* in *Doctor Faustus.*

45 Cf. Karl Maria von Weber, *Der Freischütz: Texte, Materialien, Kommentare,* ed. by Attila Csampai and Dietmar Holland (Reinbek, 1981), 85 (my translation).

46 Bergsten, *Thomas Mann's "Doctor Faustus,"* 216.

47 Letter to Agnes E. Meyer, 31 October 1944; cited in *Dichter über ihre Dichtungen: Thomas Mann, Teil III: 1944–1955,* ed. by Hans Wysling (Munich, 1981), 33.

48 Cf. Mann, "Das Ewig-Weibliche" of 1903.

49 Victor Oswald, "Thomas Mann's 'Doctor Faustus': The Enigma of Frau von Tolna," *GR* 23 (1948): 249–253.

50 Mann, "Richard Wagner und 'Der Ring des Nibelungen'," in his *Gesammelte Werke* 9:506.

51 Ibid. (I have taken the liberty of adapting this passage slightly.)

COMPOSED BY POLEBRIDGE PRESS, SONOMA, CALIFORNIA
MANUFACTURED BY CUSHING MALLOY, INC., ANN ARBOR, MICHIGAN
TEXT AND DISPLAY LINES ARE SET IN TIMES ROMAN

Library of Congress Cataloging-in-Publication Data
Our Faust?
(Monatshefte occasional volume ; no. 5)
Includes bibliographies.
1. Arts, German. 2. Arts, Modern—Germany
3. Faust, d. ca. 1540—Legends—History and
criticism. 4. Faust, d. ca. 1540—Portraits.
5. Faust, d. ca. 1540—Songs and music—History
and criticism. 6. Goethe, Johann Wolfgang von,
1749–1832. Faust. 7. Goethe, Johann Wolfgang von,
1749–1832—Influence. I. Grimm, Reinhold.
II. Hermand, Jost. III. Series: Monatshefte occasional
volumes ; no. 5.
NX652.F38097   1987   700'.943   86–40452
ISBN 0–299–97019–1

AI